The new pornographies

Manchester University Press

The new pornographies
Explicit sex in recent French fiction and film

Victoria Best and Martin Crowley

Manchester University Press
Manchester and New York
distributed exclusively in the USA by Palgrave

Copyright © Victoria Best and Martin Crowley 2007

The right of Victoria Best and Martin Crowley to be identified as the authors of this work has been asserted by them in accordance with the Copyright, Designs and Patents Act 1988.

Published by Manchester University Press
Oxford Road, Manchester M13 9NR, UK
and Room 400, 175 Fifth Avenue, New York, NY 10010, USA
www.manchesteruniversitypress.co.uk

Distributed exclusively in the USA by
Palgrave, 175 Fifth Avenue, New York,
NY 10010, USA

Distributed exclusively in Canada by
UBC Press, University of British Columbia, 2029 West Mall,
Vancouver, BC, Canada V6T 1Z2

British Library Cataloguing-in-Publication Data
A catalogue record for this book is available from the British Library

Library of Congress Cataloging-in-Publication Data applied for

ISBN 978 0 7190 7398 4 *hardback*

First published 2007

16 15 14 13 12 11 10 09 08 07   10 9 8 7 6 5 4 3 2 1

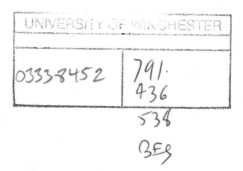

Typeset in Sabon by
Koinonia, Manchester
Printed in Great Britain by
Antony Rowe Ltd, Chippenham, Wiltshire

Contents

List of figures

Acknowledgements

An earlier version of part of Chapter 6 was published as 'Houellebecq – the wreckage of liberation', *Romance Studies*, 20:1 (June 2002): *New Textual/Sexual Perceptions*, 17–28: we are grateful for permission to use this material here. We would also like to thank participants in the following seminars and conferences, at which elements of this work were presented, for their comments: French Department Research Seminar, King's College, London; Queens' College Arts Seminar, University of Cambridge; Medieval French Research Seminar, University of Cambridge; Cambridge French Graduate Conference, April 2005; 'The world of Houellebecq', Edinburgh, October 2005. Finally, we are extremely grateful to all those who have discussed and supported this project, especially: Sarah Allport, Monique Antelme, Bill Burgwinkle, Jennifer Burris, Lucille Cairns, Jenny Chamarette, Andrew Counter, Ruth Cruickshank, Jenny Diski, Georgina Evans, Patrick ffrench, Matthew Frost, Emma Gilby, Nick Harrison, Katja Haustein, Ian James, Sarah Kay, Jean Khalfa, Hector Kollias, Jo Malt, Laura McMahon, Gerald Moore, Douglas Morrey, Ian Patterson, Beate Perry, Keith Reader, Alex Regier, Frances Robinson, Kathryn Robson, Larry Schehr, Bradley Stephens, Emma Wagstaff, Cathy Wardle, Emma Wilson, Rachel Wooller.

A note on translations

Quotations are translated throughout the text in square brackets, running on from the French. We have used published translations wherever possible; all other translations are our own.

Introduction

Don't start from the good old things, but the bad new ones.
(Bertolt Brecht, quoted by Walter Benjamin)

In November 2005, with some fanfare, the Presses Universitaires de France published their *Dictionnaire de la pornographie*, edited by Philippe di Folco with an august advisory committee, and over a hundred contributors, including many notable intellectual names. Unwitting visitors to the publisher's website were greeted by a gaudy animation advertising this publication, featuring the warning phrase 'X Attention' in flashing pink letters, miming the style of a pornographic website; when the title of the *Dictionnaire* subsequently appeared on screen, the pulsing pink 'X' remained. More spectacular evidence of the advance of pornography as a theme and as an aesthetic into the western cultural mainstream could hardly be imagined. This advance – whether it be a matter of websites, magazines, cable and satellite television, or art-house cinema – is unmistakable, and well documented. It does not in itself form the object of this study, however. Rather, it forms the cultural horizon against which this object has constituted itself.

The aim of this study is to examine that body of recent French literary and cinematic productions which have been characterised by their reference to, use of, or complicity with the aesthetics, the codes, the tropes or the world of pornography, and which have made a significant cultural impact on the basis of this dimension.[1] That it has become possible to identify such a body of work, and that an alignment with pornography should work to facilitate such cultural prominence, should already make clear the massive presence of pornography within the broader contemporary cultural field; but it is not as a symptom of this cultural dominance that these works will here be explored. Rather, our aim is to consider what issues might

1

be at stake – socially, culturally, politically and aesthetically – in the decision by a range of writers and filmmakers to use the pornographic as a key point of reference within their work. That is to say, their use of pornographic imagery and figures will be explored as symptomatic of contemporary debates, anxieties, and possibilities in such diverse areas as the status of the novel, the apparent hegemony of liberal democratic capitalism, sexual relations, the contact between films and their spectators, or the sexualisation of children. Our interest is to evaluate some of the principal ways in which it has been used, in order to gain an understanding of the roles it plays for those writers and directors who have chosen its characteristic features as the vehicle for their concerns.

We will mostly be considering works produced in France over the last decade, since approximately the mid-1990s. This is of course the period in which pornography has acquired its dominant status; a handful of typical developments during this period (chosen more or less at random from a much longer list) might include, for example: the anti-feminist backlash, and the 'raunch culture' diagnosed by Ariel Levy (Levy 2005); the blurring of boundaries between pornography and other cultural forms observable in such phenomena as 'lads' mags' in the UK, and some music videos in the US; and the increasingly easy availability in mainstream press outlets of hard-core material. With specific reference to the French context, it would also be necessary to cite the establishment of the first French adult cable and satellite television station, XXL (which by 2005 was claiming a million subscribers); the rise of the publishers Editions Blanche and La Musardine; and the prominent publication of the autobiographies of those the French call *hardeurs* and *hardeuses*, and that English has taken to calling 'porn stars' (indeed, the popularisation of the words *hardeur/-se* and 'porn star' is itself such a symptom).[2] Since 1991, French television station Canal Plus has been broadcasting *Le Journal du hard*, its monthly round-up of adult cinema, followed by an adult film; in 2005, it was estimated that 1,200 hardcore films were being broadcast per month on French television, counting pay-per-view and repeats.[3] This extension of pornographic material from its once restricted forms of diffusion to the heart of the western cultural field is, then, the backdrop against which the works we will be discussing are situated.[4] The aims of a number of those writers and filmmakers we will discuss – including, for example, Erik Rémès, Virginie Despentes, Michel Houellebecq or Bertrand

Bonello – include a critique of the reductive, empty consumerism of this world, for which the pornographic, defined for these purposes by a soulless, commercially motivated materialism, can become a kind of shorthand. At times, however, this thematisation is marked by a very contemporary ambivalence, which leaves any critique of the ways of this world, and of this pornography, awkwardly entangled with the very structures it might like to denounce.

Our object is not the commercially driven, sub-aesthetic genre of pornography as such, then. While academic and political considerations of the nature of pornography will inform our sense of the nature and stakes of the genre, therefore, and while, indeed, the development within the western academy of the discipline of 'porn studies' is doubtless not the least significant indication of its increased cultural capital, we do not seek here to intervene into these debates.[5] Definitions of pornography will of course at times be relevant to our arguments; aspects of particular significance will include, for example: the supposed sub-aesthetic literality of the pornographic; the association of pornography with effectivity (the pornographic *has an effect*); the related notion of pornography as an *act* (of hate speech or incitement to violence, in the arguments of Andrea Dworkin and Catharine MacKinnon); the defining vectors of reality and fantasy (pornography as both indexically real, and governed by fantasy). Such aspects will be of most significance here, however, to the extent that they help to identify the pornographic codes being cited in any given work, and the stakes thereby introduced. We do not ourselves intend to propose such definitions; rather, they will serve methodologically to help us to identify our object. This object is therefore, in a sense, pornography at one remove, or in quotation marks, used as a reference point in the service of some other social or sexual concern. Only 'in a sense', however: for the intermittent complicity with the pornographic evident in many of these works makes their relation to its discourses, and its world, much messier than this hygienic relation of citation would allow. Indeed, what is at stake in a number of the works we will be examining is precisely this question of critical distance, in a range of guises; and typically, the effect of the pornographic is to overspill these aesthetic boundaries, contaminating its host with its base, bodily instrumentality. Nor is this always simply a blind spot on the part of the work: in some cases, it is positively desired, assumed as a decisive element of the aesthetic in question, perhaps as part of a dialectic of transcendence (as in the work of Catherine Breillat, for example), perhaps in order to refuse the normative premises of such universalising elevation (as in that of Erik Rémès).

While we do not seek to avoid the significant issues thrown up by pornography per se, then, we do propose to address them only inasmuch as they are at stake in the use of the pornographic by particular works. This study is not, therefore, an account of the nature or aesthetics of pornography. Rather, it starts from the observation that the pornographic has become a preferred mode for the explicit representation of sexual activity in much recent French literary and cinematic output, and explores the reasons for and the effects of this preference. The use of pornography in contemporary French artworks has in fact become such a prevalent trend that the critical machinery has begun to turn in response to the phenomenon, within France and beyond: cultural journals, from *Les Inrockuptibles* to *L'Esprit Créateur*, have devoted whole issues to the phenomenon, while the *Magazine littéraire* has also discussed it in its forum for debate.[6] To give a sense of the broader field, it might be useful to identify some of the works that have cumulatively made some degree of explicit sex, particularly with reference to the pornographic, such a defining feature of recent western culture. These would include – but are far from limited to – such examples as: Lars von Trier's *The Idiots* (1999), Patrice Chéreau's *Intimacy* (2001), Michael Haneke's *La Pianiste* (2001, based on Austrian writer Elfriede Jelinek's novel of 1983), the photography of Terry Richardson or Bettina Rheims, the online diaries of Natasha Merritt, the performances and texts of Annie Sprinkle, Michael Winterbottom's *9 Songs* (2004) and Carlos Reygadas' *Battle in Heaven* (2005). There are, in addition, a number of works from the French context which touch on the sexually explicit without extensively engaging with the pornographic as such: for example, Marie Darrieussecq's *Truismes* (1996), Catherine Cusset's *Jouir* (1997), Frédéric Beigbeder's *Nouvelles sous ecstasy* (1999) or Claire Denis' *Trouble Every Day* (2002). The works that we have chosen to focus upon are those – often by some of France's more recent self-styled *enfants terribles*, such as Michel Houelle-becq, Catherine Breillat, Virginie Despentes, Guillaume Dustan or Catherine Millet – in which the conscious citation of pornography is most provocative and productive, and which have set the trend as we have interpreted it, namely for a use of the pornographic as a code that asks to be interpreted.

What concerns us in this analysis, then, are the notable and specific differences that characterise the use of the pornographic within French artworks at this particular cultural moment. The widespread citation of pornographic tropes at the end of the twentieth century is neither purely random, nor purely designed with the commercial, and cynical, intent to titillate; its aims would, however, appear to be other than those invested in it by previous generations. As Angela Carter proposed, '[pornography] can never be art for art's sake. Honourably enough, it is always art with work to do' (2000: 12). Sexually-explicit representation has, for example, often been associated with progressive politics, as in the anti-clerical satires of the Middle Ages and the eighteenth century (see Dean 2000: 27); this association even persisted in the context of the Western sexual liberation movements of the 1960s and 1970s (as in the magazine *Oz* and, indeed, Carter's *The Sadeian Woman*, in which she suggests that 'pornography is a satire on human pretensions' (2000: 16)). Perhaps most significant in the context of this study is its eruption onto the scene of the revolutionary French avant-garde in the late 1920s onwards, in which this historic association between obscenity and a progressive agenda saw authors, especially dissident surrealists such as Bataille, representing sex explicitly in order to force readers and spectators into new, recodified modes of reception. This move, which retrospectively established a whole lineage of *érotisme noir* with Sade as its great precursor, crucially depends on generally accepted notions of the status of the pornographic in relation to the aesthetic, particularly as focused around the idea of *effectivity*.

The disquieting sensation of extreme emotions – arousal, disgust, alarm, recognition – that overwhelms the spectator of graphic sex has often been at the root of pornography's resignation to the lower class of artwork (see Clover 1993: 3). Indeed, in opposition to the prevailing aesthetic tradition in the western world for the past two hundred years or so, a tradition that values art as disembodied, rational, harmonious and free from materiality (and which was itself assaulted by the various avant-gardes of the twentieth century, and before them by Nietzsche), pornography shatters the barriers between the object of art and its spectator, refuses the distance of contemplation and reflection, and highlights the relationship between art and the unethical, avid desire of the consumer. Adorno's *Aesthetic Theory* proposes that 'Perhaps the most important taboo in art is the one that prohibits an animal-like attitude towards the object, say, a desire to devour it or otherwise subjugate it to one's body'. Yet Adorno goes on to say: 'Now the strength of such a taboo is matched by the strength of the repressed urge. Hence all art contains in itself a negative moment from which it tries to get away [...] the dignity of works of art depends on the magnitude of the interest from which they were wrested' (1984: 16). So pornography, in its appeal to precisely the grasping, panting, desublimated sensuousness underlying artistic practice, is undignified art. Art whose defences have been unbuttoned; art, appropriately enough, in a state of *déshabillé*.

The avant-gardists, and Bataille most particularly, made aesthetic mileage out of this by exploring the contaminating force of the pornographic as a way of accessing fundamental but hidden dimensions of subjectivity, possibly as part of a revolutionary political project. This tradition persists until at least the 1970s: it is evident in Bernard Noël's *Le Château de Cène* (1969), for example, or in the work of many of those associated with the journal *Tel Quel*, for whom Bataille was of course a crucial figure. It is notable, for instance, that when Barthes rehabilitates a quasi-Nietzschean aesthetic of effectivity, in *Le Plaisir du texte* (1973), his key term – *jouissance* – is chosen for its suggestion of the politically ungovernable effects of explosive sexual rapture.[7] As we explore most extensively in Chapter 4, one of the issues at stake in the modern-day incarnation of pornographic citation in France is, however, the extent to which such experimentation can still be thought to be ideologically transformative – or, alternatively, whether it can still be thought of in such terms at all. One of the historical specificities of much of the material we will be considering here is its awkward relationship to literary and intellectual culture: it often fits with difficulty into the progressive political and aesthetic narratives – including this tradition of sexuality as supposedly 'subversive' – by which this culture is still largely, if uncertainly, sustained. And the engagement of this material with the codes of pornography may accordingly be seen as both signifying and enacting this lack of fit. Fifteen or twenty years ago, significant literary texts or art-house films dealing provocatively with questions of sexuality would most likely have been described as 'erotic' rather than 'pornographic'. One of the many issues at stake in this often tenuous distinction is the notion that the erotic, unlike the pornographic, offers a defamiliarising presentation of its sexual subject matter, and so can trouble the social and aesthetic conventions through which this material is more usually articulated, this troubling serving as an indicator of aesthetic quality.[8] Thus, even when works – such as the great majority of those in the French tradition of *érotisme noir*, from Sade to Bataille to Robbe-Grillet, say – might be thought by some readers to be reactionary in their sexual politics, they could still be celebrated as aesthetically progressive; often, indeed, formal progressiveness would be read as effecting progressive reconfigurations in terms of sexual identity (on this, see Suleiman 1995.) Plenty of contemporary work continues to operate in this way, of course (see for example Beyala 2005 and Roman 2005). Indeed, some of the material considered here continues to situate itself in relation to this tradition of progressive eroticism. The films of Catherine Breillat, for example, develop an avant-garde aesthetic programme which is linked to what their director understands as a confrontational and emancipatory politics. Alternatively, Guillaume Dustan situates his work in relation to elements of this tradition, but announces in this work a drastic reconfiguration of the sexual body on the basis of radical anal pleasure, thereby polemically inhabiting a progressive political position in opposition to mainstream heteronormativity (of which Breillat would not be the least significant example). And even Catherine Millet's relentless account of her sexual adventures – particularly as interpreted by her partner, Jacques Henric – asks to be read in the light of Sade, Bataille and Benjamin. On the other hand, however, a fair proportion of this recent material does not obviously inhabit any progressive tradition, let alone that of what Lawrence Schehr, in an outstanding account of this lack of fit, has called 'modernist models of the erotic and the pornographic, determined by a generalised truth' (2004a: 4); and this has introduced a large degree of ambivalence into the reception of this material, both in France and elsewhere.

The pornographic aspects of this material are an important contributor to this questionable status, for three principal reasons. In the first place, to embed the codes of pornography in a work without offering enough by way of avant-gardist estrangement is one way of provocatively withdrawing the work to some extent from conventional aesthetic consideration. Figures such as Despentes and Houellebecq, for example, produce work which both engages with the conventions of literary culture and holds itself at a sometimes parodic distance from these conventions, wilfully ducking under the bar which separates the literary from the sub-literary, the aesthetic from the sub-aesthetic. Second (as a subset of this first point): pornography is often defined as merely venal, its aims limited to the instrumental or the commercial, as opposed to the nobly subversive aims of the erotic. A tendency has thus recently appeared, in some French criticism, to bemoan the dominance of the pornographic as the primary code for the presentation of sexually explicit material, and to regret the consequent disappearance of the heroic, avant-gardist, progressive ambitions – whether aesthetic, political or existential – of the erotic.[9] Writing in a recent issue of the *Magazine littéraire*, Michela Marzano summed up the view underpinning such responses, arguing that:

> La pornographie devient ainsi une sorte de miroir des contradictions du monde occidental contemporain, c'est-à-dire d'un monde qui prône la liberté, tout en renfermant les gens à l'intérieur d'un système très normatif; qui exalte le plaisir, tout en effaçant le désir; qui célèbre l'autonomie individuelle tout en réduisant les relations personnelles à des échanges marchands. (2005: 28)

> [Pornography thus becomes a kind of mirror for the contradictions of the contemporary western world, namely a world which champions freedom, even as it encloses people in a highly normative system; which exalts pleasure, even as it eliminates desire; which celebrates individual autonomy, even as it reduces personal relations to commercial exchanges.]

Good old eroticism has been replaced by bad new pornography. On this account, those producing work which references this degenerate code would be guilty of simply reproducing the selfish, consumerist materialism of their world, without providing the ironic, critical displacement proper to the artwork. The third principal way in which the pornographic often renders such work suspect is in its relation to progressive sexual politics. Thanks to such developments as legislation on civil partnerships (the introduction of the PACS in 1999), or the foundation of the movements Les Chiennes de Garde (in 1999) and Ni Putes, Ni Soumises (in 2002) to oppose misogynistic violence, such politics have been prominently debated during the period in question. While they are, accordingly, taken as read as part of the cultural horizon by many of these works, they may well nonetheless find themselves critiqued; even when they are embraced, the works in question frequently include elements which appear incompatible with this alignment. The best example of this is doubtless Virginie Despentes' *Baise-moi*, in whose problematic celebration of female agency the refusal of phallocratic violence takes place in terms all but indistinguishable from this violence: progressive sexual politics find themselves affirmed and negated in the same moment. As in Despentes' début, so throughout the works we will be considering: the complexities of this encounter are invariably delineated through references to pornography.

One of the impulses behind this study, however, is the notion that we cannot respond to this recent cultural production simply in the mode of nostalgia. That the works we discuss have proved successful suggests that they have something to tell us, beyond the pessimism that predicts imminent cultural apocalypse at the hands of those tellingly grouped together in 1999 as 'new barbarians' (Jacob 1999). A cry of 'où est l'érotisme d'antan?' will hardly do as an attempt to interpret what is at stake in the recent success of these pornographically inflected works. Following other, less nostalgically inclined criticism (such as Baqué 2002, Ogien 2003, Schehr 2004a or Bourcier 2004), we propose, rather, to take seriously some of the questions posed by this success. Our aim is not to take at face value the presence in these works of images drawn from pornography (even if this is at times how such images beg to be received, and how they are often dismissed), but to explore instead the significance that lies behind their appropriation and deformation. Not least, we recognise the need to explore the various discourses that result from often ambivalent acts of citation and deployment. These include, for example, the entanglement of the body in competing and contradictory realms of coding that confuse the sexual, the medical, the political, and the abject; equally at stake we find the status of the image, its ability to deliver some kind of truth, to disturb and enlighten the spectator/reader with unexpected angles on this opaque and mysterious body in its moments of *extremis*. We will also seek to reflect on some of the broad cultural questions posed by the success of the works we consider. What if, for example, the properly literary novel were no longer the site of a meaningful critical engagement with its world? What if the western artwork were indeed utterly absorbed within the consumerist spectacle? If the reference to the pornographic in these works does indicate a desire to approach the sub-aesthetic, might this have to do less with the supposed deviance of this desire, than with the contemporary status of the aesthetic? Our fundamental contention here is that the recent prominence of the works we discuss is not accidental or merely craven, but rather condenses a manifold of significant issues, which deserve to be interpreted. As others have argued that the cultural prominence of pornography means the genre deserves serious consideration (see for example Gibson 1993 and 2004, and Williams 2004), so we argue here that the *uses* of the pornographic within other genres may be similarly eloquent. If we are indeed, as the title of a recent issue of the journal *L'Esprit Créateur* put it, *After the Erotic*, we will need to think hard – as do the contributors to this issue – about what this might imply.[10]

While it is important to avoid nostalgia, then, it is no less important to avoid wallowing in despair. A degree of disillusion with the subversive potential of the erotic avant-garde is indeed a defining feature of much of the material we consider here – but there is equally plenty which is continuing, creatively, to explore the possibilities of self-fashioning and social disturbance produced by the confrontational manipulation of the codes of explicit sexual representation. How, accordingly, might we define the features of modern pornographic citation 'after the erotic'? Like their avant-garde forebears, contemporary pornographic tropes may situate their protagonists at the limits of reason, sanity and civilised behaviour, and often in particular temporal and spatial locations, defined by the use of a contract or a designated erotic area, such as the ubiquitous *échangiste* club; areas, in other words, beyond, or marginal to, the everyday. Equally reminiscent of these forebears are the compulsion and the violence that often accompany the protagonists' descent into the claustrophobic world of obsessive sexual practice. But what we appear to lack today is the paradoxical positivity of the avant-garde's citation of pornography, the manic glee with which it unleashed its troubling images on the cultural arena. Instead we find, time and again, a profound melancholia inhabiting the heart of the sexual enterprise; even the element of cynicism self-consciously displayed by contemporary artworks revels its own innate despair, and the supposed collapse of narratives of liberation encoded by these artworks in their citation of the pornographic. In short, even the briefest reflection on its similarities to and differences from its previous, avant-gardist incarnation brings us back to an unavoidably unhappy conclusion: the pornography in these films and texts is no longer any fun.

Something of the specificity of the current climate may also be gauged by the necessary comparison with the work of the great progenitor of modernity's pornographic tradition, Sade. Carter points out that Sade's sexual universe is one in which the protagonists do not exist beyond their quest for extreme eroticism, and where their gratification comes only at the cost of intolerable pain both given and received: 'his imagination', she writes, 'took sexual violence to an extreme that may, in a human being, only be accompanied by an extreme of misanthropy, self-disgust and despair' (2000: 33). This description tallies closely with the representation of the sexual desperadoes of contemporary France – but again, the difference is highly instructive. The suffering of our modern-day protagonists sees their so-called pleasures inevitably accompanied by misogynistic and abject repulsion for their own bodies as well as those of others. In this respect Sade is, as Carter claims, 'the avatar of the nihilism of the late twentieth century' (2000: 34). Unlike their Sadean predecessors, however, these protagonists seem often entirely to lack any frame of reference – however perverse – by which such suffering might be given a meaning (however destructive). From these shores, even the pure loss of Bataillean expenditure without reserve shines with the happy glow of ontological authenticity and perverted existential heroism. But to repeat: we cannot simply be nostalgic for this vanished intensity, or obsessed by its supposed disappearance. If it has indeed vanished, then what, exactly, has it left behind?

The point, then, would be to read this material as symptomatic of its cultural moment. And the use of the pornographic can begin to look all but definitive of the current concerns of this moment – for example, of French literature in particular as described by Michel Crépu in his 2001 article in *L'Express*, 'Le roman français, est-il mort?'. ['Is the French novel dead?'] Crépu identifies three major preoccupations motivating literary narrative, along with what he presents as their contemporary fate:

> le moi. Ce qui reste quand le surmoi (politique, religieux, moral) a disparu. Un moi hystérique, tout en nerfs et en tripes. Misérabiliste et mégalomane, obsédé de transparence, extraordinairement puritain et pornographique en même temps. A quoi sert le moi? A avoir des états d'âme? Non: à dire la vérité. Pas la vérité d'une idéologie quelconque, mais la vérité du corps sexué, la vérité 'sociale' aussi bien [...] Deuxième source: la soif de réel. On est épuisé d'avoir tout soupçonné. Ce que l'on veut maintenant, c'est *toucher* [...] [La troisième source]: l'art du récit. *Raconter une histoire.* (Morello and Rodgers, 2002: 20)

[the self. What remains when the superego (be this political, religious, moral) has disappeared. A raw, frantic, hysterical self. Miserabilist, megalomaniac, obsessed with openness, extraordinarily puritanical and pornographic at one and the same time. What's the point of the self? To get all worked up? No. To tell the truth. Not the truth of some or other ideology, but the truth of the sexual body, as well as the 'social' truth [...] Second source: hunger for the real. Being suspicious of everything has left us exhausted. What we want now is to *touch*. [The third source]: the art of narrative. *Telling a story*.]

As we will see, Crépu's three areas of engagement correspond closely to the way pornographic tropes are cited in the works under analysis here: the cult of the individual, which in turn promotes a highly developed focus on the intimate monologue, and, subsequently, the desire to experience the real, the dream of immediacy that perpetually haunts representation but whose demands have, as we will see, become increasingly pressing in the contemporary cultural moment.

If their relation to the tradition of 'subversive' eroticism is vexed, then, the undeniable contemporary resonance produced in these works by their references to the pornographic needs also to be situated in other contexts. The language of popular culture is one of these, often used – as in Despentes and Dustan, for example – without the ironic, citational framing that might have marked it out safely as literary. Inextricably linked to this is the language of consumerism, especially the referential economy of the commodity fetish, in which the common noun ('whisky', say) is replaced by the brand name ('J & B', to take an example from Houellebecq). The use of the pornographic as an index of such contexts is unsurprising: it is par excellence a discourse in which the sexual body becomes a commodity. But this use frequently indicates a problem: as we have suggested, the relation between these works and the codes of the pornographic is not just one of ironic citation: it can, just as often, be a matter of complicitous usage. (In especially vexed instances, it can be both at the same time, as we will see in the cases of Houellebecq and Despentes.) And the risk that thereby emerges to the critical distance definitive of the artwork is particularly evident in the use in these materials of the languages of pornography and the commodity. Speaking the language of their world, that is, they may perhaps gain a kind of immediacy; this may, however, be at the price of the distance that alone might have guaranteed the act of critique.

A crucial forebear here comes not from the French context, but from recent American literature, in the form of Bret Easton Ellis's *American Psycho* (1991). The impact of this book on the generation of French writers publishing from the mid-1990s appears to have been considerable: both Houellebecq and Dustan have acknowledged its influence, for example. (See Wellershoff and Traub 2005; and Dustan 2002: 29–39, 2003: 375, and, for the significance of the same author's *Less Than Zero*, 1998: 157.) This influence seems to have been due to three principal factors. First, the use of the language of the commodity as a dominant way of articulating a relation to the world. Second, the use of graphic representation of sexual acts, especially as conjoined with extreme violence. In this work, graphic sexual detail is used pointedly, and significantly, in the service of unpleasure and anxiety. The narrative is designed to arouse discomfort in the reader because of its signalled actuality, its consumerist and pornographic dimensions symbolically pertaining to a hopelessly diseased and corrupt culture. Bateman's psychosis is not to be understood as a rogue gene, but rather as an accurate reflection of his society's values, which are thereby critiqued. Western society's adherence to images, to the celebration of the superficial, becomes the provocation for, and the justification of, nauseating acts of violence that are linked, synonymously, with misogynistic acts of sex. But if this work has proved so influential, this has above all to do with the third of these factors, in which this critical dimension is placed severely at risk. This crucial factor is the narration of events from the perspective of the psychopathic protagonist, Patrick Bateman, with an unstable use of irony rendering uncertain the position taken by the text in relation to these events, somewhere impossibly between critique and complicity. Equally, very many of the recent works we will be considering express both horror and fascination before social values and aesthetic codes they seem to want to denounce – but with which they seem to remain strangely, perhaps guiltily, entangled.

As this situation of snagged, suspended critique perhaps suggests, the current French exploration of pornographic tropes clearly also needs to be considered with reference to some of the key existential, epistemological and aesthetic tonalities associated with the notion of postmodernity. The collapse of the belief in cohering meta-narratives of science, knowledge and religion, the replacement of a sense of progress in humanity with resigned inertia, the obsession with the surface, have all had a profound impact on contemporary aesthetics, which has engaged in a lengthy process of mourning for, among other things, existential coherence and the belief in the effectiveness of collective action. Postmodernity's consequent fascination with, and insistence upon, the fragmentary, the ephemeral and the fugitive means that, frequently, sexual acts are not subsumed into a structure of significance within their artworks, but rather stand alone in their recalcitrant, troubling carnality. However, this resistance to dislocated structures of meaning also allows these moments to encode the paradoxical gesture in many of these fractured contemporary cultural forms towards contact, touch, proximity. In other words, the use of pornographic tropes in contemporary artworks can be identified both as figuring a generalised gloominess in relation to meaning-making structures, and as part of the powerful wave of nostalgia implicit within postmodern art for that which is experienced as real and immediate. As Laura Marks has pointed out, many of the cultural forms which define the contemporary moment are characterised not only by an extreme degree of mediation, but also by the desire for or promise of real, immediate contact (see Marks 2000 and 2002). The concept of effectivity, so important to the avant-gardes of the early twentieth century, here returns, shorn of its progressive potential, in the mode of a contact which – as Hal Foster has argued in *The Return of the Real* (1996) – is traumatic, impossible, paradoxical, empty and sensuously compelling. The recent good fortune of notions such as Peirce's 'index' and Benjamin's 'aura' (as discussed in Chapter 2 of the present volume) would be indicative of this tendency, in which epistemological emptiness becomes the space of a strange simultaneity of affective blankness and intensity.

We can understand this via the notion of the space–time compression that both Fredric Jameson and David Harvey present as exemplary of the postmodern. Jameson proposes that in the postmodern perspective, 'experience of the present becomes powerfully, overwhelmingly vivid and "material"' (1984, cited in Harvey 1990: 54); Harvey ties this to a breakdown in the signifying chain whose effect is 'to reduce experience to a series of pure and unrelated presents in time' (1990: 52). What could be more 'material', more intense, more vividly present and resistant to cerebral causality than the graphically depicted sex act? What better, then, both to enact and, paradoxically, to signify this rupture in the field of signification?

Žižek, in fact, proposes that explicit sexual acts have the effect of derailing the illusion of depth created in cinematic time. 'The sexual act would function as an intrusion of the real undermining the consistency of this diegetic reality' (1992: 111), he writes, which echoes Jameson's assertion that in the postmodern compression of time to a perpetual present, 'the world thereby momentarily loses its depth and threatens to become a glossy skin, a stereoscopic illusion, a rush of filmic images without density' (1984, cited in Harvey 1990: 54). It is no surprise, then, that so many postmodern images of sexuality – whether filmic or not – are in character pornographic; that they concentrate on body parts with a fanatical fetishism, relying for their imagistic power on the supposed 'reality' of the act. Nor, indeed, that the pornographic has become a favoured code for writers and filmmakers wanting to articulate the structure of feeling of their time. The ambivalent combination of critique and collusion found in many of the works we will discuss in this study perhaps has something to do with this: the attempt to articulate from within a crisis of meaning. The desirability of finding excessive and shocking forms of art to address such a crisis remains a constant in aesthetic theory: in her 1996 work, *Sens et non-sens de la révolte*, Kristeva demands a kind of political heroism from contemporary art, arguing that: 'Nous sommes aujourd'hui entre deux impasses: échec des idéologies révoltées d'une part, déferlement de la culture-marchandise de l'autre' (14), with the result that: 'Nous pouvons nous demander aujourd'hui si seule une *expérience de révolte* ne serait pas à même de nous sauver de la robotisation de l'humanité qui nous menace' (15). ['the two impasses where we are caught today: the failure of rebellious ideologies on the one hand, and the surge of consumer culture on the other; an experience of revolt may be the only thing that can save us from the automation of humanity that is threatening us' (Kristeva 2000: 7)] Kristeva's emphasis on experience reinforces the fantasy that it might be possible to pierce representation. The resultant encounter with the real that lies beyond would provide the kind of shock needed to jump-start a stagnating society. The contemporary appeal to the pornographic is clearly consonant with such an intent to shock, but, as we will consider at some length, such an appeal is fraught with difficulty, not least in its own awareness of the limits of its likely effectiveness. Precisely whether the classic avant-gardism advocated by Kristeva is currently a viable position is a question addressed by several of the works we here explore – most extensively perhaps in Bonello's *Le Pornographe* (2002) – and it will, accordingly, form one of the recurrent concerns of this study.

If the sociopolitical effectiveness of art remains a vexed question, Harvey nevertheless argues that the postmodern cultural artefact is characterised by the persistence of another kind of avant-gardist effectivity: the participation of both producer and consumer in the creation of meaning, as for example in its tendency to embrace the 'happening' or 'performance' as its privileged form. We can identify another link to the pornographic here, which references more clearly than most other cultural codes the real presence of the performer (which is exactly what is meant by the term 'performance' in 'performance art': on this, see Williams 2001), and the absolute necessity of audience participation. Alison Pease in her work on obscenity and modernism points to the way that the reader is encouraged to identify to the point of merger with the figure of the voyeur, and this 'by engaging in an act of sensual self-scrutiny, gauging the body's complicity with the mental recitation of sensational or voluptuous imaginings, and in doing so, achieving sexual stimulation and gratification. Pornography, by this account, is not so much a representation of sexuality as a specific practice of it' (2000: 6). So as an artistic practice that is also a sexual practice, pornography troubles the borderline between reality and fantasy, between the origins of sexuality and its representations – and so insinuates itself into the structures of feeling of the postmodern as a signature aesthetic, performing the collision of the real and the image.

Precisely because sexuality requires fantasy to become reality, pornography can offer itself – fictitiously, of course – as a kind of distilled concentration of sex. The interplay between fantasy and reality over the space of the pornographic will be considered in some detail in this analysis, in order to evaluate the distinction between the erotic and the pornographic in which a certain transparency and (in consequence) triviality is inevitably assigned to the latter. Michael Worton clarifies this distinction by suggesting that: 'Pornography both programmes and relies upon the immediacy of "naïve" reading, where the body engages only marginally with the cerebral activity of deciphering, decoding and evaluating. On the other hand, erotic fiction teases and tantalises through its play with content and with the problematics of sex as content, rather than treating text pornographically as mere vehicle for the evocation of sex' (1998: 94). In other words, pornography offers – disingenuously – an apparently simplistic experience, a transaction with the reader or spectator that is as uncomplicated as the sexual transaction effected between the men and women in its images. Yet the one thing we can undoubtedly say about the contemporary artworks that cite pornography, is that their urge to link explicit images of sexuality to substantive cultural, political or ethical concerns produces a far from uncomplicated picture.

However tempting it may be to assume that the graphic representation of sexuality is irretrievably depthless, and that it offers a spectacle for consumption – in the form of pure participation – that is entirely without significance (not least since this is how such representations may seek to extricate themselves from the difficult ethical and political questions they inevitably raise), its extensive presence in texts and films produced by intellectual French artists at the turn of the twenty-first century indicates the undoubted existence of sustaining fantasies, struggles, and debates that underpin these supposedly transparent and discontinuous erotic acts. Our analysis in this book sets out to prove that the fantasies underlying the representation of graphic sexuality are not in any way simplistically sexual, or trivially commercial, but that they impact upon significant issues about contemporary culture, artistic practice, and the kinds of engagement it is possible to posit between these two.

The exploration of these different areas of concern has taken place against a particular matrix of theoretical thought informing our readings. Certain theorists (Žižek or Baudrillard, for example) have written directly on pornography, while others (Kristeva or Foucault, say) have provided key terminology and approaches towards the interaction of sexualised bodies with their societies. Our interpretations of films have been informed by the work of a growing circle of theorists (Marks, Sobchack, Williams, Doane) on the power of film to extend beyond the confines of the screen and enact a form of touch upon the spectator. We have often tied together analysis of film and narrative, recognising the common fascination in both media with imposing an experience of contact or continuity upon the reader/spectator, but acknowledging where pertinent the different debates surrounding different artistic forms, including with reference to this fantasy of immediacy. We have also sought to tie together the author-centred chapters (Chapters 2, 3, 5 and 6), by organising them largely around a common thematic focus, namely the interplay of notions of distance and proximity in relation to the aesthetic. We have also decided to allow our own differences of approach to remain palpable, aiming to produce a co-authored analysis in which we have spoken from our differently gendered perspectives on an agreed corpus of material: Martin Crowley has written on Catherine Breillat, Michel Houellebecq, Catherine Millet, Virginie Despentes, Guillaume Dustan and Erik Rémès; Victoria Best has written on the battle between the sexes, the concepts of revolution and abjection in pornographic art, and the exploitation of children. This initial individual drafting has subsequently been followed by collective editing and rewriting, and we take joint responsibility for everything presented here. Our different analyses interweave and cross-refer – over such issues as the representation of the abject, or the use of the aesthetic frame, for example – and they have also been mutually influential; but we have not sought to homogenise our responses, preferring instead to embrace multiple perspectives within the overall frame of a common and, we hope, coherently conceived project.

In Chapter 1, we consider the insistent heterosexuality of most contemporary pornographic citation, exploring a range of texts and films, and taking in the female perspective on the male and the male perspective on the female. Despite the attempt that we see in these artworks to maintain a steady, concentrated focus upon the sexual act, it becomes clear that they are each informed by a wealth of fantasies about the other gender that are far from symmetrical. Using Žižek and Deleuze, we analyse these artworks in relation to the anti-pornography movement in America, to new understandings of female desire and to the age-old idealisation of woman as muse, here significantly informed by male fears and anxieties.

The enthusiastic heterocentrism of most of our corpus finds its apogee in the work of Catherine Breillat, which forms the object of Chapter 2. The most important of the cinematic auteurs to have achieved recent prominence by virtue of their use of explicit sexual material, Breillat (who, lest we forget, has been making films for over three decades) is also by far the most conventionally avant-garde of our subjects. In her work, a highly individual redefinition of the erotic and the pornographic is mobilised in the interests of an aesthetics of transcendence, in which graphic representation aims to induce in the spectator an uncomfortable but idealistic recognition of the glory of the sex act, as part of which (and in ways which recall the early work of Irigaray), Breillat seeks to reclaim the female body from its misogynistic relegation to the basely material. The aesthetics of Breillat's work receive extended consideration, with particular reference to the relation between her aim of transcendence, and the mechanics by which she seeks to make contact with her spectator.

Any discussion of Breillat must consider the ways in which her transcendent and progressive aims may nevertheless be compromised by the axiomatic heteronormativity which she shares with much of her context. Against this, in Chapter 3 we discuss the work of Guillaume Dustan and Erik Rémès, whose explicit representations of sexual activity intervene into debates about the place of gay and queer identities in contemporary France, particularly with reference to sexual practice in the light of the AIDS epidemic. Our account of their work focuses on its ethos of existential affirmation, its engagement with recent political arguments (from civil partnerships and same-sex parenting to the polemics around the rejection of safe sex), and considers identitarian questions of assimilation in relation to their use of figures of immediacy and transitivity to represent the relation of their writing to its world.

In Chapter 4, we consider the possibilities for revolution and reform that have traditionally informed the high-art appropriations of the pornographic and trace their irrevocable collapse in contemporary art. This dynamic is explored in relation to the modern fascination with the real in representation, the desire to pass beyond the limits of film and text and experience an act of supreme intensity. Using Bataille's concept of formlessness and Baudrillard's notion of the hyperreal, we explore the inevitable outcome of such overextended ambition, focusing on what has been termed by Ronald Jones a contemporary 'hover culture' of inertia and stasis (Jones 1988). As a consequence of progressive failure, we find in the place of revolution an endless fascination with revelation, with exploring the limits of subjectivity and the corporeal that may hope to provide impetus to political action, but which ultimately loses itself in the myriad dimensions of the abject.

Chapter 5 addresses two female authors whose spectacular success is inseparable from their use of sexually explicit material: Catherine Millet and Virginie Despentes. The governing aesthetics of the two are diametrically opposed: despite presenting a graphic memoir, Millet wishes to maintain a properly aesthetic distance from her reader, whereas Despentes' writing seeks to get as close as possible to the often seedy world it describes. They are joined, however, by the failure they share: predictably, Millet's hygienic distance from her reader proves highly unstable, while Despentes' desire to denounce the materialism of the world in which her texts are embedded leaves her in a highly contemporary tangle of critique and complicity.

Despentes' work, particularly in its use of sexually explicit material, thus forms a typical example of the problems facing the contemporary artist who wants to denounce the hegemony of consumer capitalism: with the artwork already thoroughly commodified, there is no external vantage point from which such a denunciation might be performed. This dilemma has been most extensively debated in relation to the work of Michel Houellebecq, considered in Chapter 6. Houellebecq's quintessentially contemporary stance sees him lamenting the miserable materialism of globalised capitalism in terms which displace this materialism to so minimal an extent that he appears unable to resist complicity with it. This is especially clear in his representations of sexual relations, in which his criticism of the pornographic reduction of human individuals to actors in a viciously competitive sexual marketplace finds expression through a combination of sentimentality and an often misogynistic repetition of precisely this reductive materialism. Houellebecq is left, we argue, dreaming of a utopian deliverance which he presents as accessible only via the very misery he longs to escape.

In Chapter 7, finally, we discuss the place of the child in these contemporary quasi-pornographic representations. While the notion of child pornography is anathema to all but a few, it is remarkable how frequently the issue of infantile eroticism occurs within contemporary texts, notably the growing number of narratives concerning instances of child abuse. The analysis here seeks to find the borderline between morally defendable exposures of child abuse and uncomfortably intimate representations of underage sexuality, constructing as it does so a different perspective on child sexuality as proposed by the work of Adam Phillips and Leo Bersani. It explores two different categories of texts; those that inhabit a supposedly ethical stance, and those that clearly abandon any ethical principles at all, considering how difficult it is to treat this topic within a culture that is internally conflicted over its own idealised images of childhood.

Our title, finally, is of course adapted from Marie Nimier's *La Nouvelle Pornographie* (2000), a witty reflection on the current cultural capital of the genre. (Nimier's text is discussed in Chapter 1 of the present volume.) It should be taken less as an assertion, however, than as an interrogation. Not all of the material we discuss in this study can be thought in any meaningful sense to be in the business of renewal, innovation, or reinvigoration, whether of the pornographic or anything else. In any case, as Nimier's ironic title tells us, parodying the endless lies of marketing, claims to innovation – especially in relation to so contested a field as pornography – might best be treated with a at least degree of scepticism. It might, that is, just be the same old naked emperor after all. But our suggestion, simply, is this: the works we will consider are producing explicit representations of sexual activity in ways that are not easily reducible to the categories of highbrow erotica as we might once have known them. Their specific differences have to do with the dominant presence of the pornographic as the code through which these representations are articulated. And their uses of this code may tell us something about the particular claims they have made, with such success, on the attention of our cultural moment. As in Brecht's advice to Benjamin, then, it is not with the good, old things, but with the bad, new ones, that we need to start.

Notes

1 It should be pointed out that the pornography in question is, over-whelmingly, heterosexual, and the works in question invariably hetero-centric, if not homophobic: the conservatism this implies is a significant indicator of the extent to which such reference has become a more or less unproblematically mainstream phenomenon. This is discussed further in Chapter 3 of the present volume.

2 For 'porn star' autobiographies, see HPG 2002 and Morgane 2003. A more critical account of life in the French pornography industry is given in Anderson 2001. For an excellent survey of these and other relevant developments in recent French culture, see Bourcier 2004, especially 13–14.

3 'Sexe et télé: La stratégie des chaînes' (online). Available from: www.leblogtvnews.com (accessed 18 November 2005).

4 On the 'mainstream' status of pornography (with specific reference to American culture), see Williams 2004: 1–2.

5 For good surveys of the recent lines of these debates, see Gibson 1993 and 2004; Cornell 2000; and Itzin 2001. The definitive academic discussion of the aesthetics of pornography remains Williams 1999; the development of the discipline of 'porn studies' is evidenced in Williams'

edited volume of this title (2004), whose introduction also provides an extremely useful survey of these debates. Very helpful definitional considerations may also be found in Dean 2000, especially 7–11.

6 *Les Inrockuptibles*, 504, 505, 506; *Sexe!* (triple edition, 27 July–16 August 2005); *L'Esprit Créateur*, 44/3 (Fall 2004); *Magazine littéraire*, 447 (November 2005), 26–8.

7 The Lacanian provenance of the term only underscores this lineage: as Catherine Clément reminds us (1981), Lacan's intellectual and biographical connections to this avant-gardism are extensive.

8 On this, see the arguments explored in the introduction to Hughes and Ince 1996, and in Worton 1998.

9 See Deleu 2002, Marzano 2003 and Mayné 2001. Baqué (2002) starts from a similar position, but develops a much less nostalgic argument. A generally less pessimistic approach to the issue may be found in Ogien 2003.

10 Lawrence Schehr's introduction to this collection (2004a, cited above) provides an outstanding account of the principal developments in question, and the issues at stake.

1

The battle of the sexes

Many of the texts and films that explore graphic sexuality through the citation of pornographic tropes maintain a focus that is resolutely heterocentric. While the sexual acts described are frequently tortuous, perverse, masochistic or simply bizarre, the authors and filmmakers who have reached prominence through this trend: Houellebecq, Breillat, Despentes, Millet, remain normatively heterosexual in their approach to the contemporary erotic. This can perhaps be explained, not as a reactionary oasis in the wilderness of modern mores, but as an inevitable consequence of the cultural concerns of such artistic practice, where pornographic tropes are consistently cited within social frameworks that are disintegrating or damaged, be they dysfunctional family structures, poverty and social exclusion, or the superficial image-dominated consumer society. Tracking the consequences of such postmodern cultural landscapes leads back to the microcosm of the family, and within that the heterosexual relation, as the focal point of social change. Our essentially heterocentric culture has regularly posited man and woman as cause and effect, question and response, yet these works set up the opposition this time in order to posit an insurmountable disjunction between them. And the pornographic relation, which is aesthetically supposed to facilitate the simplest of heterosexual transactions, is seen to be caught up in a web of demonic desires, violent drives and contemporary cultural alienation that obliges us to reconsider the very foundation of sexual identity. Ultimately, for these artists at least, we have to acknowledge the force of the 'hetero' in heterosexuality, and recognise that sexual intimacy between men and women in this contemporary aesthetic trend means negotiating non-negotiable difference.

Undoubtedly the representations we find in contemporary artworks that explore heterosexuality owe something to the significant

23

French feminist movement of the 1970s and 1980s. It is clear that woman no longer functions as a mirror to the man in contemporary narrative,[1] but it is not always clear how to define and understand her desire subsequently; women remain instead aligned with opacity and enigma, a not-so-unusual state of affairs, but one that provokes some extraordinary sexual encounters in the artworks under discussion. While pornography has traditionally been associated with male authorship, it is striking to note how many contemporary representations of explicit sexuality are produced by women, and focus on the trajectory of female erotic desire. The aim of this chapter is to explore the conflicted sexual space, considering the perspectives of men and women in turn, but starting somewhat unconventionally with women's art. The image women offer of heterosexual relations is a very particular one that provides a clear starting point for any analysis of the new pornographies.

Women on men: fantasy in practice

If we can see an important artistic trend emerging from the persistent literary appropriation of erotic and pornographic tropes, it is a movement which, for the first time in French intellectual artistic history, features as many authors and filmmakers who are women as it does men. Certainly the woman's voice is a powerful and extreme one, for we find again and again in these works a level of aggression and violence unparalleled in other eras of female creativity. For all their differing approaches and perspectives on eroticism, contemporary artworks by Catherine Breillat, Virginie Despentes and Catherine Millet (whose work will be explored in some detail in subsequent chapters) are generally characterised by a certain fearlessness and ruthlessness. They subject the current state of affairs in heterosexual relations to an unflinching and detailed dissection that knows no boundaries in the depths of emotions it will plunder, nor the furthest outreaches of sanity it will explore. Binding these texts and films together also is a continuous thread of discontent and dislocation, whereby distaste, misery and dissatisfaction are all projected onto, and worked through, the sexual encounter. Criticism surrounding these works so far has tended to emphasise their bleak and joyless nature, and one way to read these sexual acts would be to see in them the repository of all the discontent that remains unexpressed in gender relations. It is certainly the case that many of the sexual encounters appear to be undertaken by women as paradoxical combinations of revenge and recompense.[2] Yet it is also possible to trouble this simplistic reading, and to understand these representations of sexuality as offering radically alternative positions on the question of female desire that are intriguingly aligned with developments in the most recent feminist thought.

The work of Clotilde Escalle has risen to some critical prominence over the past ten years or so and provides a useful starting point in its excessively brutal and disturbing representations of hetero-sexuality. Escalle was named by the *Nouvel Observateur* as one of the original 'new barbarians' (Jacob 1999: 66), but while others have dropped from the public view or have moved on to embrace other subjects, Escalle has continued to focus on explicit sexuality with a series of texts designed to challenge erotic taboos. Incest, granny sex, sadomasochism and extreme sexual violence have all been explored within Escalle's troubling narratives, in which a lucid, simple style belies the turmoil of murky emotions that inform them. A particularly vicious and uncompromising portrait is drawn of the heterosexual arena. In her second novel, *Pulsion* (1996), the heroine, Pauline, is driven instinctually to give herself to any man who will take her. The novel opens on the aftermath of a fight with her boyfriend, and while the residual emotions from this event implicitly compel her to sex with a stranger, the fight turns out to be in any case the basic structure of emotional interaction with Frédéric: 'Sur le lit, ils se frappent. Se désirent et cognent. S'arrachent les cheveux, veulent s'étrangler' (1996: 7). [In bed they fight. Lust after each other and beat each other up. Pull their hair, try to strangle one another.] The desperation of heterosexuality, borne out of a longing to receive what the opposite sex seems unable to give, is writ large in Escalle's work. The simplicity of her style gives us to understand that we are dealing with fundamentals, with the brute (and brutal) force of desire that compels men and women to come together in what would seem to be inevitable ignorance and despair.

The man Pauline picks up subsequently, a driver who stops at the side of the road for her, is described as repulsive but she rapidly engages in dissatisfactory sex with him: 'Puis il la pénètre. Cet instant est très rapide. Elle veut le retenir, en le griffant, en le mordant. Déjà il se détourne d'elle, ouvre la portière et, le pantalon sur les cuisses, debout, de dos, jouit' (1996: 12). [Then he penetrates her. This is over very quickly. She wants to hold him back, clawing and biting at him. Already he turns away from her, opens the car door and, trousers around his knees, his back to her, he comes.] This asymmetrical coupling is symbolic of the disparity between men and women in their sexual responses, and revelatory also in the female protagonist of a troubling submission to male sexual power (visible also in the work of Despentes and Breillat). Men are represented as selfish sexual predators, ever ready to enter into loveless sexual contact with women, while women display a kind of unbalanced pragmatism, embracing whatever erotic experience comes their way. Pauline continues in her trajectory towards ever more masochistic sexual experience, becoming the abused plaything of a group of young boys on the beach. In such scenes Escalle's texts move to appropriate what has historically been a male-dominated tradition of eroticism uniting sexuality with extreme violence, as Pauline submits to a gang rape that leaves her broken and bleeding.[3] There is no sense, however, that Pauline can be termed a victim. She enters into these transactions willingly and repeatedly, clearly seeking to satisfy her own agenda, although whether she does so is less certain. In a textual move reminiscent of Bataille and Sade, the narrative moves on to the location of a locked hotel room, where Frédéric and Pauline find their liaison interrupted by an innocent third party, the hotel manager. The latter is initially concerned with their well-being and his hotel's reputation, but Pauline offers herself to him and he succumbs to sexual opportunism. The situation descends into sickening violence which, similarly to the experience of sexuality, works compulsively on the protagonists, ensnaring them in a net of intense emotions that neither resolves nor progresses the narrative. Instead sex and violence are depicted bluntly, without any attempt being made to render them significant.

However, Escalle's heroines all share a legacy of excessive maternal neglect, which impinges upon their sexual development, and offers some justification for their behaviour. Pauline's mother declares outright that 'Tu pourrais mourir, je n'en concevrais aucune peine' (1996: 17). ['You could die and I wouldn't feel any pain.'] Pauline's response to this is to 'se jette sur elle et cherche sa bouche pour l'embrasser' [throw herself upon her, seeking her mouth to kiss her]. Maternal repulsion is met and countered with a daughterly love that is sexual in its staging. Indeed, in Escalle's most recent text, *Où est-il cet amour?*, the abandoned daughter finds the comfort she craves with her nanny, Khadija in an eroticised form, lying on top of her and caressing her breasts and her sex. It is intriguing that what might in other texts be subsumed into a positive representation of homosexuality is recuperated into the heterosexual framework by Khadija's laughing cry at the start of their encounter 'Tu veux faire l'homme?' ['You want to play the man?'] (2001: 25). Rather than explore lesbian dimensions to sexuality, then, these texts literalise the Oedipal fantasy of sex with the mother. Escalle's texts manifest a fascination for Oedipal scenarios that are not abstract and fantastic, but personalised, acted out through manifestations of rage, hatred and erotic seduction in otherwise realistic family settings. This tendency to realise the structures of fantasy that underlie human relationships can be seen in the link between the title of the text, *Pulsion*, and the events within it. The term *'pulsion'* is Lacan's translation of Freud's term 'der Trieb' or what we might understand as a drive function, related to desire as its point of origin and its non-teleological dynamic force. It precedes the construction of subjectivity and, in its lack of personalisation, can be conceived of as posthumously surviving it. In Escalle's text the sexual behaviour of her protagonists can be read as a function of *pulsion*, the indestructible drive force that is beyond all meaning and all ethical endeavour, that simply compels her characters to intense experience beyond any understanding of that experience as good or bad, pleasurable or otherwise.

One way of reading these resistant texts, then, is to see them as depicting an unsignalled collapse of fantasy into reality. The apparent absence of a framework of fantasy within the text, helping to move the reader towards meaning creation by signalling the text's assumptions and responses, is in fact a consequence of the highly fantastised nature of the textual events themselves. Michael Worton proposes that 'the reader is drawn into these fictional worlds as if they are quite normal – and certainly the novels present them as such', and he goes on to argue that 'Escalle's work confronts the oppressive power of the normal by saying – simply, directly – that another world, another way of living is also normal, one in which the marginal, the silenced and the occulted become mainstream and are posited as the "norm"' (Worton and Rye 2004: 219–20). We could develop this argument by suggesting that part of what Escalle's texts stage as the 'norm' are the Oedipal and violent psychosexual dramas that underpin the erotic. In this heterosexual erotic, women are represented as choosing masochistic submission while men are sexual parasites, feeding off their compulsion to sexual activity. Inevitably this begs two questions: whether Escalle's excessive hostility between the sexes is indeed the magnification of a psychic actuality and also whether a state of declared warfare is essential to heterosexual erotic engagement.

This fantasy structure can be understood in part by an appeal to a recent feminist concept of the phallic masculine imaginary. Catherine Waldby discusses a certain representational structure of erotic relationships in which men seek 'always to be the destroyer, to refigure their women in their own interests but to resist such refiguration themselves' (Waldby 1995: 267). The support for such a fantasy is based in biology for, 'the mobile and indeterminate nature of women's boundaries renders the violation of women difficult, in the phallic imagination at least ... Specific instances of damage to women's bodily integrity do not count because women's bodies are considered to be already damaged, already transgressed' (1995: 268). Penetrative sex is the founding metaphor for the violable woman and, as a model of erotic relations, leads to the collapse of the distinction between sex and sexual violence. Moira Gatens has also argued that any work that posits the body of woman as a violable space and figures everyday intercourse as a form of rape is invariably under the sway of the phallic masculine imaginary.[4] The texts of Clotilde Escalle offer a clear manifestation of this form of heterosexual encounter and can be understood, via the theories proposed by Waldby and Gatens, as the realisation of a certain imaginative figuration of the relations between men and women. Escalle magnifies a particular understanding of heterosexuality in which biology becomes symbolism.

Such arguments come in response to the feminist anti-pornography writings of Andrea Dworkin and Catharine MacKinnon. This is not to say that their intent is in any way to promote the pornographic, but rather to clarify and critique the fantasies of heterosexual relations that underpin the Americans' perspective. It is indeed intriguing that the rush of sexually explicit artworks produced by women in France should follow so quickly on the heels of this highly visible feminist movement. At the time when *les nouveaux barbares* were being extolled in *Le Nouvel Observateur*, Carol Clover was declaring that: 'For better or worse, pornography has become the feminist issue of the decade' (Gibson 1993: 1). Dworkin and MacKinnon founded a vocal and widely publicised feminist campaign against pornography in order to bring to the light of day structures of abuse and degradation that they claimed informed women's daily lives, but which, paradoxically, were silenced in the name of free speech in America. Catharine MacKinnon argued that 'Our culture has become so saturated with pornography – the abuse of women protected as ideas – that men's sexual dominance over and dehumanization of women is reality: pornography constitutes social reality itself [...] women, too, are duped into believing in the patriarchal system that destroys their humanity and are fed illusions of moral power and sublimity to compensate for their disempowerment' (Dean 1996: 88). Caroline J. Dean suggests that this concept of relations is based on a certain understanding of men's reliance on pornography as a quest to dehumanise others in order to consolidate a sense of self, founded in an anxiety that intimacy will result in self-dissolution. She suggests that in this model, 'Pornography constructs men's emptiness as plenitude, their self-division as self-constitution' (1996: 92). It is interesting that, in the structuring fantasies of the vision of heterosexuality propounded by MacKinnon and Dworkin, women are precisely the ever-violated unboundaried body of the phallic imagination, while men, in their emptiness and insatiability, become vampiric and hystericised, troubled in their relation to power and self-possession. The pornographic interaction thus comprised a simple exchange of demonised gender images, women subsumed by a masculine fantasy of invasiveness, men revealed as a reviled image of femininity. The absolute values of the anti-pornography movement were reflected in the absolute strategies it proposed for women to combat the insidiously harmful heterosexual climate. Dean glosses it thus: 'again and again, anti-pornography feminists reiterate the idea that for women, sexuality and selfhood are entirely incompatible in our culture' (1996: 93).

Extreme as this account of heterosexual relationships may be, its structure is undeniably present in a wide range of works. Men's 'hatred' of women, and women's abject sexual subservience are fundamental to the novels of Escalle, to Virginie Despentes' revenge fantasy, *Baise-moi*, and are readily identifiable in the steady stream of sadomasochistic erotic literature that has been published recently by authors such as Florence Dugas, Marthe Blau and Vanessa Duries.[5] But the question clearly arises, how to read the French artworks that reproduce these violent, misogynistic pornographic tropes when they come, precisely, in the wake of a highly visible anti-pornography movement? Do they pose a provocative challenge to a misplaced moral code that would refuse to see the erotic in the aggressive? Or do they rather represent the inevitable outcome of misogynistic pornography in their abusive and troubling hetero-sexual scenarios? Do these texts believe in the pervasiveness of the heterosexual relationships they represent, or is their very internal contradictoriness and excessiveness the indication of an implicit critique? One way forward might be to consider them as aesthetically related to a wider, contemporary multimedia movement involving visual, installation and performance art produced by women and concerning the image of women. Artists as diverse as Orlan and Cindy Sherman have produced artworks manifesting a similar fascination with female 'degradation', and with ugliness and abject corporeality.[6] These works also signal an ambiguous challenge to masculine fantasies of women's erotic desirability: Griselda Pollock asks: 'Does Sherman's "ugly" phase instate women's internalised misogynistic revulsion? Is it aimed at culture's repressions or the whole structure of feminine masquerade? Does it inscribe a new movement, a postmodern sense of the body that oscillates between horror and frankness about mutability, mortality, dreaming of an escape from the disciplining of bodies into conventional sexualities, genders, identities?' (2003: 191). The texts under discussion here are as brutal and provocative as Sherman's photography, and they too appropriate culturally commodified images of women and play them out against disturbing images of corporeal disgust. What arises from the comparison with Sherman is the recognition that contem-porary art by women is fascinated by pervasive, negative images of women that circulate in modern culture, and the extent to which those images become incorporated in female subjectivity. They play precisely upon the ambiguity between fantasy and reality, presenting disturbing imaginary dimensions of womanhood as if they were real, in other words collapsing the (hostile) cultural and the ontological. Their engagement with pornography can be understood as entirely pertinent when we consider that it, too, is conflicted in the same way as Sherman's photographs. Caroline Dean defines this conflict, asking: 'Is pornography the actual spectacle of corporeal abasement that symbolizes ethical degradation, an image or description of that spectacle, or a fantasy about it?'(2000: 10).

There is no resolution as such to the layered, multi-dimensional space of the pornographic in works of art by French women; the difficulty of assigning truth value to their disturbing representations of women becomes one of the central aesthetic strengths of the art. The uncertain play of fantasy and reality fascinates without providing any toeholds for the construction of meaning, undermining the reader's and spectator's ability to judge and interpret the eruption of a certain misogynistic masculine imaginary into the representation of sexual women. However, other French women authors use pornographic tropes in very different ways; as an intriguing contrast we need to consider fictional works which challenge the assumption, as intrinsic to Pollock's account of Sherman's work as it is in the narratives of Escalle, that images of graphic sexuality go hand in hand with female debasement. With a change of perspective in mind, it is worth considering the altogether different texts by Alina Reyes and Marie Nimier that use pornographic tropes to explore the possibility of successful heterosexual relations in which women hope to find their subjectivity celebrated. What is at stake in these texts is in some ways more subversive than this negative, troubled vision of heterosexuality, which relies, partially at least, on a conventional contamination of the pornographic by masculine fantasy. Instead, these texts attempt to construct a new relationship between women and pornography that embraces new critical thinking on the nature of desire.

Alina Reyes was arguably one of the first literary women writers to focus exclusively on pornographic material, coming to prominence with her 1988 text, *Le Boucher*. In this very short récit, a young woman experiences sexual ecstasy with the eponymous butcher of the title, the narrative aligning male predatory sexual power with vivid and disturbing descriptions of the preparation of raw meat. Her most recent text, *Sept nuits*, details the gradual escalation of sexual game play between two new lovers who decide to postpone penetrative intercourse until their seventh night together. Reyes' aim here is to write pornographic literature from a female perspective that would serve to stimulate women. This is also the contract undertaken by the narrator in Marie Nimier's *La Nouvelle Pornographie*. Nimier's text recounts the problematic path of its narrator, an author repeatedly identified with Nimier herself, to produce a collection of pornographic tales for her demanding publisher, Gabriel. In this endeavour she receives the ambiguous help of her sexually active flatmate, Aline. The focus here is upon a more optimistic appropriation of pornographic tropes: Reyes' texts aim to articulate female sexuality; Nimier's text aims to articulate the hopes underlying and informing female sexuality. The first point to note about these texts (and in fact we can include in this artworks by Catherine Breillat and Blau),[7] is the structural dominance of the contract that binds men and women together. Reyes' artificial seven nights and Marie's publishing contract imply a need for women to stake some legal hold over men if they are to maintain male interest long enough to satisfy their erotic requirements. We may also note the extent to which the men in these texts disappear to leave the textual space free for the woman's processes of self-creation and self-analysis. While the male protagonists in *Pulsion*, and *Où est-il cet amour?* were hardly complex characters, they nevertheless provided an essential origin for hostility; they played an equal part in the representation of conflicted heterosexuality. In Reyes' texts the men are reduced to their body parts, subject to the same fetishising fragmentation as women in traditional pornography. Equally Marie's publisher, a would-be progressive who cannot quite overcome embedded conventionality, is never more than a pretext for romance, and Marie's desire crystallises around his image without any obvious motivation beyond his involvement in their contract.

While Reyes and Nimier both explore at length women's relation to the erotic, neither mentions the significance of the contract, nor the solipsistic appropriation their female characters make of the male protagonist, in terms of the fantasies they entertain and explore concerning the nature of his desire. In this way, the blind spot of women's relation to their own eroticism is to conflate the conditions for prostitution with the context for romance. Where a man's sexual engagement in a woman is required for that woman's own sense of self-creation (and here we might have to wonder whether any man would do), the commercial transaction proves to be, in these texts at least, a necessary prerequisite, as if in the absence of financial obligation, a man would not renounce the cultural world for the sake of a woman. Yet his presence in the relationship is an odd mixture of necessity and indifference. Furthermore, the concept of 'being in love' in these texts is, by implication, far from altruistic; it can be seen as a woman's strategy designed to prolong, intensify and thus illuminate the inner psychodrama provoked by the presence of the man. The inner contradictions of these texts, in their desire to combine pornographic tropes with more conventional love narratives, produce some quite extraordinary narrative consequences.

Alina Reyes' texts distinguish themselves from Nimier's by their immersion in pornographic images, and, in this respect, they are more closely aligned to the artworks by Escalle and Despentes. Both *Le Boucher* and *Sept nuits* are structured as seductions, with the notable difference in *Sept nuits* that it is the man who is the figure of restraint, who provides the legislating 'no' to the woman's rampant desire. While the butcher is the eponymous embodiment of male predatory desire, the male protagonist in *Sept nuits* is portrayed as fragile and uncertain. 'C'est nous qui sommes fendues, mais c'est eux qui sont blessés' (2005: 21) ['We are the ones with the crack, but they are the ones who are damaged'] Reyes' narrator tells us. While this is accompanied by a certain idolisation of the male, the reader is lead to wonder whether this is not also a subversive way of emphasising female strength. Looking at herself in the mirror, the heroine declares: 'Toute femme est un homme qui a sa femme en elle, une femme pour qui elle bande tant qu'elle ne sait si elle doit la cacher ou la donner à tout venant…' (2005: 63). ['Every woman is a man who has a woman inside, a woman for whom she has such a hard-on that she doesn't know whether to hide it away or to give it to anyone who comes along … '.] Indeed, the giving of the self to *le premier venu* in the aftermath of what should have been the climactic scene (in all senses), becomes the most intriguing feature of both texts, and again questions the primacy of the man in these scenarios. Once Reyes' heroine has finally succumbed to the butcher's desire, she goes to a nightclub, picks up a stranger with whom she has sex in the woods and wakes up paralysed in a ditch. The woman is by no means victimised, rather, she remains triumphant in the satisfaction of her desire. In *Sept nuits*, the final penetrative sex scene takes place on a boat; when dawn breaks the heroine slips out of her lover's embrace in order to have sex with the cabin boy, and rather than infidelity, it is represented as a kind of excessive extension of faithful desire: 'il me regardait le regarder dans mon plaisir, sachant que je ne pourrais jamais, jamais épuiser mon désir de lui, et que c'était pour nous deux une bénédiction et une malediction' (2005: 75). ['he watched me watching him through my pleasure, knowing I could never, never exhaust my desire for him, and that it was both a blessing and a curse for us'.] My suggestion here is that the desire of which the heroine speaks, referring to its object as the ambiguous and anonymous 'lui', is more likely to be desire directed towards the internalised male that was formerly glimpsed in the mirror image. Indeed, for both of Reyes' heroines, the sexuality they display is a self-powered, tireless dynamic that perpetually exceeds its objects and encompasses both gender positions. In this sense, it echoes the concept of desire elucidated by Gilles Deleuze, which has been much in evidence in the most recent writings of feminist theoreticians.

Claire Colebrook proposes that for Deleuze: 'Desire begins impersonally and collectively, and from a multiplicity of investments which traverse persons' (Colebrook 2002: 141). In consequence: 'The forces of life exceed the simple actual bodies we perceive; we repress the excess, violence and disruption of life – the creative forces that transgress the boundaries of persons or intentions' (2002: 142). In a formulation that appeals to the representation of desire so prevalent in the artworks under discussion, Deleuze proposes that:

> le désir ne menace pas une société parce qu'il est désir de coucher avec la mère, mais parce qu'il est révolutionnaire. Et cela veut dire, non pas que le désir est autre chose que la sexualité, mais que la sexualité et l'amour ne vivent pas dans la chambre à coucher d'Oedipe, ils rêvent plutôt d'un grand large, et font passer d'étranges flux qui ne se laissent pas stocker dans un ordre établi. (Deleuze and Guattari 1972: 138)

> [desire does not threaten a society because it is a desire to sleep with the mother, but because it is revolutionary. That does not at all mean that desire is something other than sexuality, but that sexuality and love do not live in the bedroom of Oedipus, they dream instead of wide-open spaces, and cause strange flows to circulate that do not let themselves be stocked within an established order. (Deleuze and Guattari 2000: 116)]

Subsequently, Deleuze and Guattari develop the significant concept of 'becoming-woman', a notion based on the recognition that the Oedipal prohibition of incest makes 'woman' what must be repressed and excluded in order to found human history. The idea of becoming-woman would thus function as 'the opening for a new understanding of desire that does not begin with the loss or repression of an original object'; it would mean 'thinking of the becoming of woman, not as a sex, but as the opening to "a thousand tiny sexes"' (Colebrook 2002: 143). This unboundaried and multiple form of desire is uncannily exemplified in the excessive cry of Reyes' heroine that 'je n'aurais pas eu assez de mille mains, de milles bouches, de mille cuisses ouvertes, pour l'aimer à fond. Et que je n'aurais pas eu assez de deux sexes, un de femme et un d'homme, pour le baiser comme je l'aurais voulu' (2005: 71). ['I would never have enough thousands of hands, thousands of mouths, thousands of open thighs to love him through and through. And I would never have enough of both sexes, one female, one male, to fuck him like I wanted to.'] The feminist engagement with Deleuzian theory has focused upon the woman as site of multiple investments[8] and upon the inside–outside border of the body as malleable and perpetually in a process of (re) creation,[9] interests that are entirely in keeping with the representations of gendered sexuality in the texts of Reyes and Nimier, in which the female sexual body becomes a site of multiple investments that play with gender relations to power. It is intriguing to note that the dominant fantasies surrounding and constructing women's image of her sexual body in these texts are once again ascribed to, and supposedly still originate from, the masculine imaginary. Unlike the texts by Escalle, however, where the eruption is hostile and abusive, shutting down the self-reflexive dimension of the narrative, this occurs often in the absence of actual male engagement and it is by no means depicted as an uncreative state of affairs.

In Marie Nimier's *La Nouvelle Pornographie*, sexual relationships are explored through a narrative that manipulates two levels of engagement; one dimension of the story representing the narrator's troubled love life, the other reflecting on the very nature of graphic sexuality. These modes can be seen interacting in the highly postmodern account the author/narrator, Marie, gives of the task set: 'ce que j'écrivais puisqu'il faut bien reconnaître que j'étais seule à tenir la plume, pouvait, d'après Gabriel, être perçu comme un objet naviguant à la frontière des deux mondes, en équilibre instable, à la fois répugnant et désirable, pour un même lecteur, et au même instant' (Nimier 2002: 102). ['what I was writing, for after all it must be admitted that I alone held the pen, could, according to Gabriel, be perceived as an object navigating in unstable equilibrium the frontier between two worlds, an object that would be both repulsive and desirable to the same reader at the same time'.] The representation of sexuality as both unpalatable and attractive is part of the contradictory impulse in the text towards the experience of the erotic. An understanding of the sexual subject as split in irreconcilable ways is maintained and developed throughout the text, in the representation of woman as torn between a traditional domestic servitude and a new sexual incarnation, in the split perspective on pornography as both sensually arousing and simultaneously clichéd and risible, and in the split in the narrator between her old, cautious *pudique* self, and the sexually outgoing, erotically adventurous woman her tales privilege. This fractured narrative is constructed from a complex interweaving of fantasy and reality, as the narrator plunders her memories and dreams and follows the train of her thoughts into sexual daydreams. The erotic subjectivity displayed by the narrator is thus unstable, uncertain and represented as engaged in a perpetual process of becoming. In sexual matters, as in authorial ones, Nimier's text articulates a paradoxical subjectivity that *in its very contradictions* finds satisfaction and release. At its basis is a celebration of the paradox of unified multiplicity that recalls Deleuze: 'Je comprends ce désir de se mettre entre parenthèses, ce besoin d'être contraint pour se dépasser. Il ne s'agit pas de résoudre quelque chose, ni de se guérir, mais de se dissoudre jusqu'à retrouver la force primordiale qui nous agit' (2002: 167). ['I understand this desire to put oneself between brackets, this need to be constrained in order to overreach oneself. It's not about resolving or curing something, but about dissolving the self to the point of uncovering the primordial force within that drives us.'] Far from attempting a resolution of this complexity, Nimier's text portrays the complexity itself as an accurate account of postmodern sexuality for women.

As the text unfolds, conventional pornographic scenarios are increasingly replaced by unusual, highly individualised encounters. Searching for personal anecdotes that would provide the impetus for an erotic tale there is actually very little in the way of graphic sex. Instead Nimier recalls a formative experience of a Chinese man falling asleep on her lap in a plane. This leads to a subsequent encounter with a Chinese stranger in Paris who reminds her of the first man and to whose hotel room she goes. Once there, although the stage is set for sex, Nimier ends up sitting on the bed, drawing on his bottom with a blue Biro. When he seems to want more she inserts the Biro into his anus and then slips quietly away. What seems new about these new pornographies is the absence of seamless, mechanical sex, and its replacement with a hesitant, fragile eroticism that pursues precisely the moments of self-shattering failed negotiation with the world that produce a sexualised response. In contradistinction to the majority of texts exploring female eroticism, Nimier's displays a salutary respect for the dangers and anxieties lurking within the intense sexual encounter. One telling anecdote concerns a close friend, an otherwise sensible, responsible girl called Lisa who suffers a breakdown provoked by a kind of destabilising immersion in the erotic. 'Elle avait commencé par aborder des inconnus dans la rue en leur proposant de coucher avec elle. Elle prétendait qu'ils la suivaient et que la seule façon de se débarrasser d'eux était de satisfaire leur désir' (2002: 123). ['She had begun by approaching strangers in the street and offering to sleep with them. She claimed they were following her, and the only way to get rid of them was to satisfy their desire.'] This state of affairs goes from bad to worse: 'Vers minuit, elle se déshabilla en plein carrefour sous prétexte qu'un automobiliste l'avait regardée de travers'. ['Towards midnight she took all her clothes off in the middle of a roundabout on the grounds that a driver had given her a funny look.'] Lisa is eventually hospitalised, and worse still, marries her analyst. This dark and troubling anecdote offers a different but utterly pertinent take on contemporary sexuality. Why create elaborate, melodramatic scenarios to summon the erotic, when the erotic is entirely inescapable? Lisa's madness is the madness of resignation to a sexuality that is never truly absent from subjectivity, that is thanklessly, relentlessly pervasive. Lisa, unlike the beaten and abused heroines of texts by Escalle and Reyes, could figure as a true victim of the contemporary erotic imagination. After all, there is a recognisable pornographic logic involved in instantly undressing the moment a man looks at you. Yet to actually do so could be understood as the disturbing consequence of transposing fantasy into reality with insufficient respect for their borderlines.

While many of the contemporary texts that cite pornography may be considered guilty of just that, Nimier's text is fascinated by the passage from normality to the bizarre and *imprévisible* world of the erotic. It is a text in which the chain of metonymic associations is repeatedly broken by the figure of the palimpsest, the underlying experience that reverberates through into the present. The confusing dynamics of the text are compounded by the surprises the erotic holds in store; its ability to be sought futilely and then to crop up when least expected. Nimier's narrative does not embrace the linear, end-oriented structure of classic pornography in which fantasy effortlessly slides into reality, instead she represents fantasy and reality as radically heterogeneous, and yet utterly seduced by one another, desperately seeking to unite with one another across a rag-bag of fragmentary, uncontrollable experience. Her text charts the chancey, destabilising moments of their collision, when the fantasy frame finally slides into place. In this way, Nimier's text is fascinated with this figure of the '*glissement*', of the slide into erotic fantasy, of the undressing of language to reveal its sexual intent. Nimier shows how this slide, or turn into eros can occur anywhere, under any conditions, and often the most banal. The madness of Nimier's friend, Lisa, can be understood as a surrender to the unbearable tension of waiting for this *glissement* to occur; a recognition of the pressing nature of the sexual whose conditions for genesis are difficult to create consciously, and equally ready to assail the individual at any moment. Much more powerful than the stagy violence of contemporary pornography, is the tiny, subversive movement of the '*glissement*' by means of which the fantasy frame of the erotic overwhelms the unsuspecting self.

Nimier's new pornography is a complex mix of differing levels of fantasy within a subject who is also irreconcilably split between dream and possibility. But how are we to conceive of the heterogeneous spaces that her text describes? As early as 1967 Foucault was arguing that 'L'époque actuelle serait peut-être plutôt l'époque de l'espace. Nous sommes à l'époque du simultané, nous sommes à l'époque de la juxtaposition, à l'époque du proche et du lointain, du côte à côte, du dispersé' (Foucault 1994: 752). ['The present epoch will perhaps be above all the epoch of space. We are in the epoch of simultaneity: we are in the epoch of juxtaposition, the epoch of the near and far, of the side-by-side, of the dispersed' (1986: 22).] Foucault had resolutely material and geographical spaces in mind, but one of the figures he draws out for special note, the heterotopia, may interest us here. This postmodern space is the site of an internal contradiction, for heterotopias encompass radically different spaces that have erupted within conventional reality, such as the prison or the clinic. Foucault provides a map of geographical space, but can we not transfer it onto gendered psychical space to account for the way that the masculine phallic imaginary erupts in the space of the female pornographic imagination? In the way that 'l'hétérotopie a le pouvoir de juxtaposer en un seul lieu réel plusieurs espaces, plusieurs emplacements qui sont en eux-mêmes incompatibles' (1994: 758) ['heterotopia is capable of juxtaposing in a single place several spaces, several sites that are themselves incompatible' (1986: 26)], might we be able to envisage the postmodern space of the female erotic as described by Marie Nimier? If we take the concept as a paradigm for female sexual selfhood, we can envisage a subject who is a composite of contradictory fantasy images, memories and experiences that exist simultaneously and in heterogeneous juxtaposition to one another. Of course this means that the feminine sexual imagination might also be composed of reactionary, self-despising and vengeful erotic images, throwbacks to a more traditional, hierarchical gender structure, but equally there is nothing to say that such internalised images might not also offer perverse and creatively stimulating pleasures of their own. What we can say is that, if we are to explore the inherent contradictions of female sexuality further, there must be some analysis of the fantasies by means of which women interact with and fantasise men, for it is undoubtedly a truth of asymmetrical gender relations that men do not write about the fantasies informing the images women create of them. By contrast there can be no theory of the female (sexual) subject that is not deeply entrenched in the tracking and creating of fantasies, that would seem to be predominantly masculine, to the point that, as Breillat declares: 'La vraie possession vois-tu, car malgré tout c'est de possession qu'il s'agit, est purement chimérique, c'est celle qu'accorde le peu de réalité de l'acte à l'amplitude désespérée de nos rêves' (2001b: 110). ['You see real possession (for despite everything possession is the key) is a pure illusion; it's the illusion that the unreality of the act accords to the desperate magnitude of our dreams.']

Men on women: the destructive muse

There is an intriguing short story by Stéphane Zagdanski entitled 'La matrice d'art' that brings together some of the tropes that repeatedly occur in the representation of women in contemporary pornographic artworks by men. In this short story our male narrator attends an exhibition of Picasso's pictures of bullfights and notices a woman, Lise, whose erratic progression around the canvasses intrigues him. His aim at first is a masterful, pedagogic one, as he believes women cannot understand painting. He intercepts her and treats her to a disquisition on Picasso and Hemingway that is highly eroticised and although 'Lise semblait épuisée par mon bavardage' (Zagdanski 2005: 00) ['Lise seemed exhausted by my verbosity'], she invites him back to her place and they make love. Once back in her own space, Lise rallies and the tables are turned. The place of male rhetoric is superseded by female vocal musicality as Lise expresses her pleasure in 'une litanie hululée, une sorte de refrain trempé dans l'aigu qui triturait mon épine dorsale' (2005: 87). ['a screeching litany, a kind of refrain that had been steeped in shrillness and that pummeled away at my dorsal spine'.] Out of this inarticulate song, our narrator eventually identifies the word 'Ipousteguy', and deeply affected by the erotic experience he has undergone he seeks its meaning. He discovers it is the name of a contemporary sculptor whose work is dominated by sex and death, and intended to be 'un rappel à la conscience, aux contradictions, aux inquiétudes et jusqu'aux erreurs de l'homme moderne' (2005: 89). [a reminder of the conscience, the contradictions, the anxieties and even the mistakes of modern man.] The narrator's fascination with Lise's song is matched by an obsession with her sex and inevitably a series of erotic encounters leads him to deduce an enigmatic union between Ipousteguy and Lise's vagina, which he is determined to resolve. His solution is to give Lise a hefty dose of sedative and to examine her sex, working from the assumption that it is somehow autonomous from the woman. Indeed he is in for something of a surprise. When he touches her, 'sa vulve se déploya comme une pliage japonais' [her vulva unfurled like a bit of Japanese origami] revealing deep within the face of a woman. Not just the face, but what turns out to be an entire 'cinématographe génital' (genital cinematography) where he sees in quick succession 'Un homme tenant un verre. Un pénis en érection. Un pénis en forme de note de musique. Une femme se caressant' (2005: 93). ['a man holding a glass. An erect penis. A penis shaped like a musical note. A woman caressing herself'.] Our narrator's first response is to feel belittled, his verbosity trivialised by her carnality. His response, however, is vengeful: he rapes her; and subsequently appropriative: he marries her.

   In this extraordinary short story we find not only a comprehensive account of the fears and fantasies that surround female sexuality for men, but also an indication of the way that the contemporary epoch has altered the male gaze. The story hinges upon the unseen work of Ipousteguy and his stated aim to represent male anxiety and error. Before the evocation of Ipousteguy, the narrator was safe and secure in his masculine, discursive mastery of art. He was able to indicate to Lise that the 'seul organe à demeurer semblable à lui-même' (2005: 84) ['the only organ to remain recognisably itself'] in all the differing representations of that most macho of activities, the bullfight, was the penis. His sexual encounter with Lise, however, destabilises not only his aesthetic ideology but also (because the two are implicitly linked) his sense of gender superiority. She has the better relationship to art of the two of them, not because she can appreciate it, but because she can embody it. The concept of rhetorical mastery, symbolised by the phallus, is replaced by the creative carnality of art, represented through the vagina. While there may still be a residual polarity here between (male) mind and (female) body, that binary opposition is undermined by the knowingness assigned to the vagina, in the image of the eye that catches out the onlooker, reminding him of his culpability. It is possible to read an allusion to Bataille's *Histoire de l'œil* here, and the reproachful eye of Marceline that stares back out of Simone's vulva at the unnamed narrator, but the context of the two narratives is significantly different in terms of gendered power relations. In Bataille's tale, Marceline has been the brutalised victim of Simone's and the narrator's sexual game play; her suffering has intensified their pleasure. In Zagdanski's story, Lise has triumphed (albeit unconsciously – in a literal sense) over the narrator and humiliated him in a field of accomplishment he thought he had conquered. As if to emphasise this, the moving art gallery of her vulva contains both male and female sexual symbols, implying that his sexual potency in art has been co-opted by the woman. Woman's relationship to artistic creation and to artists is here entirely transformed; she has become a new kind of work of art, and one that most certainly embodies and performs the narrator's anxieties and errors. In this tale the woman as erotic *objet d'art* is transformed by becoming herself an artist, the source and the site of a new form of creativity that encompasses both male and female sexuality, signalling an autonomy and omnipotence in art that women have rarely known before.

While the role of the woman has changed significantly in this tale, men have maintained some notable constants. Despite the differences between Bataille and Zagdanski's texts, what links them across almost ninety years of literary history is the impact made on the narrator by the sight of the female genitals. While in the previous section, the vagina provided a powerful influence on the female imaginary, it was often in a derogatory or pejorative sense, a 'trou' or 'gouffre' breaching the body's boundaries and inciting male violence. For Zagdanski (and for Bataille), the vulva may well remain the point of access to a woman's subjectivity, and an access often gained in unethical ways, but it simultaneously works a kind of black magic on its viewer. The secret part of a woman is fanta-sised as a kind of treasure trove; a repository of primal knowledge, or supernatural creativity that is entirely alien to men and whose absence they bitterly resent. Indeed, the site/sight of lack so influ-ential to the work of western feminists in the 1980s has altered significantly; there is most certainly something now in the place of nothing.[10] But what that something is, is still up for discussion. Marie Nimier in *La Nouvelle Pornographie* talks of the sight of the vagina in pornographic movies as 'la dimension sublime de nos corps, leur dimension sacrée, sans maquillage putassier, sans déguisement avilissant ni vaseline sur l'objectif, et qu'il s'agissait là du plus bel homage que l'on puisse nous rendre' (2002: 165). ['the sublime dimension of our bodies, their sacred dimension, free from whorish makeup or degrading disguise, or Vaseline on the lens, and that such a sight would constitute the most beautiful homage we could be paid.'] Nimier's vision is fundamentally misjudged for she imagines such images prove to men that the fearsome vagina does not in fact possess teeth. Having calmed such primal fears, the need to 'combler' (fill a gap, in the sense of making good) a woman will seem no longer necessary, with the result that there can be lucid communication between men and women by means of an untroubled and untroubling image of womanhood. Zagdanski's short story does not embrace such a utopian future, however. The acknowledgement of power invested in the female genitals provokes not a communication but an appropriation. Lise is put back in her place, back in the conventional masculine phallic imaginary that is to say, with the narrator's 'gentle' act of rape, and she is then incar-cerated in marriage and held hostage night after night to the man's solitary, egotistical *jouissance*. The acknowledgment of a specific subjectivity in women, and a hypnotic, erotic, creative one at that, has a far from calming effect on male anxieties.

'La matrice d'art' provides a contemporary view on the battle between the sexes from the male point of view, and asks us to recon-sider women in an updated version of a very old role; the artistic muse. Zagdanski's story explores the consequences of a woman taking over the traditionally male domain of artistic creation and reveals a jealous defensive impulse in its narrator to sequestrate lost power. The relationship between women and creativity has been at the heart of recent psychoanalytic research into the changing gender roles in postmodern society. Rosalind Minsky outlines the situation whereby: 'In a culture where many women no longer collude with many men's views of them as predominantly passive, lacking and vulnerable, many men suddenly find themselves without women onto whom they can project their own unconscious lack, loss and envy, and may feel overwhelmed by feelings they never know they had' (Minsky 1998: 107). Drawing on a range of classical theorists including Horney, Winnicott and Bion, Minski develops a theory of masculinity which marks a return to Karen Horney's 1932 proposition that men are fundamentally envious of women's capacity for motherhood, in the sense that the loss of identification with the mother can provide a stumbling block to development which is never fully recompensed. In the absence of an obvious compensation for foreclosure to the realm of the maternal, the boy child makes a cultural bargain instead. Minsky proposes that 'The child denies in-sight (in-visibility?) into the powerful creative meaning of the mother in favour of the sight or visibility of the phallus which is subsequently discovered to signify cultural power' (1998: 112). This is all very well while the genders agree a division of labour, with nurture assigned to woman and culture to men. Once this bargain breaks down, however, the situation for men is decidedly perplexing: 'In male phantasy, women's power threatens to run out of control as soon as she seriously enters culture as if she too is a subject and demonstrates her intellectual and creative as well as physical and emotional capacities' (1998: 119). Minsky suggests that cruelty towards women and the exclusion of women from political power are ways to prevent men from succumbing to a kind of psychic annihilation and overwhelming feelings of emptiness and envy.

The figure of the muse provides a significant position from which to view this situation, not least because it is striking just how often such a trope appears in contemporary texts and films when the masculine viewpoint is privileged. Minksy suggests that the figure of the female muse is itself a symptom of womb-envy, and indeed, Elisabeth Bronfen details the changing representation of the muse from a feminist standpoint, tracing the gradual annihilation of the spirit and then finally the actual body of the woman from classical to modern art. In its earliest conception, the relationship between artist and muse was one of reciprocity, the woman offering the man access to memory and knowledge that he lacked, the man producing an autonomous text that effaced the woman's materiality but celebrated her involvement. Such an exchange implied a lack on the part of the man that could only be filled by a momentary loss of self-possession as he was inhabited by the power and insight of the muse. Bronfen notes with a certain irony that in the historical movement from classical Greece to Augustan Rome the poet 'no longer feels himself the creature of some higher power, but assumes that his own creative potency is sufficient' (Bronfen 1992: 364). Poetic genius is now innate, rather than inspired and the muse is more of a guardian angel than a divine conduit. By the Romantic age, however, a further deformation had been wrought on the relationship with the best muse now proving to be a dead one. Bronfen reads into this twist a patriarchal act of mastery and control over the lost woman that is intended to be definitive. It also marks a significant veiling of the woman that is equally her exclusion from the realm of artistic creativity: 'With the dead beloved acting as source for poetic inspiration, what is at stake is the preference for distance, for the textual copy of the beloved, for a vicarious and mitigated Romantic experience' (1992: 365). The contemporary return to the figure of the muse troubles this ultimately safe relationship between man and woman, for, as Zagdanski's text demonstrates, the current cultural climate acknowledges an altered relationship between women and creativity in which women can no longer be assigned a purely passive role. In the masculine imagination, women's creativity is confused with her maternity, her physical role as genetrix merging with her capacity for genesis. Zagdanski's text points to Courbet's *L'Origine du monde* as his predecessor, but in his contemporary tale Romantic mitigation and mediation of the woman have been replaced most threateningly with the real thing. The contemporary fascination with the pornographic in a postmodern age of extreme visibility and high anxiety engages with the muse as erotic spectacle in a way that demonstrates both an authentic desire for truth and certainty on the part of the male author, yet draws him into a potentially dangerous relationship with the sexual woman.

We can see this dynamic in action in Cédric Kahn's 1998 film, *L'Ennui*. It tells the story of the anxiety-ridden philosophy professor, Martin, who, in the wake of his marriage break-up, meets the young, erotic, enigmatic artist's model, Cécilia. The circumstances of the encounter are important for they set up a pattern that exerts a hypnotic hold over the male protagonist. Dissatisfied with his life and his job, Martin is trawling the streets in his car one evening and follows a couple who intrigue him. At first the relationship between

the much older man and the young girl seems harmonious, but at
a street corner they brawl, engaging in a brief, physical struggle,
before the man walks on alone. Martin parks and follows the man
into a sex club. He watches the man whose face in the dingy lighting
of the club is a terrible death's mask, his eyes ringed with darkness,
as if in a hellish torment. As the man goes to leave he finds he has
forgotten his wallet and his distracted attempts at self-justification
are met with violence from the doorman. Martin rescues him, paying
what he owes, and in the guise of a bond, the man insists he takes
the wrapped painting he is carrying. When Martin tries to return the
painting, he finds the house empty and is informed by a neighbour
that the painter has died during an intense sexual act. Martin returns
home and unwraps the painting, which is of a naked woman. In a
brusque volte-face he returns to the studio to find the model for
the painting, the young woman he saw accompanying Meyers that
night, on the point of departure. Their first encounter sets the pattern
for those that will follow. Martin questions the girl closely about her
relationship with the painter, Meyers, in a tone that is demanding
and interrogative. It becomes apparent that Meyers was sexually
obsessed with Cécilia although in the early stages of their relationship he had seemed indifferent. Cécilia was attracted to Meyers
because he reminded her of her father, to whom she has a passionate
attachment. Without any signalled moment of transition, Martin
is obsessed with the ghost of Meyers and with what Cécilia represented to him. This instant identification is performed sexually in the
next scene as Cécilia enters his apartment and wordlessly removes
her clothes, before Martin pounces on her in a brutal but intense
sexual encounter. But his quest for the meaning of their relationship and his desire to resolve the enigma of the muse are destined to
be repeatedly frustrated. Cécilia responds serenely to his post-coital
questions while refusing to assign reasons to emotions, passively
resisting Martin's challenge that 'il y a toujours une raison pour
chaque chose' with her inarticulate 'sais pas' and 'ça s'explique pas'.
['there's a reason for everything' ... 'dunno' ... 'you can't explain it'.]
In the absence of enlightenment, or perhaps as a process of enlightenment, Martin's trajectory will increasingly come to resemble that
of Meyers as he becomes sexually obsessed with Cécilia, craving her
body while detesting her stolid resistance.

The lengthy scenes of sexual intercourse thus symbolise and
display all there is to know about Cécilia, the spectator sharing

voyeuristically the same relationship with her as Martin, seeing all there is to see of her, and becoming in consequence frustrated by her resistance to more profound meaning. Martin's lovemaking becomes ever more intense and demanding as her silence fuels his erotic desire for her but simultaneously becomes a source of mental torture. Of course Martin is not an artist, as Meyers was, and so his appropriation of Cécilia as muse points towards an entirely different kind of creation. As the film progresses it becomes apparent that Martin's difficulties stem from an inner emptiness that desperately seeks some kind of definition. His behaviour is remarkable for its edgy, pent-up quality, perpetually on the point of explosion in crazy driving, or lengthy, searching interrogations of Cécilia or intense sexual activity. At one point in the film, having made the sudden decision to leave his flat, he is pictured struggling into a jacket before he has fully managed to get his jumper over his head, and the tension and constraint implied by the flailing figure speaks eloquently of his headlong rush towards a manically desired self-definition. As he increasingly identifies with Meyers, living out the same trajectory in relation to Cécilia, we can see that his appropriation of the muse was necessary not in the service of some external work of art, but in the creation of a painfully absent sense of selfhood.

A similar dynamic can be identified in Chantal Akerman's film *La Captive*, a reworking of Proust's *La Prisonnière*. In this film the sickly and insecure Simon loves an androgynous young woman, Ariane, but is frustrated by her opaque quality and by his own unfounded but overwhelming jealousy. One of the most striking scenes in the film pictures Simon in the bath, separated from Ariane, who is similarly bathing but invisible, behind a frosted-glass wall. While the rest of the film is remarkable for its cool, disengaged elegance, this particular scene slides into the erotic with Simon expressing his loving admiration of Ariane's sex, glimpsed when he parted her legs while she slept. Ariane appears naked behind the glass, and Simon stands up in his bath, attempting to cover her body with his own, so that our view of the woman is elusive and fragmented. This configuration is another symbolic reminder of the lack of relationship between the sexes that infects many of the works of art that deal with heterosexual relations. The pointless, yearning gestures Simon makes to coincide with Ariane, separated as they are by the glass, symbolise their fundamental inability to communicate, to be mutually known to one another, and ultimately to make each other happy. Simon's appropriative viewing of Ariane's sex represents the most contentment he derives, with the woman sleeping and delivered to his gaze.

What this film can help us to read in *L'Ennui*, is the underlying structure of self-creation that inhabits the contemporary evocation of the muse. Proust exerts a profound influence on contemporary male writers of the pornographic, with Zagdanski declaring that 'c'est chez Proust qu'on peut le mieux trouver cette définition même de l'écriture comme un acte érotique' (Zagdanski 1999: 22) ['it is in Proust's work that we can best find the very definition of writing as an erotic act']. Proust's revelatory analysis on the subject of the unattainable desired woman revealed most about the man who longed for her. Jealousy, Proust declared, was an *apprentissage* in art, for it forced the man to search for the truth, no matter what the cost might be, no matter what the truth might reveal. Engaged in his quest, the man would find himself illuminated in his own searchlight, brought into stark relief by the intensity of his own investigation. Yet what we also find in Proust, less flatteringly, perhaps, is a feminisation of the male as he struggles against his own frailties and weaknesses, his certainties eroded by the gradual attrition of time. Both Simon in *La Captive*, and Martin in *L'Ennui* find themselves defined by a quest that obscures their own emptiness, the desire to resolve the enigma of woman, and in both cases obsessive jealousy becomes the motivating spur. In *L'Ennui*, Martin's retrospective fascination with Meyers is swiftly replaced by jealousy when he suspects Cécilia of having an affair with her actor friend, Momo. Both films are dominated by relentless questioning on the part of the man and oblique responses on the part of the woman, a structure that mimes the familiar encounter of detective and criminal, analyst and patient, but which abandons such comforting organisations of power to reveal instead a contemporary insistence on the unimpeachable barriers between the alien worlds of men and women. In *La Captive*, Ariane explains to Simon that a certain *pudeur* of the soul is necessary for her erotic engagement: 'J'aime imaginer que vous avez un monde où je n'ai pas accès. Il m'intrigue'. ['I like to imagine that you have a world to which I don't have access. It intrigues me.'] In *L'Ennui*, the less innocent Cécile responds to Martin's exasperated 'finalement tu diras la vérité' with the words 'Quelle vérité?'. ['finally you'll tell me the truth'; 'Which truth?'] Both films perform an ontological difference of knowledge that is intrinsic to the genders; men display a frantic demand for a knowledge of emotions that women refuse to give, not simply out of cussedness, but also because their approach to what might be knowable is entirely other. Yet in both films the women are utterly at one with their existences in a way that only highlights the painful division of men from themselves. Ariane's carefree *jouissance* with her girlfriends is matched by the sexual self-possession of Cécilia, and both indicate a feminine pact with the vagaries of existence that hopelessly eludes the male protagonists. The woman's inaccessibility, her autonomy and self-sufficiency, gives her extraordinary power. Minsky talks of the way that 'Modern Kleinians distinguish funda-mentally between the desire for knowledge, including the desire for emotional insight, and envious curiosity involving a wish to gain power and control over others in order to deny feelings of vulner-ability, loss or humiliation' (1998: 123). In these films the male quest for knowledge remains mired in a misplaced longing for control that cannot be achieved, with the result that the male succumbs to a kind of hystericisation, a loss of self-control that expresses a loss of cultural power and manifests itself in an excessive eroticism.

This hystericisation can be productively linked to a postmodern concept of the women's role in men's self-creation. In her discussion of the muse, Bronfen uses Cixous' distinction between two forms of libidinal economy: 'one – a masculine economy of preservation, the other a feminine one of excessive exhaustion – which, [Cixous] adds are, nevertheless, both ruled by the relation each subject has to death. The former desire to preserve implies a stasis and repeti-tion which inevitably touches what it seeks to avoid – death. The latter, the transgressive delight in risk and expenditure, inevitably appears as a form of animate mobility, despite its embrace of fatal risk' (1992: 368). Cixous' opposition is a pertinent one, suggesting that the opposing sexual economies of parsimony and extravagance require each other in a mutual play of self-definition. These films mark a reversal of these libidinal economies, with men increas-ingly engaged in exhaustive, excessive risk-taking, and women embracing a newfound capacity to protect and preserve themselves. *La Captive*, a film directed by a woman from a male point of view, plays out to a languishing, painfully slow tempo that is in stark contrast to the frenzied, over-adrenalised rhythm of *L'Ennui*. Yet it is also intriguing that Ariane's serene self-containment is proved to be ultimately untenable in the face of Simon's relentless probing, and finally she commits suicide, exhausted by his endless questioning. Woman's ability to tolerate the change in economy is therefore placed in doubt. In *L'Ennui*, however, the roles are fully reversed, with Martin's frantic self-expenditure ending in a car crash that, contrary to the opening prediction of the film, does not kill him. When he is depicted at the end of the film in his hospital bed, the spectator's expectations are confounded and what we took to be suicidal despair at the depths of humiliation he had reached in his relationship to Cécile has been transformed into an existential principle. He explains in voice-over that 'il faut se nourrir de son désespoir' as 'il faut vivre à tout prix'. ['one must feed on despair' ... 'one must live at all costs'.] Cécile has performed her function as muse, despite the odds, for Martin now has a truth he can live by, even if it is one shot through with negativity and based still in an economy of excessive expenditure.

The most extreme model of the muse as figure of creative destruction, or as force of negativity is in Yann Moix's recent novel, *Partouz*. In Moix's extremist vision the failure of women to act as an inspirational source of self-creation for men results in the most dire of historical consequences. This novel allies the events of September 11 with the contemporary state of relations between the sexes, arguing that 'le véritable enjeu du terrorisme, c'était le sexe. Le véritable combat d'Al Quaida n'était pas tant réligieux que sexuel' (Moix 2004: 24). ['What's really at stake in terrorism is sex. The true battle of Al Quaida is not so much religious as sexual.'] The narrator's viewpoint is based on the (fictional) history of one of the captains of the planes in the Twin Towers attack, Mohammed Atta (Momo), who in an act of sublimation undreamt of in *L'Ennui*, exchanges his hopeless passion for Pamela Wiltshire for a terrorist mission. Bronfen's characterisation of the original muse as 'incompletely accessible, always beyond reach' (1992: 362) has become an unacceptable state of affairs, and the consequences of this are profoundly alarming for history: 'Les femmes passent, mais les ruines sont éternelles' (2004: 30). ['Women come and go, but the ruins are eternal.']

It is not surprising that the muse remains destructive when the conception of heterosexual relations in this text bears a remarkable similarity to those in *L'Ennui*. Women are represented as highly sexed and unromantic, perpetually ready to take a man's emotions and then trade themselves faithlessly on the open market. Men are feminised and despairing, unable to possess women sufficiently either in body or spirit. This role is embodied by the narrator who, conducting the narrative from a swinger's club in Paris, searching for the woman he has fallen 'in love' with, is unable to gain any erotic action, repeatedly failing in his attempts to arouse women and be aroused himself. The pervasive sense in women's artworks of their vulnerable porosity is nowhere to be found here. Instead, in a move related to the exchange of libidinal economies, women are fantasised as utterly impermeable. In a formulation that is strikingly at odds with the conventional view of male sexual activity, and indeed with the view expressed in contemporary artworks by women, the sexual act is seen from the male perspective as actively obstructive to possessing the woman. In *L'Ennui*, Martin complains to his ex-wife that in his endless sexual encounters with Cécilia, 'je gaspille de l'energie dont j'aurais besoin pour la posséder vraiment'. ['I waste the energy I need to really possess her.'] While in *Partouz* the narrator describes a world where 'toute fille donnée était impossible à avoir' (2004: 205). ['any woman who gives herself is impossible to have'.] Man's inability to 'have' women, to possess them satisfactorily, makes their potential as muse for male self-creation painfully unreliable at best, yet man's inability to make women a possession fosters no form of respect for womankind. Instead it is seen as evidence for women's sexual insatiability and their fundamental faithlessness.

In *Partouz*, the combination of endless unfaithful women and hopelessly empty men is understood as the basis for art, but also as the provocation for history. This text reworks the conventional formula that behind every successful man one finds a strong woman, to propose instead that behind every man who made history one finds the story of unrequited love (with Proust, again, standing as a paradigm). While this hypothesis is harmless enough, the madness of this text originates from the inclusion of the terrorist as a figure of both political history and creativity: 'Un terroriste, c'est comme un peintre ou un écrivain: si vous ne l'empêchez de poursuivre son activité, il la poursuit' (2004: 88). ['A terrorist is like a painter or a writer; if you don't prevent him from pursuing his activities, he will pursue them.'] *Partouz*'s profoundly provocative celebration of the terrorist attempts to domesticate the negativity of terrorism by blaming it on thwarted romantic hopes, yet its equation of artistic sublimation with mass destruction, and its foundation in a misogynistic hatred of women's sexual freedom is deeply alarming. The argument for terrorism as a form of political creativity is represented with some degree of confusion. On the one hand it is seen as a quasi-moralistic act with fundamental Islamists seeking to impose 'de l'ordre dans le désordre sexuel qui menaçait de s'installer partout sur le planète' (2004: 24) ['order into the sexual disorder which threatens to take hold of the entire planet'], while on the other it is an act of pure vengeance against the feckless and castrating disinterest of women. This is reminiscent of the moment in *L'Ennui* where Cécilia, speaking of Meyers without truly abandoning her deadpan expression, says 'il disait que tout était de ma faute' ['he said everything was my fault'.] In both text and film, women are made entirely responsible for the actions of men and, by extension, the events of the world no matter how apocalyptic. And yet they are simultaneously represented as utterly irresponsible, given over to pleasure and the endless present without thought of the consequences. Inevitably it seems that the role of women is less one of muse than one of scapegoat, and this on a scale it is almost impossible to comprehend.

However, the very extravagance of the accusations placed at women's feet works to question the extent of women's culpability. The hysterical hyperbole of the narrator clearly renders him unreliable, and his arguments less than plausible. For while the representation of women in this text is black and bitter when extracted from the surrounding narrative, the ambiguity of *Partouz*, despite its would-be unambiguous political messages, is founded in its own jokey, ironic tone. This is exemplified by the figure of Le Lapin in the swingers' club, a man who certainly never bothers to make romantic overtures to women either verbally or manually. Instead, 'il besognait, il faisait l'amour une bonne fois pour toutes, de manière générique' (2004: 162). ['he slaved away at it; he made love once and for all, in generic fashion'.] Le Lapin's hard work wins him significant rewards, as he is by far the most successful man in the club with women, but is it possible for him to offer a role model to modern man? His inclusion in the narrative is more for comic value than pedagogical intent, and the admiration expressed by the narrator is far from untouched by ridicule, as when he describes how 'dans ses parages, ça sentait vraiment comme une odeur de caoutchouc brûlé. Comme quand on conduisait quelques kilomètres en ayant oublié de débloquer le frein à main ... ' (2004: 160). ['in the vicinity there was a distinct smell of burnt rubber. Like when you've driven a few kilometers having forgotten to take the handbreak off ...'.] *Partouz*'s pronouncements on the state of heterosexual relations are thus irreducible to a clear didactic intent, the excessive figures it creates drawn from a contemporary palette but equally intended to shock and offend.

This oscillation between apocalypse and farce, between the sublime and the ridiculous is considered to constitute an inevitable ambivalence in the representation of the sexual act according to Žižek. 'It is not simply a question of a pure ecstasy beyond rules which can never be captured by an external, disinterested gaze. The encounter between (symbolic) rules and pathos is by definition a failed one' (Žižek 1997: 176). The unrepresentable real of the act is inevitably resistant to any form of codification. Its appearance can never be guaranteed, and following any form of textbook formulation to try to tease ecstasy out into the open may lead to success or it may make the event ridiculous. The masculine imaginary seems particularly susceptible to the uncertainty and oscillation that comes from a radical inability to know whether sexuality is sublime or ridiculous. It becomes, then, a feature of works that embrace the masculine imaginary to attempt to impose radical structures or 'rules' on the sexual encounter, and a feature of postmodern texts to find these rules always open to internal collapse into the parodic. Thus Žižek says 'the "comical" is in a way the sexual act "as such", "in itself" in so far as the way we do it is by definition always a manner of learning, of rules we imitate from others'. So we can see how 'the split between the sexual act and its representation affects this act itself – which is why it is always possible that this act, all of a sudden, also appears ridiculous to those who perform it ... ' (1997: 177). Žižek draws our attention the proposition raised earlier in this analysis that the sexual act can never be freed from the representative fantasies that cluster around it, that 'sex' does not exist as such without these fantasies. What he also indicates is the fragility of those fantasies and their contradictory multiplicity. Žižek's account here bears echoes of the heterotopic spaces of fantasy that inform the erotic works by women. But while we see in women's artworks a certain paradoxical simultaneity of fantasy frameworks operating, what these works by men indicate is the possibility that one frame, one fantasy may exert an almost tyrannical force over the psychodramas of male sexuality.

This kind of tyrannical fantasy is by no means absent from women's works; in Escalle's texts, for instance, we can also see the dominance of the male phallic imaginary. But what we find in women's texts is a certain internalised recuperation of these images, in which a woman's sexual experience is measured against her own internal otherness, for instance the autoerotic gaze embodied in Reyes' texts. There is an ethical issue to be drawn here out of a psycho-sexual dynamic that would appear, on the evidence of these texts, to be differently organised across the gender divide. For in Yann Moix's text, the triumphs and failures of sexual experience are threateningly linked to the stage of world history, where the eye of a mediatised world registers the sexual crimes of women against male *jouissance*, as only such an arena will do for such an outrageous crime. We seem to reach an impasse whose lack of resolution threatens apocalyptic consequences and suggests at the very least that there should be some recognition, on either side of the gender divide, of the profoundly asymmetrical fantasies pitted by men and women against each other. Or else, as the narrator of *Partouz* half-jokingly suggests: 'L'amour, nous allons tous en mourir' (2004: 55). ['Love, we're all going to die of it.']

Notes

1 See Luce Irigaray, *Speculum de l'autre femme* for the theoretical position on this concept.
2 See Virginie Despentes, *Baise-moi* and Catherine Breillat's *Anatomie de l'enfer*, discussed in Chapters 2 and 3 of the present volume.
3 Pauline Réage's *Histoire d'O* presents a female-authored text that also subscribes to the erotic tradition. This is also an influential text for Escalle, given the sadomasochistic dimension of her sexual representations.
4 See the chapter 'Power, ethics and sexual imageries', in Gaten 1996.
5 For instance, see Florence Dugas, *Dolorosa soror* (Blanche, 2000), Marthe Blau, *Entre ses mains* (Pocket, 2005) and Vanessa Duries, *Le Lien* (J'ai lu, 2000) all extremely popular mass-market texts.
6 See Orlan's series of staged cosmetic-surgery operations entitled 'Regeneration' that challenge western concepts of female beauty, and Cindy Sherman's series of photographic self-portraits.
7 In Blau's novel, the female protagonist continually submits to rules imposed on her by her mysterious lover that closely determine what may occur between them. In Breillat's text *Pornocratie*, made into the film *Anatomie de l'enfer*, the male protagonist agrees to spend a set number of nights with the woman in order to explore her abject sexuality.
8 See the work of Rosi Braidotti, in particular *Nomadic Subjects*.

 9 See the work of Elizabeth Grosz, notably *Virtual Bodies*.
10 See Luce Irigaray's *Ce sexe qui n'est pas un* for a full explanation of
   the vagina as sight/site of nothingness. However, Françoise Meltzer in
   her analysis of Joan of Arc's virginity claims that the primal power of
   the vulva is influential in much twentieth-century theory: 'Woman as
   obscurity is a trope that has been noted many times, but I am making
   a different point here: that the obscurity of woman is a metaphor
   informed by female anatomy. The very *insideness* of her sexual organs,
   for example, lend themselves to tropes of mystery, darkness, obscurity
   and shrouding. This is the case in Levinas as well as in Nietzsche, Freud,
   Plato' (2001: 63).

2

Catherine Breillat: touch/cut

If, as Françoise Audé claims, explicit sex has recently become a prominent feature of auteur cinema (2002: 113–14), then the key figure in this trend is Catherine Breillat, in whose work relations between the sexes are just as morbid and extreme as many of those we have just considered in Chapter 1. As David Vasse writes, while she might be seen as having anticipated this trend, currently, she is its figurehead (2004: 24). In one sense, this status does Breillat few favours: her work is consistently confronted by the reactions provoked by this aesthetic choice. 'A l'étranger', she says, 'on qualifie souvent mes films de "french" [*sic*], un adjectif qui signifie intellectuel et un peu chiant' (Rouyer and Vassé 2004: 40). ['Abroad, my films are often called "French", an adjective which means intellectual and a bit of a pain.'] But also, of course, this adjective is often used as an ambivalent shorthand for sexual frankness; and the epithet to which Breillat usually finds herself entitled by virtue of this dimension of her work is, predictably, 'pornographic'. In this respect, Breillat is a perfect illustration of the tendency which forms the focus of this study. Her work cannot be understood without reference to its proximity to the pornographic; this proximity demands to be thought as both citation and entanglement; and this relation is seen as a necessary part of the articulation of key aesthetic and thematic concerns. This chapter will accordingly address Breillat's work in terms of its relation to the pornographic, exploring what is at stake for her aesthetically in this relation, and using some of the issues raised to discuss features characteristic of her filmmaking. The first section of the chapter will discuss Breillat's supposed proximity to the pornographic (including her own thoughts on the matter). The second section will consider Breillat's own conception of her art, with particular reference to questions of identification, literality and transcendence. Developing these discussions, the third section will examine Breillat's portrayal of relations between the sexes; via the figures of the touch and the cut which emerge from this, it will then attempt to get closer to the aesthetics of Breillat's work.[1]

By the time of *Anatomie de l'enfer* (2003), Breillat described her body of filmic work as a 'decalogue'.[2] Her ten full-length films return obsessively to a thematic kernel concerned with relations between the sexes, and the nature of female sexual identity. One group examines the difficult transition to womanhood of adolescent girls (*Une vraie jeune fille* (1975, not released until 2000), *36 fillette* [1987], *A ma sœur!* [2000]); another, the violent, at times murderous encounter between men and women in the sexual arena (*Tapage nocturne* (1979), *Sale comme une ange* (1991), *Parfait amour!* (1996), *Romance* (2000), *Brève traversée* (2001), *Anatomie de l'enfer* (2003)). This is not quite an exhaustive list: *Sex Is Comedy* (2002) is mostly a reflection on the power struggles and other relationships involved in filmmaking, specifically the filming of scenes of intimacy, and reprises key scenes from *A ma sœur!*. Nor are the two groups mutually exclusive: the first is, if anything, a subset of the second. Breillat is also an author: indeed, she was a published author before she was in her twenties, and had already published four books before making *Une vraie jeune fille* (which was an adaptation of the fourth, *Le Soupirail* (1974)). She has subsequently published five more, including *Le Livre du plaisir* (1999), an anthology of (for the most part) sexually explicit writing. She has also collaborated as screenwriter on a number of films by other directors. Her cinematic work is characterised by trademark long takes, and by her extraordinary, painterly way with light, colour and composition, features which have become only more evident with the increased production values of her later films. She has a gift for producing performances of compelling emotional intensity and complexity from her often young leading actresses, and situates her work in a tradition of filmmaking, including such figures as Kazan, Bergman and Buñuel.

To consider Breillat's work solely in terms of its relation to questions of pornography is clearly reductive, therefore. Such consideration may, however, be necessary, for the following reasons. In the first place, rightly or wrongly, the idea of the pornographic is repeatedly invoked in discussions of Breillat's cinema. Furthermore, this is not a question Breillat avoids: on the contrary, she conceptualises her representations of sexuality according to what she understands by notions of pornography and eroticism. Finally: its relation to the pornographic has been a major factor in the international success achieved by Breillat's work since *Romance* (1999). The explicit representation of sexual material in this film – while it is more limited than some excited responses might lead one to believe – situated Breillat in the wider cultural trend, in France and beyond, which this study seeks to address; if her work has insistently been discussed in terms of its representation of sexual material, this is no doubt because in this respect it has resonated with its broad cultural context. Consideration of her work will also serve as a clear example of how the reference to the pornographic in recent works articulates other concerns – in this case, from aesthetics and sexual politics. The following discussion is, accordingly, deliberately limited to those films in which the pornographic is most extensively engaged by Breillat. It should be remembered, however, that her confrontational approach to questions of sexuality and gender relations is hardly limited to these works, and indeed is elaborated across a number of films and written texts in which the question of the pornographic is hardly if at all present.

Refreshingly, perhaps, for a contemporary artist, Breillat insists that her films have something to say; and that something, she claims, is of the order of a truth. She wants to take hold of her viewers and, by means of a violent confrontation, reveal to them something transcendent. She wants to touch us; and that touch is inscribed in various compelling ways in the body of her films. From the concepts she uses to discuss her work to some of its smallest, most fragile details, let us now begin to consider how she does this.

Eroticism, porn, pornography

Partly because of the relative infrequency of material in her *œuvre* to justify such a claim, then, it would be a hasty critic who would unquestioningly classify Breillat's work as pornography. Such a classification could perhaps be justified by its relatively explicit sexual content, graphic genital close-ups, and occasional scenes of unsimulated sex; or, more tenuously, by what could be claimed to be its intermittent depiction of female sexuality as bound to an existential assumption of victimhood. And Breillat's work is repeatedly described in terms of pornography. This association is not just erroneous: confronted with the degree of explicit sexual material which characterises certain of her films, it is impossible to avoid at least negotiating the question of the pornographic. Indeed, elements such as her use of Italian porn star Rocco Siffredi in both *Romance* and *Anatomie de l'enfer* are clearly a provocative engagement with this question (see Price 2005 and Vasse 2004: 91). Such elements are, however, also part of the general strategy of these films, which, working within the terms of their cultural horizon, necessarily invoke pornography as the major code for the explicit representation of sexuality. The stakes of Breillat's enterprise are these: wishing to engage with what she sees as the truth of human sexuality as her core thematic, she finds herself obliged to encounter – dialectically and critically – what she considers to be the pornographic deformation of this truth, in order to arrive at its potentially redemptive intimation. To understand more fully how Breillat conceives of this approach, we have to explore the complicated, idiosyncratic discourse she deploys to discuss these matters.

This discourse is structured around the terms 'érotisme', 'pornographie' and 'porno'. It is important to state at once that Breillat's understanding of these terms is not that of most cultural commentators. Indeed, her use of these terms runs directly, and surprisingly, against their usual senses. In most accounts (including recent French studies of the contemporary rise of pornography, as discussed in our Introduction), 'pornographie' describes everything bad, instrumental and commercial in the explicit representation of sexuality. 'Erotisme', by contrast, names work which does not pander to the pleasure of the consumer, but interrupts and problematises this pleasure; which subversively pushes social or artistic boundaries; and which demands a real and supposedly dangerous subjective investment on the part of its creator as much as on that of its recipient. Breillat's use of these terms is quite different.

For Breillat, 'érotisme' is the enemy: it represents a reductive, hackneyed and hygienic lie designed to objectify and alienate female sexuality. That is to say, Breillat uses 'érotisme' to mean what most other contributors to these debates understand by 'pornographie'. In the first place, the – invariably masculine – spectator at an erotic spectacle is sheltered, says Breillat, protected from any meaningful involvement (Rouyer and Vassé 2004: 36); this insulating distance allows the objectification of the female performer (Puaux 2001: 68).[3] The erotic, for Breillat, designates the combination of misogyny and cliché that dominates our culture's explicit representations of sexuality, which she sums up in a memorable, withering dismissal: 'L'érotisme, c'est une femme mystérieuse avec des porte-jarretelles, qui écarte les jambes et qui fait bander les hommes. Car l'érotisme est toujours du côté des hommes' (Clouzot 2004: 164). ['Eroticism is a mysterious woman in suspenders, spreading her legs and turning men on. Because eroticism is always on the side of men.'] Not just clichéd and misogynistic, however, the erotic is also for Breillat hypocritically hygienic: it both alienates female sexuality and pretends – humiliatingly, she says – that the image it creates is acceptable, positive, attractive (Vallaeys and Armanet 2000). Humiliation, in Breillat's universe, results not from specific sexual acts, but from this combination of objectification and aestheticisation. As she says, 'je préfère qu'on puisse montrer une femme qui se fait prendre à quatre pattes, si ça lui chante, parce que la dignité, ce n'est pas le respect de la pudeur, mais l'intégrité des droits de l'homme. C'est-à-dire l'intégrité du droit à disposer de soi-même' (Clouzot 2004: 165). ['I find it preferable that one should be able to show a woman being taken on all fours, if that's what she fancies, because dignity is not about decency, it's about respecting the integrity of human rights. Which is to say, respecting the integrity of the right to do as one sees fit with oneself.'] An art which worked on these principles could not be called 'erotic', she insists: 'ça me met hors de moi quand on me classe dans les œuvres érotiques. Je ne trouve pas qu'il y ait d'art érotique, voilà, si l'on veut savoir! L'art compromet. Il est subversif. Donc il ne peut pas être érotique' (Rouyer and Vassé 2004: 36–7). ['it drives me crazy when my work is classified as erotic. To be honest, I don't think there's such a thing as erotic art. Art compromises you. It's subversive. So it can't be erotic.']

Breillat's understanding of 'érotisme' thus mostly targets what others generally understand by 'pornographie'; but her hostility to aestheticisation and to the recuperation of representation within a progressive agenda does strike home with the interests of those who maintain 'érotisme' as a positive term, most of whom celebrate the aesthetic and progressive value of the works they group under its heading. Breillat shares with such critics a belief in the subversive engagement operated by the truly artistic. But unlike them, Breillat has, she says, at times been tempted to use the term 'pornography' to affirm this subversion, inasmuch as, for her, this term maintains the authenticity evacuated by the hypocrisy of eroticism (Rouyer and Vassé 2004: 36). In Breillat's use of the terms, the value of subjective

investment reserved by most others for the term 'érotisme' is associated with its bad other, 'pornographie'. This is because, for Breillat,
'pornographie' can name works which refuse the prettification she
identifies in the erotic: 'La pornographie, c'est laid, moi je préfère
le laid' (Vallaeys and Armanet 2000). ['Pornography is ugly, and
I prefer ugly.'] What for others saves the erotic from mere pornographic instrumentality – namely the aesthetic interference it introduces into its reception – can for Breillat be a sign of bad faith. She
would doubtless agree with Federico Ferrari and Jean-Luc Nancy,
who draw our attention to the tendency of erotica to recycle the
supposed interference introduced into the viewer's pleasure as a
further dimension of this pleasure, and so define 'érotisme' as just a
hypocritical version of pornography (2002: 122).

Breillat recognises, however, that the massive development of
commercial pornography nowadays makes it hard for the term to
denote anything subversive whatsoever. In order to distinguish her
use of the term from what more or less everyone else understands it to
mean, therefore, Breillat attempts to maintain a distinction between
'porno' and 'pornographie', with the latter retaining the status of
heroic, modernist ordeal, evacuated of the miserable commercial
instrumentality evacuated into the former (Rouyer and Vassé 2004:
38–9). 'Pornographie', then, would for Breillat designate the fragile
space within which the genuinely subversive is created, hemmed in
by 'érotisme' on one side (too pretty, too alienated), and 'porno' on
the other (too commercial, too instrumental).

This space is so narrow, in fact, that 'pornography' might not
actually work as a name for what Breillat wants to do. Culturally
speaking, she says, 'there is just one view of sex, and it is pornographic. And I think that that is just the point of view of a very bad
industry, and artists have the responsibility to represent sex from
another point of view' (Murphy 2005; see also Devanne 2005).
What Breillat had wanted to designate by the term 'pornography' –
an explicit vision of sex which produces a profound existential and
even metaphysical engagement on the part of the spectator – might
have to go nameless, perhaps. At which point, we are free to agree
that, in her terms, her work is indeed not pornographic, after all.
In her text 'De la femme et la morale au cinéma' (an address given
in Tehran on 28 February 1998), Breillat categorically removes
exploitative, 'streetwalking' films from consideration: they are, she
says, quite simply not films, and are of no interest (1999: 8).

But Breillat cannot entirely dissociate herself from the pornographic, nor does she. Even in this text, she describes pornography in traditional avant-garde terms derived from Bataille and Genet, as a matter of sanctity and initiation (1999: 20). Hoping for a transcendent outcome unusual in this tradition, Breillat espouses – to some extent – the explicitness of pornography, but seeks to hijack this to radically different ends. From eroticism, she wants to take the aesthetic interference, but refuse the alienating prettification; from pornography, she wants to take the 'ugly' explicitness, but refuse the reductive, commercial instrumentality. This means that, as she acknowledges, she must verge on the pornographic if she is to surpass it (see Devanne 2005). At this point, Breillat might be accused of using the techniques of an industry she denounces (see Spoiden 2002); alternatively, the relation may also be described in terms of proximity or citation. For if the pornographic dimension of her work is irreducible, her work is equally irreducible to the pornographic. Françoise Audé (2001), Julien Chastel (2002) and David Vasse (2004) have therefore all described *Romance*, for example, as both using and exceeding the codes of pornography. Whether this odd relation be configured as complicity, proximity, or citation, it is clear that, if Breillat is going to do what she wants to do, her work is going to have to veer perilously close to the pornography she repudiates. What she wants to do, however, is something quite different.

Art, identification, reality

Simply, Breillat sees herself as making art, not just pornography or erotica; and critics have often backed her in this. There are clear grounds for this, notably in the formal textures of her films, and the impairment these may be read as introducing into the visual pleasure of the more or less protected spectator of the erotico-pornographic.[4] Breillat wants to interrupt this pleasure – but seriously, not hypocritically as in the eroticism she denounces – in order to implicate the spectator in the work, to touch the viewer via an identificatory recognition of the truth this work conveys. This section will, therefore, begin by exploring what Breillat understands to be the nature of this truth, before considering the questions of transgression, transcendence and identification it raises, and its aesthetic consequences for the relation between Breillat's films and the reality they represent.

Breillat sees herself as communicating the truth of human sexuality, hidden under moral, aesthetic and religious codes. 'Religion would have us believe that sex is simply about the flesh when in fact it's something higher and more idealistic', she says; her aim is to show what supposedly cannot be shown – the supposed truth of sexuality, represented conventionally by the female sex (as discussed in Chapter 1, pp. 41–2) – in order to question the misogynistic interests served by this prohibition: 'I wanted to confront this forbidden image, to present a close-up of the female sexual organ – that which can't be seen, which can't be watched – so as to ask if this is really what sexuality is really all about' (Macnab 2004: 22). If pornography pretends to effect such a revelation (as in Nimier's reading, for example, as discussed in Chapter 1, p. 42), it fails to engage with what is ontologically at stake, and so is merely the objectifying flip-side of prohibition: 'le film porno résulte de la culpabilisation, il en est le pendant, c'est pareil, c'est pareil' (Gaillac-Morgue 2005). ['porn films are the result of guilt, the two go hand in hand, they're the same thing, the same thing'.] While pornography may show that it is possible to travesty sexuality into a business transaction, then, this misses the point, the meaning of human sexuality as an existential project of self-transcendence. With a quasi-Bataillean anthropology, Breillat cites human sexuality as a 'language' which cuts humanity from the realm of the animal, instigating the possibility of a transcendence which forms the truth towards which our existential projects tend. But in contrast to Bataille's base materialism, which permits only an empty transcendence of irrecuperable negativity, Breillat is an idealist. Categorically, she declares: 'J'aime la transcendance, et la transcendance, c'est une sublimation. Je pense qu'il n'y a que cela d'intéressant de toute façon' (Clouzot 2004: 177). ['I like transcendence, and transcendence is a form of sublimation. That's the only thing that interests me, in any case.]

Contrary to a postmodern aesthetics of affective and epistemological flattening or displacement, Breillat is, effectively, a Modernist, whose approach to her art is characterised by the high value she attaches to the artwork as disruptive and revelatory. The heavenly revelations she accordingly seeks are made possible for Breillat by what she sees as the identificatory mechanisms proper to all fiction. What she calls the 'mask of fiction' means that 'on regarde une histoire qui officiellement n'est pas la nôtre', but that 'on s'y reconnaît, mais secrètement' (Gaillac-Morgue 2005). 'On se reconnaît dans des gens qui ne sont pas nous', she says (Devanne 2005). ['we are watching a story which, officially, is not our own'; 'we recognise ourselves in it, but secretly'; 'we recognise ourselves in people who are not us'.] The notional acknowledgement of this contact represents, as seen above, the value that Breillat is prepared to accord to pornography; Breillat seeks to exacerbate this contact, to confront and engage the viewer with moments of immediate, even physical contact, both in film and in writing. At this point, her aim coincides – if only briefly – with that of the pornographic, as she seeks to make work which will provoke a physical or affective response in its recipient. Introducing her anthology *Le Livre du plaisir*, she states: 'Ecrire sur le plaisir, c'est décharger dans le corps du lecteur' (2005: 9). ['Writing on pleasure is a way of coming in the reader's body.'] This belief is at the root of one of the distinctive features of all Breillat's work: namely, its production of intense, unsettling moments which the viewer or reader experiences as a sudden, unsolicited touch, or blow. 'Quand on touche quelqu'un', she says, 'il n'est pas forcément content. Il y a une sorte du viol du spectateur' (Clouzot 2004: 90). ['When you touch someone, they're not necessarily happy about it. There's a kind of rape of the spectator.'] This contact then serves as the channel for the identification which allows us to realise the truth of what we are reading or watching; at this point, her aim exceeds that of the pornographic, in the direction of transcendence. We will explore in detail the mechanics of this operation in our discussions of specific films, below (when we will also relate it to other theories of film, and art more generally, as a form of contact). For now, let us note its structure, and the fact that for Breillat, it makes her work the vehicle of indisputable truth. As she declares: 'Mes films révèlent aux gens ce qu'ils sont' (Clouzot 2004: 140). ['My films reveal to people what they are.']

For it is indeed a truth that Breillat sees herself as delivering. Just as the sex act supposedly transcends its physicality to become metaphysical, so, in Breillat's aesthetics, does the reality of what is represented go beyond literality, to attain the status of poetic truth. The business of cinema, she says, is not to film reality, it is to offer up truth, defined as the transcendence of realism (Devanne 2005). The status of this 'truth' is highly debatable, of course. We might like to think that the glorious transcendence of the sexual body is indeed a truth which has been repressed by discriminatory discourses of shame; we might be less happy to agree that this transcendence is necessarily to be pursued via the particular heterosexual ballet of

male violence and willed, knowing female submission which seems
to be an indispensable part of the truth Breillat has to communicate
(which will be discussed further in this chapter). We might indeed,
with Foucault (1976), be highly suspicious of this discourse of a
hidden truth in relation to sexuality, and the obfuscations involved
in constructing a discourse of supposed 'repression' which might be
opposed by pornographic 'revelation' (on this, see Harrison 2000).
But it remains the case that this is the oracular status she claims for
her work; and it is this status that her explicit representations of the
sexual body seek to secure.

Despite her insistence on her art as productive of transcendence, however, the characteristic referential structure of Breillat's
cinema derives from the fact that it remains tied to the reality it
also transcends. Take, for example, her use of a *fait divers* as the
starting point for *A ma sœur!* The film's violent ending is, says
Breillat, inspired by a real event (as was also true of *Parfait amour!*);
but what interested her in this was, predominantly, the significance
of the ways in which this story was related, which all represented
attempts to neutralise its force (see Breillat 2001a: 5; and Vincendeau 2001: 20). Her interest, that is, lies in representing this piece of
reality so that its truth – where it touches on profound, disturbing
concerns – might be confronted. But intriguingly, the catalyst for
this transformation was another piece of reality: a plump young girl
seen in a hotel swimming pool, swimming lengths and talking to
herself 'comme si elle déclarait son amour à des garçons imaginaires
[...]. J'ai alors commencé à imaginer cette petite fille dans ce fait
divers' (Breillat 2001a: 5). ['As if declaring her love to imaginary
boys [...] Then I started imagining this girl in that news story.'] We
are presented with an entanglement of reality and its reworking,
perfectly figured in the equivalent scene in the film. Here, the actress
Anaïs Reboux swims back and forth between metal steps and
wooden deck, talking softly to each, the poignancy of her imaginings
brushing against the emphasis Breillat places on the materiality of
metal and wood. Material reality interrupts the fabric of her fantasy,
rendering this fabric more delicate and more moving by virtue of the
contrast with its brute presence. Throughout the film, however, it is
Anaïs herself who has this role, as the material reality of her body
serves to articulate the encounters between the real and the imaginary in the scenes around her. She lies inert in her brand-new dress
in the edge of the sea (reprising a scene from *Une vraie jeune fille*),

while Fernando and Elena embrace in the dunes: her macabre song, with its imagery of carrion, encourages a disturbing vision of her body as just so much flesh, which punctures the sentimental holiday romance of the young lovers. Most memorably, Anaïs's face – either in tears, turned away, or half-covered by her fingers, unable not to watch – is what we see as Fernando persuades Elena to have sex with him. Here, Reboux's magnificent indications of turmoil and fragility mark precisely the point at which reality – her body, and those of the other actors – is being translated into truth. Her body, that is, both commands the specifically cinematic framing of these scenes, and operates as the more general interpretative frame which allows the viewer to receive their force, lifting them into the realm of meaning by its implication of an irreducible critical distance. This operation accordingly depends on the material presence of the body not being effaced: this body produces transcendence only to the extent that it simply remains there, interrupting the stories around it with the troubling urgency of their truth.

Breillat's aesthetic thus engages with the irreducible indexicality of the cinematic image (certainly the pre-digital image, and arguably also the digital image: see Marks 2002: 163). 'Index' is Charles S. Peirce's term for the type of sign which attests to the actual presence of what it signifies: classically, smoke indicating fire, for example. As in André Bazin's 'ontology of the photographic image', cinematic representation may be thought of as tied in this way to the real presence of the object it represents, whose image is the mark made by light really cast from this object onto film (Bazin 1958: 11–19; and see Wollen 1998: 79–106). Although this way of thinking about cinema became understandably unfashionable, in favour of a necessary emphasis on the complex mechanisms and cultural determiners according to which films and their narratives are constructed, it has recently undergone something of a revival, notably in the work of Mary Ann Doane (2002), Vivian Sobchack (1992, also discussed in Chapter 4, pp. 127–8) and Laura Marks (2000 and 2002). As Doane argues, the index is essentially without content: rather than signify, all it does is point (2002: 25, 94). Like the *punctum* discussed by Barthes in *La Chambre claire* (2002d), the index interrupts the continuity of signification, narrative, and so on, by which it is surrounded: in Doane's words, 'it appears as a brute and opaque fact, wedded to contingency' (94). As both 'sign and not-sign', the index is, as she puts it, 'perched on the threshold of semiosis' (101).

This seems a perfect description of the operation of material reality in Breillat's films: it is precisely the structure we have just identified in *A ma sœur!*, for example. With her usual Modernist rigour, however, Breillat herself wants nothing to do with indexicality, which is too close to the literality she refuses. Insisting on the fundamentally illusory quality of the cinematic image, for example, she says: 'Le cinéma, ce n'est pas voir, c'est croire voir'. Accordingly, the cinematic image is severed from any indexical or referential role: 'On pense que l'image est une preuve, or, l'image n'existe pas' (Clouzot 2004: 153). ['Cinema is not about seeing. It's about thinking you're seeing.'; 'People think the image is evidence of something; but really, the image doesn't exist.'] Such statements work for Breillat to ensure the artistic dimension of her cinema, as the transcendence of mere reality in the direction of truth. Her work may, however, be more complicated – and also more interesting, and more timely – than they suggest. For, as we saw above, the particular transcendence she achieves takes its bits of reality with it as it opens onto truth. In *A ma sœur!*, the wood and metal of the swimming pool are not meaningful as such: the meaning they help to produce (the pathos of Anaïs's daydreams) depends upon them remaining irreducibly material within the scene woven around them. In such cases, what matters is our negotiation as viewers *between* what we see and what we think we see, *between* real and imaginary – and, structuring this negotiation, the persistence of these bits of reality.

At which point, the question of the pornographic again arises. For in as much as it is in part defined by the reality of what it represents, pornography condenses the indexicality of film, disavowing its own extensive paraphernalia of framing, staging, editing, coercion, and so on, in favour of a promise of brute literality. Despite what this promise would have us believe, pornography is no less in the business of re-elaborating reality than any other genre, of course. Nevertheless, its constitutive disavowal of this fact establishes the pornographic as a zone in which the aesthetic frame (which includes but is far from limited to the specific techniques of cinematic framing per se) is placed under maximal strain, or presents itself as maximally disrupted by the reality of the object. And so Breillat, interested despite herself in maintaining an irreducible contact with reality even while reworking it, traverses the zone of pornography not just because she is interested in sexuality as a theme, but also because its extreme tension between real bodies and their fictional representations offers a crude but unavoidable analogy to her own aesthetic.

The use of Siffredi in *Romance* and *Anatomie de l'enfer* needs to be considered in these terms: his bodily presence means that these films touch on the very genre defined by the myth of immediate, affective contact between spectator and real spectacle. But they operate this proximity in order to undo it: for Siffredi is incorporated into an aesthetic structure which enfolds this myth in order to surpass it. What matters is not the presence of Siffredi's body: it is the explorations of sexuality produced by the scenes marked by this presence. But the presence remains necessary, as the point of indexical contact with the reality being explored. And so Breillat maintains after all – and, arguably, despite herself – a referential literality which cannot avoid the pornographic. The risks which her actors encounter, for example, are the risks of exposure resulting from the extended graphic presence of their real bodies: of Amira Casar in *Anatomie de l'enfer*, Breillat says

> Si elle n'avait pas pensé que le film était mythique, si elle avait pensé que c'était juste une femme nue sur un lit en train d'écarter les jambes, elle n'aurait pas fait le film. Mais il y avait le risque que ça finisse par n'être que ça, quand même. C'était un vrai risque. Elle l'a quand même pris et je dois la remercier. (Devanne 2005)

> [If she hadn't believed the film was of the order of myth, if she had believed it was just a naked woman on a bed spreading her legs, she wouldn't have done the film. But there was always the risk it might end up being no more than that, even so. It was a real risk. She took it nevertheless, and I have to thank her for this.]

The risk is real because the banality is irreducible, is not effaced by its symbolic transcendence.

This awkward relationship between banal, pornographic reality and its artistic translation runs through Breillat's *œuvre*: it is already strikingly present in her first film, *Une vraie jeune fille*. Take, for example, the considerable role played in this film by Charlotte Alexandra's underwear. Breillat devotes a good deal of attention to the white knickers of her schoolgirl heroine, Alice (played by Alexandra), often in ways which would seem entirely consistent with a pornographic representation. When, on her return home towards the start of the film, Alice briefly masturbates with her teaspoon (slipping it inside her underwear), the furtive angle from which this scene is shot does nothing to reduce its pornographic dimension. But the negotiation between this banal investment in the supposed reality of the image, and Breillat's desire to convert this investment into something more artistic, is evident in the subsequent treatment of this pornographic cliché. In the sequence in which Alice walks from the fields back to her home with her knickers around her ankles, for example, Alice's awkward impeded gait itself trips up any attempt to recuperate the scene for pornographic purposes. As she stops outside her door to dirty her underwear with soil from around a rosebush, this interruption of simple pornographic visual pleasure seems to be sustained, here by the celebration of a kind of Bataillean base materialism. But Bataille, of course, also celebrated the shameful erotic passion inspired by such materiality, challenging art-lovers to demonstrate as much attachment to a canvas as a foot fetishist does to a shoe (1970: 273).⁵ And so, immediately, the shot of Alice's dirty knickers makes them available again for recuperation into a fetishistic repertoire. This recuperation is, however, made possible by the irreducible materiality of their presence: which also remains, therefore, to interrupt the instrumentality of the appropriation in question. (This is why Bataille's emphasis is on the *shame* of the fetishist's passion, which disqualifies the fetishist from a proprietorial relation to the object in question.) The entanglement is complex, to say the least. When Alice subsequently drapes her knickers over the skeleton of a dog, their pornographic appropriation is maximally disrupted; but across their appearances considered as a whole, the force of this resistance varies, and an unintended contact can here and there be produced, by disavowal of the insufficient displacements of the aesthetic frame. Strongly thematised, the knickers attain the status Breillat desires (as one of the symbols of Alice's magnificent adolescent complication); but their passage to this status is snagged on the other, less elevated uses to which they might here and there be put, uses both disallowed and made possible by their persisting literality.

Breillat's representations are not *simply* beyond the reality they elaborate, then: they are *also* beyond it, the artistic translations of a reality that also persists as such. Perhaps the most eloquent example of this – certainly the one Breillat has most illuminatingly discussed – concerns the presence of the female body in *Anatomie de l'enfer*, a film in which the visceral, humid presence of this body exerts a powerful centripetal pull. Breillat says that, making the film, 'I couldn't find an actress who would play explicit sex with Rocco

Siffredi – not one. They all refused, perhaps because we are living in a very repressive time (Murphy, 'Hell's angels'). Breillat's solution to this problem indicates well the negotiations between reality and its representation which mark her work. As she had done less extensively for Caroline Ducey in *Romance*, she used a body double for the explicit scenes Casar would not perform in *Anatomie de l'enfer*. This means that in such scenes, the literality of the explicit representation is maintained, but framed by the knowledge that this literality is also being performed. Appropriately, given the thematic focus of the film on the misogynistic hatred of the material female body, this question is centred on the visual appearance of the two actresses' pubic hair. Discussing her choice of Casar's double, Breillat says, 'J'ai pris exprès une fille qui avait beaucoup plus de poils. Ce qu'il voit est – entre guillemets – beaucoup plus horrible que ce qui est' (Gaillac-Morgue 2005). ['I deliberately chose a much hairier girl. What he sees is – in inverted commas – much more horrible than what is really there.'] This decision works thematically, exaggerating the woman's hairy physicality to signal the man's oppressive disgust; but it also works aesthetically, as the obvious use of the double signals the poised articulation between reality and its transcendence at the film's most irreducible moments of intimacy. At such moments, as the trimmed pubic hair of the former Helmut Newton model unmistakably gives way to that of her double, Breillat plays on contemporary western ideologies of feminine beauty in order to invite the spectator to view something more brutely real than reality; at which point the reality of this something wobbles, without for all that being effaced. This point is made with some elegance by Breillat in the declaration which prefaces the film, in which her belief in cinema as illusion is again affirmed:

> Le cinéma est une illusion et ne procède pas de la reality-fiction ni du happening, mais de la réalité de l'œuvre. Dans ce film, l'intimité du corps de la fille a été interprétée par une doublure. On ne saurait y voir l'actrice mais la construction fictionnelle du corps de la fille.

> [Cinema is an illusion and is based not on "true stories" or some kind of happening, but on the reality of the work. In this film, in the most intimate shots of the girl's body, she is played by a body-double. In these scenes, there is no question of seeing the actress, but rather a fictional construct of the girl's body.]

This disclaimer was apparently forced upon Breillat: Casar, she says, 'required by contract that I preface the film with the disclaimer that she didn't have actual sex with Rocco. I wrote especially heavy-handed wording designed to be vague for the viewer' (Murphy 2005). But Breillat's response also allows her to signal her aesthetic – which, again, is more complex than her insistence on film as artistic illusion might suggest. This aesthetic insists that film is not literal transcription. The body you will see intimately is suspended within a fiction. But you will see a body, intimately. In the relation between 'intimité' and 'interprétée', between physicality and its symbolic translation, Breillat gives us the aesthetic which defines this dimension of her work.

Breillat works, then, with an intricate negotiation of the status of the extensive aesthetic apparatus by which reality is brought into representation. In Breillat, this apparatus is mostly constituted either by the manipulation of point of view, or by a filmic construction which introduces a critical or self-conscious dimension into the presentation of the image; in either case, it is this element of aesthetic framing which seeks to lift the literality of the image towards some transcendent, truthful plane. Throughout Breillat's work, as we have seen, the use of such framing techniques consistently produces a complicated arrangement, in which material reality is both maintained as such, and transcended. This difficult structure (a present reality *plus* its symbolic transposition) itself works to engage the spectator, making contact by this harnessing of the immediate and its mediation. Take, for example, the use of mirrors in *Romance* and *Anatomie de l'enfer*. When Robert positions Marie before a mirror in the early stages of her initiatory sadomasochistic experience in *Romance*, we are placed in her position: we see her reflection as if we were her (see Hottell and Russell-Watts 2002: 77). When Siffredi looks back at Casar in the heavily tarnished mirror in *Anatomie de l'enfer*, we are placed within a visual field from which we are absent. In both cases, the mirror's role as a self-consciously embedded frame also works to realise the viewer's implication in the image. As in Foucault's reading of Velasquez's *Las Meninas* (Foucault 1966), I am positioned where I cannot be: both implicated and expelled. The aesthetic frame – which defines the necessary distance of the artwork – also effects the collapse of this distance, my sudden sense of dizzying proximity. And so artistic communication, as Breillat conceives of it – the shock of contact which provokes the realisation of a truth – becomes possible.

Distance, contact, traces

Breillat's aesthetic and thematic concerns thus come together with rare harmony, as questions of contact and separation are indeed her signature preoccupations. This section will, accordingly, explore this conjunction, first by an account of Breillat's thematic vision of sexual difference, and subsequently by exploring in detail the aesthetics of the cut and the touch in her work.

Anatomie de l'enfer, Breillat says, was conceived partly as a direct refusal of the doctrine of the untouchability of the female body, particularly the menstruating female body, as part of Breillat's general determination to refuse the shame into which this body has falsely been forced. The film is, in this sense, a development of the position Breillat had already asserted in her Tehran address, in which Breillat identifies an unjust culpability projected onto women by men who – in a move that articulates a significant preoccupation in her work – lack a lucid understanding of their strengths and vulnerabilities (see Breillat 1999: 12–13). Breillat elaborates on this position in numerous interviews given around the release of *Anatomie de l'enfer*, denouncing what she calls the 'fundamentalist' view of the female body, but praising Christ and Mohammed for what she presents as their advocacy of equality and respect between the sexes (Gaillac-Morgue 2005; see also Murphy 2005 and Devanne 2005). This is thematised explicitly in the film in the words spoken by Casar's character to Siffredi's, when she challenges him to drink her diluted menstrual blood: 'Tu vois, tout est là. A cause de ce sang, ils nous appellent impures […] En réalité, ils ont peur de ce sang qui coule sans qu'aucune blessure soit faite'. ['You see, it's all there. Because of this blood, they call us impure. The truth is, they are afraid of this blood which flows without there being any wound.'] And after they have both drunk, she develops this in terms of touch: her tampon must have been designed by a man, she says, to interpose a hygienic, technological interval between the woman and her sex, to prevent her touching herself, so that she remain 'intacte'. This is a move which dates back at least to second-wave feminism, and which recalls in particular the early work of Luce Irigaray, reclaiming the female body from its exclusion as 'impure', a materialist gesture confronting this exclusion with its lack of foundation (see Irigaray 1974 and 1977.) Deploying a rhetoric of intimacy and interiority, Breillat renders the 'unwatchable' body tactile, to refuse the invisible 'mystery' which, as its supposed content, serves to keep it hidden (and which is at the origin of the fantasies of Bataille and Zagdanski, as discussed in the previous chapter). When Casar's character (the body of her double) expels her stone dildo before the man's gaze, the abrupt cut to a close-up of the emerging mineral surrounded by the organic contractions of her body produces an effect of extreme defamiliarisation, a brief moment of monstrosity (this is a petrified transposition of the vision of childbirth from *Romance*) which enforces a self-conscious interrogation of what exactly it is the female body is cloistered for supposedly containing. Marie's expression of the wish at the root of her sexuality in *Romance* may, partly, be read in these terms, as a confrontational desire on the part of a latter-day Lulu to expose the vacuity of the male gaze, and so to explode the myth of interiority from within: 'Je désire être ouverte jusqu'à l'intérieur et puis quand on voit que le mystère n'est qu'un amas de tripes, la femme est morte! A la limite, mon désir c'est de rencontrer Jacques l'Eventreur'. ['I want to be opened right up, and then, when they see the mystery is just a pile of blood and guts, the woman's dead! Ultimately, my desire is to meet Jack the Ripper.'] As these phrases indicate, however, it is of course the case that Marie's desire stands in a more problematic relationship to progressive narratives of sexual liberation than this partial reading would suggest. If Breillat here seeks to refuse the 'untouchability' of the female body, elsewhere she enshrines separation and distance as the law of absolute sexual difference, in terms which reinscribe the alienation she wants to denounce. For Breillat, the terms of the law are these: there are two sexes, cut off from one another by the absolute difference between two natures, which imposes a kind of solitude for each (Gaillac-Morgue 2005). (Not the least problem with this position is its heterocentricity, which it shares with the works considered in Chapter 1: on this, and the homophobia it programmes, see Chapter 3, pp. 90–1.) The only communication possible is that between two positions of isolation: discussing *Romance*, Breillat says, 'What I find very beautiful is that these two beings [Marie and Paolo] find it absolutely impossible to communicate. And that in their total solitude, however, from the very bottom of it, each understands the solitude of the other' (Joyce 2005). Less elegantly, Siffredi's character in *Anatomie de l'enfer* tells Casar's that he blesses the day he was born apart from her species.

Breillat in fact sets up a pattern of asymmetrical invasions between the sexes, whereby the emotion and attention that women seek from men is seen by these men as an unacceptable intrusion, whilst men selfishly penetrate women's bodies with little regard for their partner's pleasure or pain. When, in *Romance*, Paul impregnates Marie, he does so without ejaculating: symbolically, union does not quite take place (their sex is interrupted as he throws her aggressively to the floor), or takes place minimally, accidentally; contact – in this world of abyssal, unattainable interiority – is reconfigured as leakage. This jolting asymmetry is complicated by the outright disgust Breillat's men show with regard to female bodies, internalised in the self-abasing, self-harming stance of a woman like Marie. When Marie is propositioned and then assaulted by a stranger, what makes this scene troubling (and reminiscent of Escalle, as discussed above) is the complicity with which Marie greets this encounter. Her earlier fantasy of anonymous sex is rapidly and seamlessly degraded to 'se faire prendre par un mec, n'importe qui' ['being taken by some guy, any guy']. Marie's attitude is profoundly influenced by her biology: 'J'ai envie d'être un trou, un gouffre', she says (picking up an image used in *Parfait amour!*, when Frédérique likens orgasm to a 'gouffre'). 'Plus c'est béant, plus c'est obscène, plus ça doit être moi, l'intimité de moi, plus je me désiste, c'est métaphysique [...] Je m'évide. C'est ça ma pureté.' ['I want to be a hole, a pit'; 'The more it gapes, the more obscene it is, the more it has to be me, the most private part of me, the more I withdraw, it's metaphysical [...] I empty myself out. That's my purity.'] (On this, see Audé 2002: 117; and Chastel 2002: 215.) In this abyss, Marie embraces an abject and worthless sexual self-image (and so falls short of the more affirmative ethos of Escalle's heroines): 'Ça c'est mon rêve. Quand, pour un mec, je sais très bien que je suis juste une chatte qu'il a envie de bourrer'. ['That's my dream. When, for some guy, I know full well I'm just a pussy he wants to screw.'] Marie does not appear to be motivated by a determination to enlighten the men around her. The prime motivation for her immediate discontent is a lack of love from Paul, yet Marie's sense of degradation seems intrinsic to her eroticism. Indeed, Breillat may be suggesting it is intrinsic to all female sexuality The complex character of Marie combines without resolution a quest for transcendence ('J'ai une exigence incroyable d'absolu'), a profound and disturbing sense of her corporeality ('je désire être ouverte jusqu'à l'intérieur') and a hopeless need to be rescued from this paradox by a man ('Il aurait pu me réconcilier avec mon corps'). ['I have an unbelievable desire for the absolute'; 'I want to be opened right up'; 'He could have reconciled me to my body'.]

According to this vision, then, male and female are separated by the absolute cut of sexual difference; they do, nonetheless, touch. Indeed, one might configure Breillat's account of (hetero) sexual relations as the drama of this touch, its possibility or otherwise, its intermittence and its brutality. Male desire, it seems, is irreducibly murderous: Robert expresses to Marie his theory that 'la seule possibilité d'amour avec les femmes passe par le viol'; in *Anatomie de l'enfer*, when Siffredi's character acknowledges his desire to kill the woman, she claims already to have known this, since 'c'est le désir de tous les hommes'. ['The only possible route to love with women is via rape'; 'It's what all men desire.'] The misogyny which inhabits most of Breillat's male characters – Maurice in *36 fillette*, for example, or Deblache in *Sale comme un ange* – is exacerbated in the more explicit works until it becomes plainly murderous. In *Anatomie de l'enfer*, Breillat elaborates upon this, presenting male violence as a defence mechanism, a way of refusing the unknowability of women and the male weakness this implies. Fundamental to the vision Breillat here expresses to perfection is a hatred of weakness that is almost mutual: that is to say, it is physical weakness that men find so detestable in women, and psychological weakness that proves the insurmountable failing in men. Despite (or maybe because of) the extreme corporeal intimacy of their encounter, enlightenment and recognition between Siffredi's and Casar's characters prove elusive. Their sexual union may seem to be a harbinger of a new harmony, but the encounter ends with the woman's violent murder, symbolised through ghostly memories which are fittingly indicative of the unimpeachable barrier of representation that divides men from women throughout Breillat's work. No matter how present their bodies may be to each other, their mutual handling takes place through prosthetic fantasies. Indeed, Breillat's work details the very process by which the asymmetry of biology produces fears and anxieties that serve to veil the actuality of the sexes from each other. The more they view each other, the closer and more intimate they become, the more rampant and destructive are the fantasies that tear them apart. In *Anatomie de l'enfer*, Casar's character bemoans the fact that, in sexual relations, 'il y a une éternité entre l'offre et la demande'; later, Siffredi's comments, 'on espère que l'intimité d'une chambre rapproche. C'est pire'. ['there's an eternity between supply and demand'; 'you hope the intimacy of a bedroom will bring you closer together. It's worse'.] Indeed, what is confirmed by their intimacy is, precisely, separation, the impossible space of their violent (non-)relation.

Two male responses to this impasse are presented as possible: the misogynistic travesty of sublime unknowability into mere licentiousness (as in Siffredi's character's account of his experience to the stranger in the bar), violence attempting to stave off impotence; or an acceptance of this weakness, of tenderness, of the fact that 'la faiblesse est plus forte que la force' (Gaillac-Morgue 2005), ['weakness is stronger than strength'] implied in the tears of Siffredi's character which flow at the end of the first night, and again during this attempted misogynistic account. There is an ambivalence here in Breillat: it is not clear whether this male violence, and the bad faith on which it depends, are to be thought of as universal and inevitable, or whether we are to take seriously the notional consciousness-raising implied by the possibility of an honest openness to the power of fragility. Equally, it is not clear what role women might adopt in the face of this violence: that of educational martyr, as in *Anatomie de l'enfer*, or that of enlightened masochist, as in *Romance*? Is Marie's increasingly masochistic trajectory in *Romance* to be read as the expression of her individual psychopathology, or is she a sort of Everywoman, running the gamut of available male types? It may be that Breillat's mythic view of the transcendent truth of sexuality remains beholden to the misogynistic power relations she also deplores, and that, in this view, the only possibility of female liberation from these power relations is via a supposedly sublime assumption designed to transcend, but not displace them: small wonder that this aspect of her work has met with criticism. (See for example Audé 2002: 117–18; and Vincendeau 2001: 19.) For all her desire to reclaim the female body, Breillat's work sits well in a tradition of avant-garde representations of sexuality (from Sade to Bataille to Robbe-Grillet, say) whose charge derives in part, perversely, from their refusal to trouble a dominant economy in which the female role is to be celebrated as an excessive, saintly victim. In Breillat's homeopathic conception of her work, its mission is to 'soigner le mal par le mal' (Rouyer and Vassé 2004: 40). ['to treat disease with disease.'] The risk of this is that – like the works we looked at in

Chapter 1 – it may also result in a false sense of the universality of the disease in question.[6]

In her portrayal of sexual relations, then, Breillat both refuses untouchability and maintains the cut of separation. This play between the touch and the cut, proximity and distance, is, moreover, found throughout her work, and has some claim to constituting its signature aesthetic.[7] Alongside her use of sexually explicit material, this aspect also makes a crucial contribution to the timeliness of Breillat's work. As Laura Marks has argued, many of the media which shape the contemporary western cultural moment, along with the works they transmit, are defined by their paradoxical promise of a kind of immediacy, even in the midst of their extreme mediation: defined, that is, by their odd articulation of contact and distance (see Marks 2002, especially 177), what Foster calls 'the paradox of immediacy produced through mediation' (1996: 222). This promise not only invokes the return of the notion of the index (as discussed above): it also resonates with a history of phenomeno-logical discussions of the relationship between vision (classically a figure of distance) and touch (classically a figure of immediacy), for example by Merleau-Ponty (1999), Blanchot (2000) and, recently, Jean-Luc Nancy.[8] As Blanchot shows (2002: 28), what is at stake in the conflation of vision and touch is a challenge to the distant mastery of which vision is the pre-eminent figure, this challenge posed by the ungovernable immediacy conventionally represented by touch. This challenge is what Laura Marks has designated by the term 'haptic visuality': filmic moments when the viewer feels, often very suddenly, that she or he is in immediate, sensuous contact with the image (Marks 2000, especially 162, 188; and 2002, esp. xiii, 8, 12–16).[9] Breillat, too, as we have seen, frequently discusses the relationship of her work to its viewer in terms of a kind of touch. Indeed, her own understanding of this work depends crucially on the exact definition of the kind of touch it does or does not effect. Again, the question of the pornographic will be vital here, with its mythic promise of actual contact. This discussion will accordingly now conclude by exploring the kinds of touch proposed by Breillat's sexually explicit films.

In the aesthetics of Breillat's filmmaking, the cut – the constitutive punctuation through which montage articulates filmic struc-ture – itself emerges as form of touch. Breillat is rightly celebrated for her use of the long take, uninterrupted shots in which the intensity of particular scenes is heightened by the absence of the familiar rhythm of editing. But no less central to the construction of her films is her often dramatic cutting. According to Pasolini (whom Breillat repeatedly celebrates as a crucial influence), the cut equates to an existentialist conception of death: it is the punctuation that allows what would otherwise be an endless narrative to be articulated, to become meaningful.[10] One key way in which the cut articulates continuity into meaning is through juxtaposition (as is most famously argued by Eisenstein, who emphasises the dialectic of conflict this entails: see 1998a and 1998b). This use of juxtaposition might in fact be seen as a defining compositional technique in a range of early twentieth-century avant-gardist aesthetics (from Apollinaire to the Surrealists, in one lineage; but also including Cubism, and Eisenstein himself, of course): and, faithful to her Modernist avant-garde inheritance, Breillat exploits this possibility to outstanding effect – as shown notably in the most unequivocally hardcore sequence of *Romance*.

This sequence begins with the concrete realisation of separation in terms of sexual identity: in Marie's fantasy, she finds herself with other pregnant women in a strangely circular hospital room, each woman's body divided by a wall, on the other side of which their lower bodies are penetrated by unknown men. Earlier in the film, paraphrasing Alice from *Une vraie jeune fille*, Marie had said, looking at her sex in a mirror: 'Ce con ne peut pas appartenir à ce visage' (Alice's words, two decades earlier: 'Je ne peux pas admettre la proximité de mon visage et de mon vagin'.) ['This cunt cannot belong to this face'; 'I cannot accept that my face and my vagina should be so close together.'] In her fantasy, accordingly, the two bodies are divided, the acceptable, reproductive body cut off from the obscenely sexual lower body (see Martin 2005). This fantasy sequence has come to be known as the 'fantasme de la femme coupée en deux', ['the fantasy of the woman cut in two'] and its interpretation is of considerable significance for how we position Breillat's cinema as a whole. For when Breillat wishes to distance her work from pornography, she states that, unlike in her films, 'Dans le X, il n'y a que des corps coupés en deux, sans âme' (Clouzot 2004: 74). ['In porn, there are just bodies which have been cut in two, without a soul.'] She recognises that this therefore exposes this sequence from *Romance* to the charge of replicating mere 'porno', but rejects this – and rightly: the pornographic is here plainly framed, cited. But the structure is a difficult one. Marie is not 'cut in two', alienated, in the pornographic fashion, because it is her subjectivity that is at stake here (this is her fantasy). But the structure of her subjectivity is that she is, indeed, 'cut in two' (this fantasy divides her). Separation, here, is also a form of continuity. This is also true of the presence of the pornographic: indisputably framed, it is for all that an irreducible part of this sequence, precisely to the extent that it is pornographic. Again, separation is also continuity.

This awkward structure is represented physically in this sequence by the wall which divides the two halves of Marie's body. For this is not a divide: it is a caesura, an internal division, a cut within the body which is exposed to itself as to its own outside. The cut halves are sutured; and the resulting, articulated structure makes the cut the structure of their relation, the fault-line on which they meet. Separation and/as contact. And this is, crucially, taken up in the film's syntax. With consummate wit, in place of the usual hardcore climax of male ejaculation, Breillat cuts abruptly out of the fantasy to an actual clinical space, specifically to the jelly squirting onto Marie's belly prior to a scan (see Hottell and Russell-Watts 2002: 74). The intellectual montage effected by this cut not only pokes fun at the mechanistic pornographic scenario the film has just embraced – it also, by its metaphorical connection to this scenario, maintains a spaced relation to the carnality it has just abandoned. The brute literality of the pornographic sticks to Marie's tactile belly, which thereby transcends it without losing touch.

In *Romance*, then, Breillat cuts parodically away from the sperm that is the inevitable end point of the conventional pornographic narrative, in order – like the derisory version of this trope in Bonello's *Le Pornographe*, as discussed in Chapter 4 – to debunk its inflated status. In *Une vraie jeune fille*, she allows it to become visible: but not in the moment of ejaculation, rather as it is subsequently smeared on Jim's fingers. In both cases, she displaces the fetishism of visual pleasure by means of something else – and this something else is well captured by Marks's notion of 'haptic visuality'. The crucial edit in *Romance* suddenly fills the screen, disorientatingly, with sticky clear jelly: for a moment, the impression of this stickiness is everything. *Une vraie jeune fille* is full of such moments, startlingly and wonder-fully tactile (making this, arguably, still Breillat's most avant-garde work). Early in the film, shortly after Alice has arrived home, there is a memorable shot of fly paper, the sticking of the flies to the paper offering a nice *mise-en-abîme* of the contact with the viewer's sense of touch this image effects. (This is echoed later with a shot of a fly in jam, and then a fly on Alice's lips in her dream-like sequence of frankly unusual sex in the sand with Jim.) Subsequently, Alice writes her name by smearing her vaginal secretions onto a mirror at her boarding school, touches the resin seeping from a tree, cleans out the wax from her ears with a finger, crushes an egg in her hand. In all of these examples, the film emphasises the abject tactility of the image, either by close-up or by lingering on the shot. But the crucial, classically haptic moments in the film occur when Breillat cuts to a disorientatingly close image, which the viewer initially struggles to decipher. This occurs notably with the insect bite on Alice's arm which initiates the sequence in which she walks home with her knickers around her ankles, and with the shot of the cold water splashed onto her breast with which her mother returns her from an afternoon reverie. In both cases, Breillat startles the viewer by a combination of a swift edit, and the excessive proximity of the subsequent, fleshly image. In the first, the extreme, shadowy close-up of Alice's hand rubbing her arm lasts only just long enough for the viewer to work it out. In the second, the cut to the close-up of Alice's flesh tears us out of one order (her dreamy beach fantasy) and back to 'reality' (the diegesis). The texture of Alice's flesh is in each case experienced as uncomfortably close to the viewer, its tiny lines (in the first instance) or tiny hairs soaked with heavy water droplets (in the second) reconfiguring visual pleasure as a phenomenology of haptic contact. The cut touches.

It is this structure, then, that Breillat takes up again in *Romance*. The later film's two most startling edits both cut to close-up, haptic images: the jelly on Marie's stomach, and, most dramatically, the emergent baby's head in the birth scene. By the time we see Casar's double expel the stone dildo in *Anatomie de l'enfer*, therefore, we are not merely watching a disturbingly mineralised reprise of this birth scene (which it recalls by its content and its composition): we are also watching the latest example of a technique Breillat had first, and most extensively, developed in her debut film. It is not just the grotesque transposition of baby's head to stone that disconcerts: it is also the startling (and, here, expressly confrontational) touch of haptic visuality.

Across Breillat's *œuvre* as a whole, however, such moments are rare. (*Une vraie jeune fille*, in which they abound, might accordingly be considered her most ambitiously avant-garde work.) For this is not quite the kind of contact Breillat wants to establish with her viewer. In Marks's analysis, haptic visuality entails the risking of the spectator's subjectivity, and the privileging of bodily contact over psychological identification (for example 2002: 3, 13). Breillat, for all that she may wish to engage or confront her viewer, needs this subjectivity to remain in place. Explicitly, as we saw above, she wants to create moments of identification between the viewer and what is represented on screen. Her viewers are, as she says, 'atrocement priés de se reconnaître' (Frodon 2004) ['appallingly asked to recognise themselves']: and both halves of this structure are vital. It is appalling, we are put to the test – but this is part of a process of recognition, in which our psychology therefore also remains intact. The striking contact Breillat seeks, and achieves, serves an aesthetics in which it is transcended by the re-establishment of psychological mechanisms; we are grabbed by the image, but this is so that we might be moved elsewhere, to a higher order.

While it works tremendously well as a description of certain crucial moments in her most sexually explicit work, then (*Une vraie jeune fille*, *Romance* and *Anatomie de l'enfer*), Marks's 'haptic visuality' does not offer a key to Breillat's aesthetics as a whole. Seeking to describe this aesthetics, we will have to find a position which manages to embrace the desire for contact it evinces, but also maintains the pathos of separation which paradoxically sustains the possibility of identification. Such a position might be found by considering Breillat's images of traces, most especially traces on the skin of her actors; and it is with such a consideration that this chapter will draw to a close.

As discussed above with reference to *Une vraie jeune fille*, Breillat often presents us with images of the body's secretions or excretions, those abject substances which cannot be assimilated. Breillat likes the disgust these images provoke, for the contact it facilitates; but the point of these images is not just the physical effect they are likely to provoke. The point is also that, in representing that which has *fallen from* the body, such images entertain with these bodies the odd relationship of spaced contact which defines the existence of the residue, or the trace. These substances are base, *dejected*, because the body has *rejected* them: they are what has been left behind. And Breillat also likes the pathos they thereby introduce. For the trace is the index at its most mournful, bearing witness to a presence which by definition has departed. Accordingly, this pathos of the trace is most evident not in these confrontationally abject images, or in the extreme disorientation of the haptic, but rather in the less dramatic, more tender dimensions of Breillat's aesthetic. Pre-eminent here is the attention paid by *Anatomie de l'enfer* to marks on the skin. When Casar's character first undresses for Siffredi's, she sits with her back to the camera, showing the ghostly, more or less red imprint of the bra she has just removed. Breillat holds this shot for long enough for us to register its layers of significance: she is undressed, has been dressed but now is not, her clothing – the quintessentially feminine garment that is the bra – still declaring the persistent presence of the social in the trace of its presence, which is also the confirmation of its absence (see Clouzot 2004: 91). Later, on the fourth night, as Casar's bare foot slides down Siffredi's left shoulder, we see a long scar at the top of his chest, just below his collar bone. We are reminded that this is a body: but the body of unknown, painful experience, not the plastic body of pornographic hyper visibility. The body bears the traces of what has been: what is no longer there, but whose absent presence is marked, intimately. These traces visualise the gap which both separates from and links to the event or object that left them; as such, they figure the pathos of Breillat's particular version of spaced, articulated contact. The real body and its various marks insist on their fleshy presence; but this presence is defined by its melancholic relation to a now departed impact. Breillat's aesthetic conjures up *both* presence *and* absence, *both* visceral shock *and* transcendent truth.

Traversing the touch as the space of a cut, joined by the cut in the space of separation, we experience Breillat's world as one in which the terms bleed, staining each other, but not fusing. Her images touch us inasmuch as they are *both* witnesses to the reality of their objects, *and* the aesthetic symbolisation of those objects. Her actors, in the explicit works (and including the body-doubles), become *performers*: their bodily presence is irreducible, even as its artistic disposition produces its truth (see Marks 2002: 207 and Williams 2001: 22). Performing the role of Alice in *Une vraie jeune fille*, for example, Charlotte Alexandra urinates into the sand: the reality of the act itself is beyond qualification, whatever this scene might also be taken to mean. Just as the pornographic use of any image persists to haunt its symbolic ascent, so does the base flesh we watch – a meaningless index, the irreducible, resistant, literal body – here remain mutely, pulsatingly present, even within its filmic elevation (or, indeed, its instrumental appropriation for the guilty pleasures of fetishism). And this residual presence allows us to draw together what is effectively Breillat's *unintended* aesthetics of performance, which consists of a complex tangle of elements. First, the image effects a kind of physical contact with the viewer, possibly by virtue of its haptic qualities. Then, as Breillat desires, this contact is transcended in the direction of truth, as the scene takes on meaning, and we become bound to it not by physical contact, but by identification. Contrary to Breillat's wishes, however, the literal index remains, incompletely sublimated by this transcendence. Worse, this persisting literality is also what makes some elements available for a reductive, fetishistic, pornographic appropriation. The meaningless indexicality of such elements also resists this appropriation, however: it will no more be fully taken up into this instrumental economy than it will be swept away on the wings of Breillat's desired sublimation. And so, finally, Breillat makes her distinctive kind of contact: with the viewer who is caught up in this complex of immediate reality and its articulation into meaning. It is now spectators, and not characters, who find themselves in the position of Hal Foster's 'dysfunctional' postmodern subject, 'suspended between obscene proximity and spectacular separation' (1996: 222, as quoted in Chapter 1): split, yet somehow asked to make this meaningful.

Breillat's art is left both intact and punctured – and this may well be a considerable part of what makes it so compelling. Her hard-line Modernism – anti-indexical, anti-literal, transcendent and revelatory – fails to account for the texture of her works, which are fascinating and timely inasmuch as they give us *both* sublimation *and* its failures. Refusing the objectification created by what she denounces as the false distance of eroticism, entangled despite herself with the literality of the pornographic, Breillat celebrates an art of intermittent, real, transcendent, seeping contact.

Notes

1 The following account is greatly indebted to Laura McMahon's outstanding work on Breillat's treatment of these issues, as well as to her 'Touching intact: Sophie Calle's threat to privacy' (2005).
2 Interview with Breillat by Gaillac-Morgue, on UK DVD release of *Anatomie de l'enfer* (London: Tartan Films, 2005).
3 Breillat's discussions are invariably heterosexual, a point to which we

will return in Chapter 3, pp. 90–1.

4 See for example Hottell and Russell-Watts 2002; Vincendeau 2001; Murphy 2005; Price 2005; and Vasse 2004: 89–90.

5 Thanks to Patrick ffrench for hunting down this reference.

6 For contrasting views of the possibilities offered by *Romance* in terms of female subjectivity and gender politics, see Wilson 2001 and Phillips 2001.

7 The figure of the cut deployed here is greatly indebted to its elaboration in ffrench 1999.

8 Nancy's thinking of touch is to be found throughout his work; the ideal exposition is to be found in Derrida 2000, which also includes Derrida's critique of what he takes to be the faith in immediacy and continuity which often subtends the metaphorical conflations of vision and touch in phenomenological discussions. (On Merleau-Ponty, see also Derrida 1990: 56–7.) These issues are admirably discussed in Cathryn Vasseleu 1998.

9 For an outstanding example of how Marks's approach can contribute to the reading of specific films, see Wilson 2005.

10 See Pasolini 1988 (and, on this, Gordon 2000) and Doane 2002: 105.

3

Inside, outside: Guillaume Dustan and Erik Rémès

In 1971, considering the Sadean libertine's preference for penetrating his female victims anally rather than vaginally, Roland Barthes argues that this preference allows the libertine to produce the transgressive meaning of his act: choosing anal intromission in a body which also offers vaginal intromission as a possibility, the libertine refuses the values of productivity, futurity and vitality conventionally symbolised by the act of heterosexual vaginal penetration (2002b: 809–10). In Barthes' provocatively formalistic reading (similar to the one he had earlier proposed in relation to Bataille's *Histoire de l'œil*, of course), anal rape is thus refigured as the playful manipulation of symbolic codes. His reading has its point, though: for within the Sadean schema, the female body does indeed function just as he says. Sade thus privileges heterosexual anality as the principal element in his attack on the (re)productive economics of investment and return, that ancient metaphorics which in its sexual guise sees the paternal seed invested in the maternal bodily matrix, where it grows before returning to the father, with interest, as either his property or, alternatively, his privileged relation to futurity.[1] It is not necessarily clear, however, and *pace* Barthes, that the attack on this economics must be confined to the realm of *heterosexual* anality. Indeed, precisely this question of reproduction, and the investment in futurity it implies, are often at stake in a range of debates over the relation between various gay or queer identities and the heteronormative mainstream (for example Bersani 1996, Edelman 2004). And it is certainly the case, as will be seen in this chapter, that both the homophobic dismissal of homosexuality, and its defiant, resistant assertion, sometimes rely on the figure of anality as a kind of shorthand for their arguments about the relationship between desire, productivity, anatomy, futurity, community, and so on.[2] The question of whether the rectum is indeed, in Leo Bersani's memorable phrase, a grave (Bersani 1988), turns out here to be vital in more ways than one.

This chapter will look at the work of Guillaume Dustan and Erik Rémès in the context of the increased cultural presence of sexually explicit writing, and will explore in particular the existential stakes and writing strategies involved in their respective approaches to the identity politics of being a seropositive gay man in Paris at the turn of the twenty-first century. The work of both writers has generated extreme controversy for its depiction and apparent celebration of extreme sexual practices in a context defined by AIDS and HIV: this chapter will discuss their writings and other cultural interventions in terms of their deployment of various problematics – social, sexual, physical or textual – relating to figures of containment, boundaries, limits, and so on. After a brief initial presentation of the two authors, the chapter will begin by setting the general context against which their work needs to be interpreted: first, recent French legislation with specific relevance to same-sex relationships; second, the monotonous homophobia and apparent exhaustion of much of the more mainstream material considered elsewhere in this study. Their work will then be addressed more closely, with analysis first of the existential issues they raise in relation to seropositivity, and then of the particular ways in which their work engages with its world. As sexually explicit life-writing, this work does not particularly *cite* the codes of pornography: rather, it refers to the use of pornography as part of sexual activity, and to its role in articulating scenes of desire, and itself approaches the pornographic in its graphic descriptions. It is, moreover, in their negotiation of the quintessentially pornographic qualities of transitivity and literality, that these writers most urgently confront the possibilities and responsibilities facing their work. Two of the most frequently cited definitional aspects of pornography are its status as *act* (the reality of its indexical representations, or its performative effectivity) and as *incitement to act* (as a stimulant, possibly nefarious): as we will see, these aspects are at the heart of the debates generated by the sexually-explicit writings of these two authors.

It should be noted, finally, that this chapter discusses texts authored by, and dealing predominantly with the lives of, gay men. This should not be seen as suggesting that lesbian-authored material addressing in explicit terms the identitarian issues raised by new forms of sexual practice does not exist: the work of Cy Jung, for example, would deserve particular mention in this light. If such lesbian-focused work is not analysed in our study, this is for two reasons, both relating to the criteria which have generated our corpus. This study is concerned with material which has achieved cultural prominence by means of its reference to the codes of pornography. In the first place, then: these codes seem not to form an especially significant reference point in the relevant French lesbian material, quite possibly owing to the relative scarcity of French pornography by and for lesbians. (References to pornography in Jung accordingly take the form of critical references to the formulaic representations of pseudo-lesbian activity in hetero-sexual – and so heteronormative – pornography: see for example Jung 1998: 60, 204.) Second: this material is primarily produced by small publishing houses, and has not enjoyed comparable promi-nence even to that of Rémès (published by Balland and the Editions Blanche), let alone Dustan (POL, Balland, the mass paperback series 'J'ai lu', and latterly Flammarion). This situation is anything but a comment on the quality and interest of this work; but it may well testify to the relative cultural visibility of lesbians and gay men in this recent French context.[3]

Contexts

Guillaume Dustan was the *nom de plume* of William Baranès, who, after an education taking in the prestigious institutions of Sciences-Po and the Ecole Nationale d'Administration, and an early legal career, turned to writing after discovering that he was seropositive. The first of his books was published in 1996; seven more followed – the melancholy *Je sors ce soir*, the hard-core *Bildungsroman Plus fort que moi*, and generically mixed, politically inflected, and increas-ingly melancholy works including *Nicolas Pages*, which won the 1999 Prix de Flore – before his death in October 2005, at the age of 40, from what the autopsy referred to as 'accidental intoxication'. Dustan became a prominent cultural figure, founding the first gay collection by a major publishing house (the 'Rayon Gay', then short-ened to 'Le Rayon', published by Balland), appearing on radio and television, and, most notably, detailing the most controversial aspects of the social and sexual life of his community in the most immediate kind of autofiction. Most significantly, Dustan's writings present – in a variety of tones, from the celebratory via the melancholy to the sentimental – a life including frequent and often extreme sexual activity, of which the most important elements are anal fisting, and, especially, the refusal of safe sex in the practice known as 'barebacking' (anal penetration without the use of a condom). The prominence in his early work of this last element earned him the censure of those for whom preventing the spread of HIV remains a priority, most notably the organisation ACT-UP and one of the principal founders of its Paris branch, Didier Lestrade. On Dustan's death, responses were divided between those for whom his supposed promotion of bareback sex amounted to extreme irresponsibility, and those who wanted to celebrate either this confrontational position, or the writings – much more varied than this polemic would suggest – of which it forms a significant part.[4] Dustan, for his part, had given his definitive account of this debate and its ramifications in his last text, *Premier essai* (2005: 158–87).

Erik (also Eric) Rémès completed Master's degrees in philosophy and clinical psychology, before moving at the start of the 1990s to work as a journalist for such publications as *Gai pied hebdo* and *Libération*. His first book – the strikingly titled *Je bande donc je suis* – was published by Dustan in his series at Balland in 1999; it was followed the next year, in the same series, by *Le Maître des amours* and, in 2003, continuing Rémès' preference for memorable titles, by *Serial Fucker: Journal d'un barebacker*.[5] (He is also, it should be noted, the author of a handful of sex guides.) As this last title suggests, Rémès is also concerned with the identity politics of extreme sexuality, again most intensely focused on debates around barebacking; like Dustan, he also has a liking for the genre of autofiction, his first and third texts being narrated by the alter ego 'BerlinTintin', and folding into their texture various real-world characters, places, events, and so on. Like Dustan's *Nicolas Pages*, *Serial Fucker* is also notable for its use of collage as a compositional technique; Rémès appears to be developing a form of writing in which the supposed immediacy of emails and blogs takes on – and places in severe crisis – the safeguards of literary form. Together, their work constitutes a considerable description of and intervention into a more or less extreme form of gay male sexuality as lived in Paris at the start of the twenty-first century.

The decade from the publication of Dustan's first book in 1996 until his death in 2005 saw major developments in the status of homosexuality in French culture. In 2001, Paris elected as its mayor

Bertrand Delanoë, France's most prominent openly gay politician to date. This event symbolises the key trend during this period: namely, towards the increased visible presence of lesbians and gay men, recognised as such, in the mainstream of a French society still defined by its attachment to the republican ideal of a universalist indifference to such identitarian groupings. As we will see, this movement is contested (on both sides), and it should certainly not be taken as a sign that homophobia, and its associated violence, no longer form a cause for concern. Some changes have nonetheless achieved the kind of legal solidity which confers upon them landmark status. The crucial instance of this is the introduction in 1999 of the PACS, a legal instrument offering a kind of halfway house between marriage and cohabitation. Its provisions allow adult couples, regardless of gender, to register their civil partnership and, as a consequence, to enjoy some – but by no means all – of the benefits and responsibilities deriving from marriage, with regard to such areas as social security, housing, employment, financial liability, income tax, and so on. The PACS does not address itself specifically to same-sex couples: in the classic French universalist tradition, it presents itself as 'blind' to anything other than the civil status of those involved. It does, however, give such couples a degree of legal recognition and security they had previously lacked, while falling short of – and, according to some, actively blocking – the introduction of same-sex marriages in France. Most often at stake in these arguments is the supposed 'holy trinity' family model of father, mother, and child, and the heterosexual investment in (or colonisation of) futurity this implies; at the time of writing (April 2006), debates over same-sex parenting ('homoparentalité') continue, with legal judgements seemingly inching towards a degree of de facto recognition.[6]

The relation between mainstream French culture and gay and lesbian identities has thus, over this period, been articulated along the lines which have also defined other notable identitarian debates: namely, the interrogation of republican universalism by the claims of specific minority, oppressed or oppositional groups. The specific issue may be ethnicity (as in the debates over the principle of *laïcité* in schools, or in the riots of late 2005), or gender (as in the movement in favour of the principle of *parité*, namely the equal representation of women and men in public bodies) or, as here, sexuality: at stake is the same clash between a republican tradition which insists on considering each citizen as an abstract individual, and the voices of those whose experience has led them to view this claim as at best laudable but empty, at worst an insidious form of discrimination.[7] The argument is the familiar one encountered by various forms of identity politics over at least the past half century: integration versus separatism, egalitarian invisibility versus specific recognition; in the terms of the French debate, 'le droit à l'indifférence' versus 'le droit à la différence'. Both David Caron and Frédéric Martel (in the interests of otherwise opposing analyses) have argued that one effect of the AIDS crisis was the formation of the French gay community as a distinct agent within the political field at large (see Caron 2005, and Martel 1999a: 335–45), of which the most spectacular culmination would be the Gay Pride march in Paris on 24 June 1995, attended by some 60,000 participants. For some (of whom Guy Hocquenghem doubtless remains the most prominent emblem), greater integration equals the loss, even the betrayal of the specific qualities of the community: in this case, these qualities are associated with the challenge to heteronormative family life embodied in queer identities. On this reading, the PACS, same-sex parenting, and so on, would represent a misguided desire for integration into what should, rather, be exploded. Anne Garréta, for example, witheringly describes the PACS as 'a good old-fashioned edict of toleration' (2001: 165); and the section of Rémès' website devoted to his blogs opens with the following quotation from Françoise d'Eaubonne, one of the founders in 1971 of the Front Homosexuel d'Action Révolutionnaire (FHAR): 'Vous dites que la société doit intégrer les homosexuels, moi je dis que les homosexuels doivent désintégrer la société'.[8] In this context, debates about safe sex have major resonance beyond questions of individual or public health. For Dustan and Rémès, polemically, the assertion of seropositivity, which they ally to the refusal to condemn barebacking and other extreme practices, is also the assertion of a specific, distinct, identitarian position. In this climate, this assertion, and the emphatic celebration of anal pleasure it entails, constitutes a defiant rejection of a universalism dismissed as merely a cover for the propagation of familial, reproductive heteronormativity.

A case for the figure of anality as a rejection of – and as provoking the panic of – universalist and nationalist discourse is made forcefully by Marie-Hélène Bourcier, in her trenchant reading of the furore surrounding the film of *Baise-moi* (see Bourcier 2004). In this reading the murder, by means of a bullet in the rectum, of the miserable male swinger named only in the credits as 'la truie' ('the sow', an appropriation of a standard misogynistic insult) symbolises the anality that universalism cannot assimilate. But the example is problematic: for the scene has also, with some justification, been interpreted as enacting a primary homophobic fantasy, in which the reference points would be the deaths of Lorca and Edward II, for example (see Reynaud 2005). And, unlike in Dustan and Rémès, it is hardly anal pleasure that is here in play, but rather a familiar association between anality and death. The problematic example is suggestive, however. For it points in two instructive directions. First, although its own specific instance may not be quite exact, the notion that anality, in its refusal of heteronormative reproductive futurity, is a threat to mainstream culture, will bear further consideration in the case of Dustan and Rémès. And second – inadvertently, perhaps – this example serves as a reminder of the homophobia which defines even some of their most progressive contemporaries.

As we saw in the previous two chapters, much of the sexually explicit material we are considering here is emphatically heterocentric, obsessed with *fixing* relations between the sexes. The perfect example of this is the work of Breillat, who elevates anatomical sexual difference into a metaphysical principle, thus making an ontological claim for the primary division of humanity into the two categories of man and woman. This is in order to challenge the dominant phallocratic order, in the name of its repressed female materiality, of course; but as a consequence of this heterocentricity, same-sex desire finds itself cast as miserable, complicit and deviant. Siffredi's character in *Anatomie de l'enfer*, for example, is presented as the ideal incarnation of murderous masculinity inasmuch as he is gay, which fails to distinguish between the homosexual and the homosocial, imagining that it is possible to take the former as a synecdochic figure of the former. In this interpretation, the gay man is just the ultimate embodiment of the masculine, in that he seeks to exclude the feminine and spend his time wholly in the company of men. Any admission of the reality of same-sex desire would make this a nonsense, of course, as it would force the recognition that, as Eve Kosofsky Sedgwick (1985) demonstrated in her decisive formulation of the notion of homosocial desire, the homosocial has same-sex desire not as its ultimate expression, but as its constitutive repressed term. At which point, ironically, such attempts to condemn the homosocial become, in their homophobic repression of same-sex desire, continuous with its violent exclusion of the gay otherness it dare not think.[9] The homosocial is thematised extensively in *Parfait amour!*, as Christophe's relationship with his friend Philippe becomes the object of explicit discussion in terms of its sublimated same-sex desire; at this point, a critical discussion of the homosocial seems possible, as the film recognises that this formation is constituted by the *repression* of homosexuality. Unfortunately, Frédérique's subsequent relentless taunting of Christophe for not being a 'vrai mec' (one who likes women, and who can get it up properly), and her repeated homophobic abuse of him (for example as a 'sale petit pédé de merde') ['real man'; 'dirty little queer bastard'] close down this potential critical dimension, and the film slips into a heterocentrism that affirms the homosocial it seeks to critique.[10]

In Breillat, then, gay desire is negated, invoked only to facilitate a reactionary vision of heterosexuality as metaphysical truth. It does not fare much better in other work we consider here, either. In Houellebecq, lesbian desire is rolled on as familiar male pornographic fantasy (see especially *Plateforme*); if Despentes adds to this a critical account of the mechanics of this fantasy (in both *Baise-moi* and *Les Jolies Choses*), she leaves its heterosexual matrix untroubled. Houellebecq's only real references to gay sexuality as such are in *Les Particules élémentaires*: first in the character of Desplechin, whose desire is as exhausted as that of most of Houellebecq's male characters; and then in the characteristically ambivalent mention (both snidely reductive and genuinely envious) of the enviable liveliness and heroic dignity of a gay life made up of sex in backrooms followed by a 'militant' death from AIDS (2000b: 18–19; 120). Stereotypical reduction, relative invisibility, or homophobic assimilation to a generalised, murderous masculinity: these seem to be the positions granted to gay sexuality – and even this is overwhelmingly gay male sexuality: lesbian desire is almost entirely invisible from this cultural field, it would seem – in this recent sexually explicit work. Such would be the world into which Dustan and Rémès seek to intervene. Perhaps, rather than *fixing* the heterosexual order, it would just be better to *explode* this order?

Living on

In much of the exhausted mainstream, existential and sexual ambition are definitively off the menu. Its tenaciously heterosexual imaginary repeatedly pays tribute to a phallocentrism it thinks it is subverting, by lamenting more or less desperately the ubiquity of erectile dysfunction: as we will see throughout this study, nobody, be it in Houellebecq, Despentes or Breillat, say, can get it up any more. (With the signal exception of Rocco Siffredi, ever the professional.) And this appears to encode a persistent fidelity to the symbolic equivalence of phallic projection and existential project: for nobody seems able to grasp the space of their existence as a potentially meaningful narrative, either. (For the suggestion that phallic projection constitutes a form of perceived existential advantage, allowing the little boy to project himself beyond himself while also fearfully keeping the world at a distance, see de Beauvoir 1949.) In the classic existentialist paradigm, an active relation to one's existence is of course made possible by the fact of death: it is because I know I will die that I can grasp my existence in advance as a potentially meaningful totality, and so resolve to fill it with meaning. In much of the material considered elsewhere in this study, such an attitude seems hardly to register as a possibility. It persists, however – including in Dustan and Rémès. And in their case, this has something to do with a changed, and vexed, relation to mortality.

As Lawrence Schehr has argued (2002, 2004 and especially 2005), the history of AIDS writing in France records a shift from the works of mourning of which those of Hervé Guibert would be the best-known example, to others, such as those of Dustan and Rémès, which document and celebrate a seropositive life no longer dominated by imminent death. As Schehr explains, the development in the mid-1990s of antiretroviral combination therapy has meant that diagnosis as HIV-positive may now lay down the marker of a death to come, but deferred by ten years or so, the suspended death sentence of a more or less manageable chronic condition (2002: 183–4; 2004: 101). As Dustan says pithily in *Dans ma chambre* : 'Ils sont presque tous séropositifs. C'est fou ce qu'ils durent' (1996: 74). ['They are, almost all of them, HIV-positive. It's crazy how they last' (1998b: 55).] This scenario clearly lends itself to interpretation via the classic existentialist paradigm, as Dustan says in *Génie divin*: 'être séropo ça redouble la condition humaine, la condition humaine c'est savoir qu'on va mourir, sauf que quand tu es séropo, tu sais vraiment que tu vas mourir' (2002a: 52). ['being seropositive gives you the human condition twice over: the human condition is knowing you're going to die, but when you're seropositive, you really know you're going to die'.] Seropositivity imposes an unavoidable relation to mortality, but suspends to some extent its advent, thus creating both the final term and an interval, which, together, make possible an active campaign of self-realisation. (See Schehr 2002: 184–5.)

Accordingly, Rémès' *Je bande donc je suis* articulates its identity politics almost entirely by a playful hijacking of the lexicon of Sartrean Existentialism. The queering of the Cartesian *cogito* in the work's title already proposes an existential assumption of sexuality as constitutive of meaning; its prologue twists this further, into 'Seropo ergo sum' (2004: 11). What is at issue is indeed the creation of my existence as the space of possible meaning on the basis of my anticipated death: but the existential dialectic of Sartre's *L'Etre et le néant*, in which the negativity of this being-towards-death is converted into the constructive nothingness of my perpetually forward-flung existence, is here pushed to a closer embrace of this negativity as such, in the affirmation of desire as sole existential principle: '*Libido ergo sum*. Je désire donc je suis. Je bande donc je suis. Une âme qui quête, une essence qui roule à sa perte, un être à la mort' (15). ['*Libido ergo sum*. I desire therefore I am. I get it up therefore I am. A questing soul, an essence on the road to ruin, a being-towards-death'.] The opening of *Je bande donc je suis* in fact consists of a magnificently witty *tour de force*, a pastiche of Sartre in which a coffee cup is envied for the simple, self-sufficient facticity of its *en-soi* existence:

> séropositif, au petit déjeuner, cette tasse remplie de café me paraît beaucoup plus lourde que d'habitude, plus compacte et consistante que lorsque j'étais séronégatif. Une tasse pâteuse, collante et moite, inébranlable [...] Elle me renvoie à mon être, à la mort; elle m'insulte cette vilaine sartrienne. Elle n'est pas séropositive, elle! [...] Oui, pourquoi ne suis-je pas une tasse à café idiote, hétérosexuelle et séronégative dont la seule raison d'exister est de recevoir du café? (11)

> [seropositive, at breakfast, and this cup full of coffee seems to me much heavier than normal, more compact, of greater consistency than when I was seronegative. A lumbering cup, moist, tacky, unshakeable [...] It returns me to my being, to death; it's insulting me, in its nasty Sartrean way. It's not seropositive, is it! [...] Yes, why am I not a stupid, heterosexual, seronegative coffee cup, with no reason to exist except to have coffee poured into me?]

Rémès is indeed no idiot, though; and this is far from a simple dismissal of the existential model. The core of *Je bande donc je suis* is in fact this interrogation of the relation between existence and

death, sometimes faithfully existentialist, sometimes not. Death is
first of all the rhythm of a collective experience, which beats through
the text as a polemical denunciation of the homophobic indifference
of the world at large. Rémès regularly accompanies a date with a
statistic giving the number of cases of AIDS declared in France at
that time, and quotes as epigraphs the homophobic vitriol of political figures. Despite his at times witty, playful tone, Rémès never
reduces the epidemic to an apolitical opportunity for individual self-
contemplation. This existential quest takes place in world of T-cell
counts, opportunistic infections, and the relentless loss of loved ones.
'La mort est notre culture', he writes (118). ['Death is our culture'.]
The death of others – the only access we have to our own unavoidable death, for the Heidegger of *Being and Time* – inevitably throws
the seropositive existentialist back to the anticipation of his own
death, however; and as the effectiveness of treatments improves, the
notional removal of the suspended death sentence that has defined
his life accordingly leaves our narrator in a panic: 'Vais-je survivre à
mon infection?', he wonders (179). 'Oh! mon virus, ce n'était pas la
mort, loin de là; mon virus c'était la vie [...] Ce virus était ma raison
d'être. Je suis une pédale radicale séropositive' (180–1). ['Am I going
to outlive my infection?'; 'Oh, my virus wasn't death, far from it:
my virus was life [...] That virus was my *raison d'être*. I'm a radical,
seropositive queer.'] The idea of the removal of the death that had
made possible his existential self-assumption, leaves him only with
an anonymous, indifferent death that might be anyone's, the dying
that cannot heroically be assumed as my virile destiny: 'La retraite et
sa maison, l'arthrite et la zézette molle à jamais. Quelle horreur alors
la vie' (180): ['retirement, the house that goes with it, arthritis, and a
limp dick for evermore. What an awful life'] wrinkled, incontinent,
for all the world like a heterosexual.

   BerlinTintin moves beyond this panic, however, reaches the final
stage of his dialectic: for the heightened awareness of death brought
by seropositivity, he concludes, was but an intensified version of an
existential attitude he had already found:

> Oui-oui, pourquoi grandir si on sait que l'on va mourir? Parce que la
> contamination était censée me responsabiliser, donner tout son poids à la
> vacuité de mon existence? Parce que condamné à mourir précocement, il
> me fallait remplir ma vie au plus vite? Pour bourrer la vie de sens? Que
> t'chi! J'ai toujours pensé que la vie était faite pour jouir et que toute autre
> approche rationnelle était un leurre. (210)

[Why yes, why grow up if you know you're going to die? Because infection was supposed to make me responsible, fill the vacuum of my existence with its share of substance? Because, condemned to an early death, I had to fill up my life at top speed? Cram it full with meaning? Balls! I have always thought that life was made for pleasure and that any other rational approach was a trick.]

The existential truth in question is not restricted to what he calls the 'pathos' (179) of a death brought closer by infection: it is, simply, that 'La vie, c'est un sacré long travail sur soi-même' (211). ['Life is one long process of working on yourself'.]

The existential narrative of Rémès and Dustan is, accordingly, the paradigm of self-fashioning to be derived from Nietzsche (an incessant reference throughout these texts), especially as refracted through the later Foucault. The assumption of an oppressed identity is already, of course, a defiant act of self-creation and self-affirmation: as Dustan puts it, this is 'le sens de la vie: devenir soi' (2003: 386) ['the meaning of life: becoming oneself'] which in his case, as he indicates in *Plus fort que moi*, entails rejecting the high-achieving, bourgeois, hypocritical path of conformity open to him (1998a: 16–17). The writing of this assumption thus becomes, after Rousseau and Nietzsche, the account of how one becomes what one is: these explicit texts become, in Dustan's term, 'autoporno-biography' (2002a: 2). Sexuality is to be assumed *and* continually (re)constructed. The self is there to be formed; and this exercise has as its primary site, the body of the individual, there to be modified prosthetically, cosmetically, chemically, athletically, and so on, in what BerlinTintin calls, 'ma putain de vie en échafaudage perpétuel' (Rémès 2000: 19). ['this fucking life of mine, permanently under construction'.] In the lineage of what Dustan presents as a still-unfolding liberal individualism, human nature becomes a 'supernature' (2003: 255; the reference is also to Cerrone's 1977 Eurodisco classic of this title), open to continual reinvention. In this perspective, sexual experimentation acquires an ontological significance: as Dustan writes in *Nicolas Pages*, 'je me dis que les hétéros feraient bien de s'intéresser à ce que nous sommes en train d'inventer' (2003: 70). ['I say to myself that heteros would do well to find out about what it is we're inventing'.] Ontological, and also political, these 'new pornographies': 'Nous réclamons les religions de la jouissance. Nous le sommes: raves, backrooms, saunas, c'est cela la politique nouvelle. La nouvelle pornographie. La nouvelle vie' (2002a: 336).

['We demand religions of ecstatic pleasure. It's what we are: raves, backrooms, saunas: this is the new politics. The new pornography. The new life.']

The key reference in this context is, then, the later Foucault; the Foucault who, in addition to devoting volume three of his *Histoire de la sexualité* to the ancient doctrine of the 'care of the self', made explicit in interviews the links he saw between the possibilities of creative existential self-fashioning opened by oppositional sexualities, and specific gay sexual practices, particularly forms of sadomasochism such as those which find themselves at the heart of the backroom culture of Dustan and Rémès. In a key interview from 1982, for example, Foucault famously argued that sexual subcultures were the site primarily of *innovation*, of the invention of new forms of pleasure, the remapping of the sexual body, and the displacement of erotic activity from the telos of genitally focused orgasm (1994: 737–8). The sexualities documented by Dustan and Rémès may not follow Foucault in his celebration of a displacement of sexual pleasure away from the genitals: erection and ejaculation remain absolutely central. But they are central within a field which exceeds by far the conception of sexual activity in which the genitals would be primary, and in which invention is a value in itself. As BerlinTintin says: 'si je ne parle que de fist et de trucs bizarres, c'est que les êtres humains se baisant depuis des lustres, il me semble plus intéressant et créatif de parler d'autre chose que de ces basiques intromissions' (93). ['if all I talk about is fisting and other weird stuff, it's because since human beings have been fucking each other since the dawn of time, it seems to me more interesting and more creative to talk about something other than those basic insertions'.] In *Le Maître des amours*, indeed, Rémès cites Foucault on fisting (2000: 213); in their celebration of a sexual *ethos* of constant, oppositional becoming, Rémès and Dustan are faithful to Foucault's insistence that sexuality should be about the creation of new possibilities, not the 'liberation' of some mythical essence. Hence Rémès' playful relation to Sartre: while this Foucaldian self-fashioning shares obvious similarities with its existential version, it has – as Foucault points out (1994: 617) – no need for *authenticity* as a core value. As Judith Butler has most famously argued (1993, 1999), developing the Foucaldian paradigm, the self being created is *both* a multiple, shifting, process of reinvention *and* a significant point of resistance to the discourses and practices of power in relation to which it is constituted.

What is created above all in this world of invention is a new sexual body, and a new relation to the sexual body; most particularly, a reconfiguration of notions of inside and outside, as produced primarily by expertise in anal fisting. As *Dans ma chambre* makes clear, there are important reasons to develop such expertise, to avoid internal injury (Dustan 1996: 34); but the knowledge it brings goes beyond such pragmatic concerns, and becomes a reinvention of the self and its relations to others. In the same text, the character Stéphane is described as having 'une compréhension parfaite de mes entrailles' (35); the narrator later states that 'Je suis devenu très conscient de mon corps, de son extérieur comme de son intérieur, grâce à ça, je pense' (73). ['a perfect comprehension of my entrails'; 'I've become very conscious of my body, of its exterior, of its interior, thanks to all this, I think' (1998b: 22; 54).] Dustan insists that the cultivation of one's bodily pleasure should be taught in schools (see for example 2003: 179–80): for the enlightened, guilt-free relation to one's sexuality brought by such expertise in the Foucaldian *cara sui*. Not just new knowledge or new pleasure, though: ultimately at stake in these sexual practices is the development of a new site of pleasure, and a new field of knowledge: the body's internal membranes become externalised, redefined as a surface to be caressed. (See Schehr 2002.) Anal pleasure is, as Dustan writes in *Nicolas Pages*, in a formulation dear to the later Foucault, an *ascesis*: a discipline, a training of the self – and the subject who has learned this will have reinvented himself, in the process of forming a brand-new mode of relation to the other(s) with whom he has undertaken this voyage of discovery (Dustan 2003: 442; cf. Foucault 1993: 383–411). (And anality, in the process, is wrenched away from its reductive Freudian association with sadism and aggressive control.) In *Serial Fucker*, BerlinTintin represents a scene of anal fisting in which his hand, as he puts it, plays with his partner's internal organs, reaches into his stomach, feels his beating heart (2005: 212); in *Je bande donc je suis*, Thierry caresses BerlinTintin in this way, masturbating his aorta, as he puts it, massaging his spleen, moving his fingers so that his partner's stomach moves in and out (2004: 219).[11] New practices invent new relations, new sexual organs displaced from inside to outside, the body's interior folded out to form the map of a *terra nova* of rebel pleasure.

For it should be emphasised again that all this inventiveness is not merely the privatised leisure activity of consenting adults. It is also, and immediately, political. Bodily boundaries invariably map political limits; and rebel anality is in this respect already socially transgressive. (On this, see Dean 2000; and Butler 1999, as discussed in Bersani 1996: 46–7.) Both authors are explicit in their insistence on the institutional dimensions which surround the life they depict, the deaths strewn throughout this life, the political decisions and legal structures which determine the status of its defining activities. At one point in *Nicolas Pages*, Dustan, as he puts it, remembers that he is also a lawyer, and introduces a six-page section of social, cultural, political and legal demands (2003: 286–91). These range from the trivial (cheaper drinks) via the serious (a 24–hour helpline for gay adolescents) to the concretely legalistic (residence rights for gay partners, same-sex marriage). Echoing the Foucaldian notion of 'bio-politics' (most extensively developed recently by Giorgio Agamben), Dustan makes the point that the body, especially the sexual body, is the privileged site of late twentieth-century political struggle, citing as evidence legal developments affecting divorce, abortion, homosexuality, and transsexuality, including the PACS. There follows a four-page discussion of the legal implications of the 1997 verdict of the European Court of Human Rights in what became known as the 'Spanner' case, which upheld the conviction of consenting British adults for inflicting injury upon each other as part of their sadomasochistic sexual practices (2003: 288–91). Dustan dismantles the legal reasoning behind the verdict, arguing on the basis of what he presents as a tradition of liberal individu- alism for the right to free disposition of one's own body, limited only by the principle of not harming anyone else (with the excep- tion of other legally competent adults who have explicitly asked to be so harmed). The self which creates itself also belongs to itself, irreducibly: '*je m'appartiens*', affirms Dustan, his italics emphasising this as axiomatic (2003: 291). ['I belong to myself'.] As Rémès puts it, 'c'est moi qui reste le propriétaire de mon être' (2004: 228); ['I remain the owner of my being'] and the most graphic example of this emphasis on the self-possession of the self-constructing rebel – and consequently on the absolute right to use one's body according to one's desires – comes in *Serial Fucker*, when Rémès' *alter ego* BerlinTintin establishes a relation with a slave (on the basis of contracts agreed by email, and included in the book) which extends to the circumcision of the slave's necrotised foreskin, his subsequent eating of this foreskin, and the sharing of their blood (2005: 204–8). Dustan's legal arguments make it plain that this is not mere provocation: this is the limit of the doctrine of individual freedom of which the west is so fond, challenging the mainstream to find a basis on which to reject it which would not resolve to a simple preference for one form of sexual behaviour, a preference itself unjustifiable in terms of this doctrine. It is in this sense that porn performers are, in Dustan's extravagant formulation, today's true politicians (2002a: 180): if contemporary politics is essentially bio-politics, these extreme performances are negotiating some of its emergent truths.[12]

Just as the inside of the new sexual body opens out to become a new erogenous surface, so does this presentation of marginal sexual experiences open immediately onto the question of social structure. Dustan and Rémès both celebrate the extension of various reproductive and familial rights to those sexual groups beyond the heterosexual mainstream (see for example Dustan 2003: 286–7; and Rémès 2005: 250 and 274–5); but equally, they want to maintain the values of these groups which in their view provide a welcome critique of and alternative to this mainstream. Having stated that 'Je vis dans un monde merveilleux où tout le monde a couché avec tout le monde', Dustan continues, affirmatively: 'On a le choix. Beaucoup de choix. Et personne ne souhaite fonder une famille' (1996: 70; on Dustan's communautarianism, see Caron 2003). ['I live in a wonderful world where the whole world has been to bed with the whole world [...] Take your pick. You've got a lot to pick from. And nobody's looking to start a family' (1998b: 52).] The extensive reflections on his place in the barebacking controversy, and on gay politics in general, which form the most developed section of *Premier essai*, include Dustan's clearest formulations of this anti-normative position: what he calls a model of dual belonging, 'Homos et Français, comme juifs et Français, voilà tout' (2005: 171). The problem, he argues, arises when this dual belonging encounters heteronormative reproductivity: 'Si homo et Français signifie en réalité homo et parent, nous avons un problème' (171). ['Homos and French, like Jewish and French, and that's that'; 'If homo and French really means homo and parent, we have a problem.'] The solution, he suggests in a more utopian vein, would be a generalised – universal, indeed – queering: the Republic could be blind to our strange particularities because we would have all acknowledged the strangeness within (172).[13]

Rémès, for his part, delights in mocking the dull, sexless world of heterosexual conventionality, often in bravura pieces of ironic ventriloquism (see for example 2004: 134–6), a world whose undisturbed good health has led to existential sclerosis. This vanilla world is what must be exploded, not infiltrated. 'L'homosexualité est forcément une force créatrice, flamboyante et subversive, déstabilisante pour la société', he argues, claiming inspiration from the FHAR. 'Anar, je suis pour la République du désordre, la démocratie de la sodomie' (2004: 178) ['Homosexuality is necessarily a creative, flamboyant, and subversive force, which destabilises society. I'm an anarchist, in favour of a Republic of disorder, a democracy of sodomy.'] In which we might note in particular the use of the figure of anality as an inassimilable, radical queering of republican values; elsewhere, anal sex with respectable, straight, family men is referred to as 'enculer Chirac, baiser Mitterrand, sodomiser l'ordre établi' (2000: 102). ['buggering Chirac, fucking Mitterrand, sodomising the establishment'.] Integration and assimilation, the traditional 'blindness' of republican universalism, are rejected as just part of the heteronormative infrastructure – against which this world of dizzying anal invention maintains itself as irreducibly in revolt, what Bersani calls 'the politically unacceptable and politically indispensable choice of an outlaw existence' (1996: 76). As Rémès has it, perverting not Descartes, not Sartre, but rather Camus' own rewriting of the *cogito* ('Je me révolte, donc nous sommes') into queer identity politics: 'Je bande, nous sommes' (2005: 115; cf. Camus 1965: 432). ['I rebel, therefore we are'; 'I get hard – we are'.]

Inside the body politic

This queer resistance stands in stark contrast to the political exhaustion on offer in some of the more mainstream materials we consider elsewhere in this study: in Despentes, for example, or Houellebecq; or, in its paradigmatic example, in Bonello's *Le Pornographe*, a miserable 'activism' which can amount to nothing more than the paradoxical promotion of silence as a form of political refusal. (See Chapters 4, 5 and 6 of the present volume.) This is a world, however, in which – as the best-known ACT-UP slogan has it – 'Silence = death' (see Rémès 2005: 309), and in which language accordingly has a particularly transitive quality, indisputably a form of action in the world. At which point, the figures of barriers and limits, of inside and outside, which necessarily organise the representation of sexual activity in these texts (since it is a matter of safe sex – or not – and the eroticisation of the body's internal surfaces), begin to acquire an unavoidable metaphoricity when it comes to considering both the position of the world of queer revolt in relation to the mainstream, and that of these texts in relation to this world, their world. The world within which these texts are set is very clearly delimited: it is the world of bars, clubs and backrooms which the community has claimed and marked out as its own space – what Schehr calls a 'closed utopia' (2002: 194; see also Schehr 2004: 97–8). There is a sense in which the transitivity of these texts – their ability to project a more or less immediate insertion into their world – is facilitated by the unambiguous delineation of the specificity of this world; the implied cordon *around* the identitarian space allows the absence of such barriers *between* this space and the writing which inhabits it, in a dialectic whose structure repeats that between self and community (see Caron 2003). As Hugues Marchal puts it, 'Les textes bâtissent ainsi dans le champ du roman l'équivalent du Marais dans l'espace urbain' (2003: 57). ['The texts thereby build within the field of the novel the equivalent of the Marais in the space of the city.']This section will, accordingly, explore first the ways in which the texts configure this 'closed utopia', before considering the relations they seek to establish to it, and what these have to say about the possibilities or otherwise for engaged cultural production at the start of the twentieth century. In these discussions, the quasi-pornographic dimensions of these sexually explicit texts will be central. For at issue here is the notion of writing as an act, and as an incitement to act. The pornographic is, as we discussed in our Introduction, generically distinguished by its associations with effectivity: as acting on the body, or (as in Dworkin and MacKinnon's arguments) as violating those whose exposure it documents, and already an instance of hate speech; this effectivity takes in the ability to incite action (to stimulate sexual activity, or to incite to rape). As Dustan and Rémès address the relation between their writing and its world, these will be the stakes. Does this writing act on its world? Does it – as its critics have maintained – constitute an irresponsible incitement to the unsafe practices it represents?

Rémès has a genius for *détournement*, the displaced citation of cultural material in a manner productive of hitherto unforeseen political effects. A favourite target is advertising slogans. Here, his manipulation of images of bodily fluids takes on a magnificently oppositional quality: for the world of advertising is itself already expert in a bastardised form of conservative *détournement*, now so culturally embedded that it can only be interrupted by a real sense of the inassimilable, of that which can still – and how rare this is – resist commercial recuperation. After the detailed narration of an evening of scatological experimentation in Eindhoven, it is the notoriously kitsch Ferrero Rocher advert that forms the target, in BerlinTintin's parting words: 'Très réception de l'ambassadeur tout ça, hein?' (2004: 221). ['Very "ambassador's reception", all this, isn't it?'] A repeated object is L'Oréal's globally recognizable slogan, 'Because I'm worth it'. Addressed to men, as the company tries to find new markets, this has now become 'Because you're worth it, too': but BerlinTintin has a more confrontational change in mind. First, describing his transformation into a 'Drag King' (a queer female-to-male transvestite: in his case, male-to-female-to-male), he declares that he has given up make-up and other feminine pursuits, 'parce que je le vaux bien' (2004: 190–1): the aim of the original slogan is pretty much irretrievable from within this magnificently queer tangle. In *Serial Fucker*, he connects this iconoclasm to the politics of AIDS: under the sub-heading, 'Le Sida, parce que je le vaux bien', he provides a pastiche of instructions for the application of a face-mask – the particularity here being that the face-mask in question is of course made up of sperm (2005: 36–7). Rémès' parody blocks the world of commerce, interrupting its spectacular, hegemonic expansion with the rebellious celebration of an outlaw sexuality it cannot incorporate.

The specific context of this resistance is Rémès' hostility to the perceived commercialisation of the gay scene, what Schehr calls 'the Hollywoodisation of male homosexuality as a commodity', 'the McDonaldisation of gay sex' (2002: 182). For Rémès, the assimilation which threatens the subversiveness of queer sexualities is accompanied by the reduction of these sexualities to the status of commodities, the force of their fetishism diluted to the serial sameness of the commodity fetish. In this logic, 'L'autre est un produit, à consommer. Sur place ou à emporter [...] Nos lieux de vie, vénaux. Nous, des marques' (2005: 304). ['The other becomes a product to be consumed. Eat in or take out [...] The places where we live our life become venal. We become brands.'] (Although the hostility to consumer culture is markedly absent from *Le Maître des amours*, in which BerlinTintin is an enthusiastic brand fetishist.) Dustan, by contrast, celebrates this commercialism, in the very same terms. Potential partners can indeed be evaluated as possible products to be consumed: casting his eye over the action in the toilets of a bar in search of attractive possibilities, he says: 'J'ai examiné la marchandise' (1996: 136). ['I inspect the goods'.] This is not surprising: as Houellebecq insists, for example (see Chapter 6, pp. 188–9), the doctrine of individual freedom of choice through which Dustan articulates his belief in sexual freedom can easily be translated into an affirmation of choice along consumerist lines. (On condition that one forget the exploitation of unconsenting others which sustains the global market, that is.) We might recall that Dustan's celebration of the fact that, in this scene, 'personne ne souhaite fonder une famille', is based on the statement, 'On a le choix. Beaucoup de choix' (1996: 70). ['nobody's looking to start a family'; 'Take your pick. You've got a lot to pick from' (1998b: 52).] Pornography, in fact, offers one medium in which the self can – literally, concretely – become a commodity, fusing the commercial and the sexual: Dustan mentions dildos modelled on the penises of porn stars Jeff Stryker and Kris Lord, and named accordingly (see 1996: 95 and 135; and on this, Schehr 2002: 198). And commerce in general, and in particular its presence as part of the gay life he depicts, meet with Dustan's approval. He is fascinated by the ultra-preparedness of the food on sale in Marks & Spencer, and pleased that soon, he will no longer have to travel across Paris to find it (1996: 65). The wilful simplicity of such declarations shows that Dustan knows this consumerism could be accused of superficiality, and that he is prepared to assume this: in a more theoretical moment, he even goes so far as to make the ludicrous claim that 'les courses sont un moment essentiel d'exercice de la liberté dans une société surpolicée' (2003: 63). ['Shopping is an essential moment of the exercise of individual liberty in an ultra-policed society'.] His language is accordingly, more often than not, the contemporary language of the commodity, in which the name of the object is replaced by its brand name. It's not a car, it's a Twingo or a Panda (2003: 117–18); they aren't trainers, they are my New Balance (80); these aren't swimming trunks, they are 'les maillots Hom taille 4 que j'achetais aux Nouvelles Galeries' (472); this isn't a pair of jeans, it's 'mon 505 néo-punk' (81) or my '501 usé' (1996: 29; on this, see Boisseron: 2003, 84). ['size 4 Hom trunks I used to buy at the Nouvelles Galeries'; 'my neo-punk 505s'; 'my distressed

501s'.] Dustan here develops a technique which may be traced back at least as far as Georges Perec's *Les Choses* (1965), in which the increasing presence of consumerism is documented by the text's citation of consumer goods and brand names. But whereas Perec provides enough ironic framing to suggest a polemical intent, Dustan, celebrating a world in which consumerism has attained hegemonic status, presents the brand as if it were simply the name of the thing. It is of course the distinguishing aspiration of the commodity fetish to float free of its use–value in just this way (it's not a watch, it's a Rolex): and so, citing brand names to create a recognisable cultural landscape, the referential economy of Dustan's texts is as one with that of the world they represent.[14]

It is important to avoid the naivety of nostalgia here. It is not as if, for all its critical distance, Perec's text managed to effect any meaningful resistance against the spread of the consumerism it critiques. If this consumerism has indeed attained hegemonic status, there is by definition no language which might resist it – including the language of the artwork, which once offered itself as heroic, avant-garde redeemer. As Dustan points out (the reference is to Hegel's lectures on aesthetics), 'Faire de l'art moderne c'est faire l'histoire au sens le plus hégélien du terme' (2003: 403) ['To make modern art is to make history, in the most Hegelian sense of the word']: the notion of the artwork as a meaningful, active participant in the world is itself out of date. A clear objection formulates itself here, however: did we not see above that Rémès could use his texts as a form of *détournement* to subvert the dominance of advertising? Indeed. Two qualifications are needed, however, which will allow us to get closer to the specific status claimed by these texts. First: this transitivity has to do with the delimited world into which the texts are intervening. Secondly: inasmuch as they intervene, they may well not be artworks at all.

Throughout these texts, we find the familiar notion that the relatively closed world in which they are set, bounded culturally and geographically within a few streets in the Marais, might be described – positively, even – as a 'ghetto'. Dustan calls part of *Dans ma chambre*, 'Living in the ghetto' (1996: 67), and celebrates the autonomy and lack of compromise this delimited world permits. The helpful (and playful) index to Dustan's *Nicolas Pages* defines 'ghetto' as 'plus qu'un lieu, un esprit, une culture, des codes, des savoirs, une façon de vivre' (2003: 524) ['more than a place, a spirit, a culture, codes, forms of knowledge, a way of life']: the 'ghetto' is, in this sense, an *ethos*. And must be protected as such: when, in 1997, the Paris police closed down five gay clubs on the grounds that illegal drugs were being consumed there, the successful protests against this measure included a petition – 'on a fait signer le tout-ghetto', says Dustan – and demonstrations featuring the slogan: 'On-est-chez-nous!' (157). ['we got the whole ghetto to sign'; 'This is our home!'.] For this is also a place of safety: being with 'mes frères du ghetto' means, for Dustan, occupying 'Un endroit où je n'ai plus à être sur la défensive' (1997: 18). ['my brothers of the ghetto'; 'A place where I no longer have to be on the defensive'.] Within the space that has thus been claimed – in part by polemical speech-acts, note – there is no interest in small talk: language is eminently performative, constructing a way of being, and of relating to others: in the hyper-civilised, nocturnal world, writes Dustan, 'On agit seulement. La parole est action' (1996: 118). ['You only act. Speech is action' (1998b: 92).]

And these texts are conceived of as just this: a form of action. In a 1998 text destined for an edited volume on gay literature, Dustan writes: 'L'art, j'en ai jamais rien eu à foutre [...] C'est ma vie qui m'intéresse' (2003: 383). ['As for art, I've never given a flying fuck [...] What interests me is my life.'] If gay literature has a specificity, he claims, it would be here, in this autobiographical immediacy: 'La littérature homosexuelle dit je. Ce faisant elle se donne pour sujet le sens même de la vie le sens de la vie [*sic*]: devenir soi' (386). ['Homosexual literature says "I". In so doing it takes as its subject the very meaning of life the meaning of life [*sic*]: becoming oneself.'] The ironic, citational, formal displacement definitive of the artwork has no place here, argues Dustan: 'la littérature gay retranscrit l'expérience de ses auteurs' (391). ['gay literature retranscribes the experience of its authors'.] It is a matter, bluntly, of telling the truth. To the criticism that the plot of *Dans ma chambre* consisted solely of the narrator being penetrated by a series of ever-larger dildos, Dustan responds: 'Un peu réducteur, mais très to the point. Je voulais dire la vérité' (394). ['A bit reductive, but very to the point. I wanted to tell the truth.'] Dustan is no fool: he knows that every verbal confection is also a distortion, the product of a process of selection and elaboration: *Je sors ce soir*, he says, was 'un livre calibré pour ne pas faire peur'. In his dialectic, though, this artistry can nevertheless efface itself in the service of complete truthfulness: the book was, he says, 'évidemment complètement sincère' (401). ['a book judged so as not to frighten people'; 'obviously completely sincere'.] Whence its aesthetic of complete referential fidelity, noting the minutiae of a single night out, including trips to the toilets and the cash machine, and even blank pages when the narrator falls asleep. This is a choice, of course, a form of writing calculated to create the *impression* of immediacy; but for Dustan, once its purpose is served, the process of aesthetic elaboration evaporates, leaving, precisely, the *impression* of the experiences recounted: their trace, the mark of their occurrence.[15]

Rémès also sees his writing in this immediate light – at least, when it suits him to do so. He often insists that words are acts: with reference to the spread of the term 'bareback' in France, he writes: 'Ce sont les mots qui créent les choses, les font naître' (2005: 57). ['It is words that create things, bring them into being'.] Accordingly, Rémès affirms the transitive reality of what he is writing, its refusal of any literary critical distance: in the preface to the 2005 edition of *Serial Fucker*, he writes: 'Je ne fais pas de différence entre littérature et témoignage mis à part le travail d'écriture pur du roman et d'orfèvrerie des mots [...] Tout mon travail tourne autour de cela: "l'obligation de vérité" [...] Je ne bénéficie pas du "prétexte littéraire", j'assume pleinement ce que j'écris' (2005: 5–8). ['I make no distinction between literature and testimony, apart from the pure work of writing that goes into a novel and the fine crafting of words [...] All my work revolves around one thing: "the imperative to tell the truth" [...] "Poetic licence" is of no use to me: I take complete responsibility for everything I write'.] Sex, for Rémès, is all about immediacy, the unmediated, visceral proximity of the other, 'ce contact de la viande' (2005: 29) ['this meaty contact']: this is for him, of course, one of the central aspects of the polemics about safe sex. And his writing aspires to a similar condition. Its refusal of the safe-sex doctrine is an act, for which he takes responsibility (2005: 72). *Serial Fucker* acted, he says, as a 'bomb' in the gay community (8), and was written as an intervention, a response to the criticism directed at *Je bande* by those concerned to maintain the emphasis on safe sex (9). This is, moreover, how his writings are received by those who criticise them (as was also the case for Dustan): as incitements to irresponsibility. (See especially the polemics with Didier Lestrade reproduced throughout *Serial Fucker*.) Rejected or affirmed, then, Rémès' writings are evaluated not for any 'literary' qualities, but rather for their effectivity, their transitivity: the likely consequences of the act of truth-telling to which they lay claim. As he writes in *Je bande*: 'je continue à éjaculer ma logorrhée sur du papier. Cela revient au même' (2004: 76). ['I keep on ejaculating my stream of words onto paper. It's the same thing'.] Speaking on gay literature in Fribourg, 'J'ai dit qu'un écrivain homosexuel, c'est un écrivain qui écrit sans préservatif. Et qu'un écrivain homosexuel radical, comme moi, c'est un écrivain qui avale' (2000: 178). ['I said that a homosexual writer is a writer who writes without condoms. And that a radical homosexual writer, like me, is a writer who swallows.']

Rémès complicates matters, however. *Le Maître des amours* (in which BerlinTintin has become a bisexual masseur and prostitute) is the book of separation, emphatically in favour of safe sex, with prophylactic declarations such as, 'Les capotes, c'est bien, ça met une distance', and 'Le sperme, parfois, c'est répugnant. Il faut que je me défende, me protège' (2000: 23, 44). ['Condoms are good, they introduce distance'; 'Sperm, sometimes, really is disgusting. I need to defend myself, protect myself'.][16] And the definition of writing as akin to the immediacy of sexuality is similarly interrupted, by Rémès' equally insistent statements to the effect that his writings are not in fact acts, not the raw, polemical transcription of reality. In the preface to *Serial Fucker*, he describes the work in now classic *autofiction* style, as *based on* personal testimony, but irreducible to reality, as mixing real people and events with their imaginary counterparts (5–6). This kind of insistence is usually motivated by the author's need to affirm the labour that has gone into the work (as we have in fact seen Rémès do); in this case, there is in addition a more pressing dimension. For Rémès needs to argue that his works are not open to the charge of incitement to irresponsibility; and he does so, accordingly, by playing down the transitivity he elsewhere talks up. To his friend Nina, BerlinTintin says, 'Même si c'est ma vie, ces textes demeurent des œuvres de fiction. Inspirés de la réalité certes, mais de la fiction tout de même. Ils n'incitent pas à baiser sans capote' (2005: 54). ['Even if it is all about my life, these texts are still works of fiction. Inspired by reality, sure, but fiction all the same. They are not trying to incite people to fuck without a condom.'] The suggestion is that fiction is by definition incapable of incitement: that to define something as fictional is to remove it from consideration – and possible condemnation – as an act. In response to criticism from the magazine *Têtu*, Rémès writes on his website: 'Que je sache, la littérature n'a encore tué personne' ['As far as I know, literature has not yet killed anyone'], leaving it safely intransitive, back within the protective boundariers of the literary. Rémès' writing is now defined in standard, inoffensive, liberal terms, as offering material for reflection, asking readers to question their attitudes, and so on (see for example 2005: 6); even as written to spread information and prevent infection (2000: 168).

Rémès thus ends up seeing his writing as indeed active, but at one remove. It is a kind of information service, raising the consciousness of its readers, and challenging them to make informed choices about their sexual behaviour (see 2005: 102, 107–8). At which point, Rémès – who had rejected what he considered the increasing consumerism of his community – espouses the logic of the market after all: his readers become the classic rational actors of free-market economic theory, making reasoned choices based on full, transparent information. And Dustan, who espoused this theory in cultural terms, rejects it aesthetically: for him, there is indeed no distance between text and reader, the text is defined as action – of which the clearest example is the work of Renaud Camus which, he says, saved his life (2003: 451–3). And this chiasmus may offer an instructive position from which to begin concluding this discussion of the work of Dustan and Rémès. For the oscillation at its heart is, very precisely, the crux of their work: between immediacy and mediation, contact and prophylaxis, inside and outside. Take, for example, their use of collage as compositional technique, particularly in *Nicolas Pages*, *Génie divin*, and *Serial Fucker*. Dustan, for example, includes all sorts of texts in his books, from the label from a jar of honey (2003: 59–60), to an interview with Bret Easton Ellis (2002a: 29–39), to a seemingly endless list of real names (2002a: 108–14), his CV (2002a: 98–101), an inventory of his many illnesses and the medicines used to treat them (2005: 219–20), and even, in *Nicolas Pages*, the proposal submitted to Balland for the 'Rayon gay', the collection in which *Nicolas Pages* was itself first published (2003: 227–33)! Rémès, similarly, includes in *Serial Fucker* a book proposal (2005: 230–1), numerous emails, contact ads, web addresses, tracts, newspaper articles, and a transcription of the definition of 'sperm' from the *Petit Robert* (56). On the one hand, this signals their works as pre-eminently postmodern, refusing the dialectical juxtaposition of modernist montage (as discussed in Chapter 2, pp. 77–9) in favour of a flattened textual space in which all materials attain a kind of entropic equivalence. A habitual critical reading of these various embedded mini-texts would, accordingly, emphasise the *mise-en-abîme* they create, and the irreducible self-consciousness this produces, insisting on the ironic, citational, heavily mediated quality thereby communicated throughout the texts as a whole. This reading is unavoidable, and encouraged for example by those moments in *Nicolas Pages* when Dustan, having apparently taken the reader into his intimate confidence, appears to bail out, as when he 'censors' a particular item, leaving, in place of revealed truth, just a blank (2003: 173, 182). With consummate wit, therefore, the entry for 'moi' in the work's 'Index' reads: 'en toute simplicité. Circulez, y a rien à voir!...' (523). ['pure and simple. Move along please, nothing to see here!...'.] Along with the insistent use of levels of framing discourse to create a vertiginous pattern of embedding, such moments render the idea that a 'truth' is here being communicated all but laughable.

On the other hand, though: some of these same moments import not only this mediating self-consciousness, but also direct contact with real people and events. Names and places are, simply, real. Web addresses function. When Rémès appears in *Nicolas Pages* (2003: 74, 517), or *Génie divin* (2002a: *passim*) or Dustan in *Serial Fucker* (2005: 25), they are not simply thereby rendered semi-fictional: the works are also tied inextricably to the real. However much a critical protocol may insist that (say) emails to Rémès from Didier Lestrade might be fictionalised, there can be no guarantee of this. It is always possible that this bit of text is just a fragment of the world, no more no less – what Rémès calls 'Que du réel en somme', 'du réel brut qui tache' (2005: 25–6), 'ce réel qui colle' (2000: 84). ['Ultimately just a bit of the real'; 'a raw bit of the real, leaving its stain'; 'this sticky real'.] Quoting the world, the text also impinges upon it. As BerlinT-intin says: 'Je veux seulement m'inscrire dans le réel' (2000: 79). ['All I want is to write myself into the real'.] Against this, our critical protocol is determinedly prophylactic, striving to resist the stain of the real, and it might always be right: as Rémès' frequent references to Lacan would remind us, the stain of the real is never visible as such (see 2004: 58, 64, 122). But it is not absent, for all that: we can never be sure that this is not in fact real. When Dustan quotes song lyrics, then (as he does constantly, turning his work partly, as critics point out, into a kind of sampling: see Schehr 2002: 186–7, and Caron 2003: 166), or references a particular track from a particular

CD (1997: 115); or when Rémès queers Gainsbourg (2004: 137; 2005: 14) or quotes Les Rita Mitsouko (2005: 258), this does not simply open an abyss of endless reflexivity: it also makes contact, really, with a world to which these songs form the soundtrack. If Dustan ceaselessly constructs his sexual experiences with reference to scenarios from porn films (see for example 1996: 54, 61, 81), or indeed Genet (1998a: 26), in what sense, exactly, are these experiences less real? The 'pornoself' (Schehr 2002: 196) they create is the self of the *performer*, the flip side of the coin from Charlotte Alexandra in Breillat's *Une vraie jeune fille*: role and reality coincide in one bodily representation. The quasi-fictional 'corps étranger au réel' (Rémès 2000: 15) ['foreign body in relation to the real'] is also within the real, even when this presence is only the trace of an expulsion.

If Dustan chooses as his literary reference point Marguerite Duras, then, calling her his 'permis d'écrire' (2003: 530), this is not to introduce a self-referential eternal regress: it is because 'la littérature moderne (c'est-à-dire échappée au patriarcat autoritariste) en France date de Duras', the Duras whom he loves 'pour la première personne et le mauvais français, le mal écrit des livres des années quatre-vingt [*sic*] et quatre-vingt-dix, quand elle s'est libérée' (2003: 376–7). ['writer's licence'; 'in France, modern literature (i.e. liberated from patriarchal authoritarianism) dates from Duras'; 'for her use of the first person and her bad French, the badly written books of the 1980s and 1990s, when she found freedom'. The high point of literature, that is, comes when it abandons its literary status, and approaches immediate self-expression. If it is true that at the bottom of all this *mise-en-abîme* there is a void, it is also true that in the void, there is something of the real. As Rémès puts it: 'Et à l'intérieur de rien: moi, nous!' (2005: 32). ['And, inside nothing: me, us!']

Throughout this chapter, when discussing Rémès, we have slipped indeterminately between his name and that of his *alter ego*, BerlinTintin. Not out of carelessness, though; nor in order to suggest the irrecoverable hybridity of reality and fiction. Rather, to make the point that, if Rémès is always more or less mediated through BerlinTintin, so BerlinTintin is always also Rémès – even when, in *Le Maître des amours*, he becomes a bisexual masseur and prostitute, his biography and publications are also, still, those of Erik Rémès. When BerlinTintin refers to having had to rework *Je bande* for its publication by Dustan (2000: 55–6), who, exactly, is speaking? But this is not just a nice literary game, what Dustan punningly calls in *Dernier roman* 'Loto Fiction®' (2004: 144), a knowing suspension *between* author and character. As Dustan says (in English) in *Génie divin*, 'It's not just a matter of style, it means much more than that' (2002a: 46). For it is *both* Erik Rémès *and* BerlinTintin who speak in *Le Maître des amours*, impossibly together in the same place at the same time: not *either* author *or* narrator, nor an undecidable oscillation – the fictional narrator, yes, and *also* (not *only*, but *also*) the real author.

This kind of supplementary dynamic is, of course, also part of the characteristic aesthetic of the pornographic per se: inasmuch as its representations are, somewhere, *also* irreducibly tied to the real, either by the bodies they represent, or by the bodily responses they produce. The boundary in question – between representation and world – acts as a semi-permeable membrane, blocking some forms of contact while allowing others. And so the work of Dustan and Rémès, in which prophylaxis and the body's internal organs are more than usually at stake, articulates its relation to its world by means of a demanding, affirmative, and at times inconsistent arrangement of various figures of interiority and exteriority, mediation and immediacy, irreducible boundaries and indisputable presence. In the new sexual body they propose, inside is also outside: internal membranes and organs become another surface to be caressed, in what it is tempting to read as a postmodern refusal of depth. Penetrating to the very centre of their bodies, their partners find, in one sense, nothing: there is now all but no inside, more or less everything has been externalised; there is no mystery to discover. ('Circulez, y a rien à voir! ...'). Equally, however, these partners find everything: this radically externalised body has not somehow ceased to be the real body of this real partner. The endosexual body may have no insides; it is no less corporeal for this. And by the same token: the self-conscious textual collage may offer abyssal reflexivity; it is no less in contact with the world, intervening as act and – perhaps – as incitement, with all the supposed transitivity of the pornographic. And, crucially: mapping the unfoldings of this world. Dustan's hope, from *Premier essai*: 'On attend l'essai brillant du critique pas trop universitaire qui consacrera la part maudite de la littérature française des années quatre-vingt-dix en nouveau réalisme. Et fera oublier la mauvaise affaire de l'autofiction. Ladite autofiction ayant bien plus à voir avec un certain effet de réel' (2005:

123). ['We await the brilliant essay from a not excessively academic critic, who will sanctify the *accursed share* of the French literature of the 1990s as a new form of realism. And make us forget the bad business that was autofiction. Said autofiction having more to do with a kind of reality effect.']

In Gaspar Noé's *Irréversible*, anality is linked to gay male desire in a profoundly homophobic vision of hell. The central catastrophe on which the film turns – the rape of Monica Bellucci's character – is an act of male-on-female anal rape: recalling the Sadean libertine with whom we began, this act is supposedly especially terrible for its absolute negation of the happy futurity of heterosexual vaginal penetration (itself situated in the carefree past towards which the film's reverse chronology ironically propels us, making clear this vision of heteronormativity as the now-negated realm of future possibility). The film opens, of course, with the dreadful final consequences of its male protagonist's quest for revenge: in a world of appalling violence and pure, unproductive negativity. And where is this, exactly? A gay club, of course. A gay sex club, to be more precise. A hardcore gay sex club, to be still more precise, with anonymous men eager to be fisted by any passer-by. The film's reverse chronology means that this is the very end, the final circle of hell, from which nothing good can possibly come: extreme gay anal eroticism in its standard role as the very embodiment of a threatening sterility. And the name of this club? *Le Rectum*, of course. If there is one reason to retain the possible transitivity of the work of Dustan and Rémès, it is surely this: that their insistence upon the real existential integrity of the acts they describe, and their polemical determination to put these descriptions out there as forms of engagement in the world, expose this reductively homophobic mainstream imaginary, and its axiomatic heterocentricity, as traced in Chapters 1 and 2 of the present volume, as miserably exhausted. In *Homos*, Leo Bersani forcefully celebrates the sterility classically figured in anality – its refusal of productivity and futurity – as paradoxically offering a chance to rethink community along the lines of 'a revolutionary inaptitude for heteroized sociality' (1996: 7).[17] The magnificently real creations of Dustan and Rémès allow at least the hope that, if the rectum is indeed, in Bersani's phrase, a grave, it might at least be the grave of the crumbling heteronormativity they so effectively denounce.

Notes

1 For the classic critique of this metaphorics, see Irigaray 1974 and 1984.

2 On the anus as site of oppositional psychosexual and political activity, as theorised by Hocquenghem after Deleuze and Guattari, see Morrey 1998: 386 and Caron 2001: 77.

3 For an excellent account of relevant lesbian-authored texts from this period, see especially Cairns 2002b. Many thanks to Lucille Cairns for very helpful discussion of these questions.

4 For criticism of Dustan in these terms, see the documents at www.actup-paris.org, accessed 4 April 2006.

5 Dustan says he turned down *Serial Fucker* for 'Le Rayon', fearing that the inevitably violent reaction to this text would destroy the collection (2005: 165–6).

6 For details, see www.apgl.asso.fr, accessed 11 July 2006.

7 For excellent accounts of the history and recent fortunes of French universalism, see Garréta 2001 and Schor 2001. With specific reference to the relation between this universalism and debates over gay identity in the context of AIDS, see particularly Pratt 1998; Martel 1999a (a compendious if contested account), esp. 347–59; the conclusion to Caron 2001 (in which Caron explicitly disputes Martel's anti-communautarian thesis); and Boulé 2002: 11–13.

8 See http://ericremes.free.fr/weblogs/index.php?A-lire-en-premier, accessed 5 April 2006.

9 Breillat is hardly alone in this. Kristeva, for example, makes a disgraceful equation between homosexuality and fascism, on the frankly flimsy grounds that they both, apparently, deny otherness (Kristeva 1974: 27). On Kristeva's heteronormativity, as programmed by her attachment to a particular form of psychoanalysis, see Cairns 2002a: 16–19.

10 For an excellent analysis of Breillat's essentialism and heteronormativity, see Spoiden 2004.

11 Interestingly, a similar (if more self-evidently fantasmatic) description of lesbian vaginal fisting occurs in Anne Auboneuil's *Le Rendez-vous du 29 février*, suggesting that it is not just the male body that might be remapped in this way: see Auboneuil 1999: 48, and, on this, Cairns 2002b: 99–100. In *Le Maître des amours*, Rémès folds into his text instructive material in the style of the sex guides he has also written, and broadens the span of ascetic self-construction to include the heterosexual body, introducing straight men to anal pleasure and, especially, straight men and women to the details and the anatomy of female sexual pleasure.

12 In similar vein, Martin Amis has described porn performers as 'gladiators': see Amis 2001.

13 In which position Dustan oddly rejoins the Kristeva of *Etrangers à nous-mêmes*, albeit via a non-psychoanalytic route.

14 This is also a distinguishing feature of the aesthetic of Virginie Despentes: see Chapter 5, pp. 167–9.

15 Accordingly, the quasi-literary generation of the mid-1990s with whom Dustan aligns himself, and whom he references repeatedly throughout *Dernier roman* and *Premier essai* (Angot, Beigbeder, Despentes, Houelle-becq, Ravalec, etc: the generation of 'la trash littérature', many of whom are featured throughout our study), are, he claims, distinguished above all by their sincerity (2004: 136).

16 http://ericremes.free.fr/fenetre.php?editoID=3, accessed 11 April 2006.

17 For the extended formulation of this argument, see Bersani 1996: especially 113–81. It is worth noting that the very scene from Genet's *Pompes funèbres* which becomes for Bersani emblematic of this refusal, is one of those taken by Dustan as the template for one of his sexual encounters: namely the scene in which, as Dustan puts it, 'les deux mecs baisent sur un toit' (1998a: 26) ['the two guys fuck on a roof'].

1.1 *L'Ennui* (Cédric Kahn, 2000): Cécilia (Sophie Guillemin) and Martin (Charles Berling), in one of their various sexual encounters.

1.2 *L'Ennui* (Cédric Kahn, 2000): Meyers (Robert Kramer): the consequences of overindulgence.

2.1 *Romance* (Catherine Breillat, 2000): Robert (François Berléand) and Marie (Caroline Ducey) before the mirror.

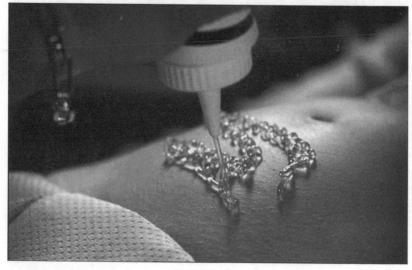

2.2 *Romance* (Catherine Breillat, 2000): the jelly for Marie's scan.

2.3 *A ma sœur!* (Catherine Breillat, 2000): Anaïs Reboux kisses the swimming-pool steps.

2.4 *A ma sœur!* (Catherine Breillat, 2000): Anaïs watches through her fingers.

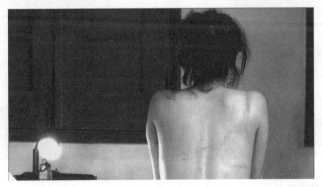

2.5 *Anatomie de l'enfer* (Catherine Breillat, 2003): Amira Casar's back, and the traces of what has been.

3.1 *Le Pornographe* (Bertrand Bonello, 2002): 'an important scene'.

3.2 *Le Pornographe* (Bertrand Bonello, 2002): Jean-Pierre Léaud, Ovidie and some kitchen roll.

4.1 *Baise-moi* (Virginie Despentes and Coralie Trinh Thi, 2000): Karen Bach makes contact with the viewer.

4.2 *Baise-moi* (Virginie Despentes and Coralie Trinh Thi, 2000): Karen Bach in iconic pose.

4

From revolution to abjection

'Tout livre a pour référent général, non pas un objet, mais un moment historique où se croisent la biographie de son auteur et l'état de la société' (Noël 1990: 155) ['Every book takes as its general referent, not an object, but rather a historical moment at which point in time the biography of its author intertwined with the state of society'], wrote Bernard Noël in *L'Outrage aux mots*, a brief text published in 1975 that set out to justify and defend his classic pornographic novel *Le Château de Cène*. Noel was taken to court on charges of obscenity against his novel, which charts the initiatory journey of a young man through a fantasy land and in particular on a forbidden island ruled by a beautiful but savage countess. For all its folkloric qualities, the novel contains scenes of extreme violence and disturbing sexual practices, most notably the rape of the young man (which ultimately becomes a consensual act) by guard dogs. *L'Outrage aux mots* provides a particularly interesting commentary on the text as it links the intellectual appropriation of pornography to the act of political revolt, or as Noël expresses it: 'le roman érotique m'est apparu comme une arme contre la bêtise politique – la seule arme contre cette société satisfaite et puante' (1990: 172). ['the erotic novel appeared to me as a weapon against political stupidity – the only weapon that could be used against this self-satisfied, stinking society'.] In other words, it claims that pornography, particularly in its most intellectual framings, is not there simply to titillate – or at least not titillate in any simplistic, unreflexive way – but that it has a political purpose, a revolutionary aim.

Noël argues that certain scenes correspond to certain traumatic experiences in his own past that find themselves conceptually metamorphosed. Active service in Algeria, and the experience of an attack by police at a meeting campaigning for freedom of the press, produced in him a sense of outrage so great that any direct representation of the political situation seemed entirely insufficient. Not least because: 'Il y a une police jusque dans notre bouche' (1990: 149). ['Policing extends even to our mouths'.] For Noël, as for the majority of French intellectuals in the sixties and seventies, political action began at the level of language; from this perspective modes of expression are contaminated by authority-ridden structures that question our very ability to express limit experiences, be they political, cultural, psychological or historical. Noël's solution to the frustration he feels facing the judge at the trial of his novel is radical: 'Il aurait fallu n'être là qu'un corps – l'un de ces corps que censure tout ordre moral. N'être qu'un corps, et simplement chier là, devant le président' (1990: 151). ['One would have needed to be nothing other than a body – one of those bodies that moral order censures. To be nothing but a body and simply be there, shitting, before the judge.'] Noël's anger produces a fantasy here that clearly ties the representation of obscene material into political or cultural dissent. If the organising principles of language allow no room for radical subversion, then the natural response is to effect a symbolic leap into corporeal disgust in a political reversal of hysteria, where the body is used to express an extreme and unambiguous message. Revolution can therefore be ably served by the revolting.

The origin for such a line of argument developed out of, initially, the Surrealists' preoccupation with the erotic as weapon of subversion, but is nowhere more evident then in the work of Bataille, as analysed by poststructuralist theorists such as Jacques Derrida, Philippe Sollers and Julia Kristeva. When Bataille died in 1962 he was known to a relatively small intellectual minority, however the decade that followed saw his work taken up by the highly influential Tel Quel group, and after May '68 he was raised to prominence and widely esteemed as an authority in many areas of cultural interest to French theoreticians; notably sexuality, the ludic and representation. Part of the appeal of Bataille's work lay precisely in the quirky, highly original way that it traced their interaction in the notion of *l'informe*, or formlessness, a concept that had a significant impact on French visual art as well as literature. *L'informe* provides a pertinent example of Bataille's fascination for the power of transgression, and of the link that transgression effects between pornographic material and subversive forms of discourse.

As Rosalind Krauss explains it: 'It is too easy to think of *informe* as the opposite of form. To think of form versus matter [...] Inside versus outside, vertical versus horizontal. Etc. Chaos as the opposite of form is chaos that could always be formed, by the form that is always already there in wait for chaos. Instead, let us think of *informe* as what form itself creates, as logic acting logically to act against itself within itself, form producing a heterologic'. Krauss points to the French verb 'déjouer' to capture the dynamic at the heart of the *informe*; a way of playing destabilises the game by the very act of following the rules, a kind of mis-play, 'but one that, inside the system, is legal' (Krauss 1993: 166–7). The example she uses to clarify her reading is that of Bataille's pornographic novel *Histoire de l'œil*. In this text, as Roland Barthes famously argues (2002e), the story is not about the characters but about an object – the eye – and what happens to it. What happens is that the eye is 'declined' through a series of playful linguistic combinations, so that it is substituted at times for an egg or testicles or the sun. As partly composed of fluid, the eye is linked to another chain of metonymical objects – tears, sperm, urine, and an infinite number of images are thus produced. These images are cross-fertilised from the different signifying chains that Bataille sets in motion across the text, systematically dismantling the 'proper' constructions of metaphor, and perpetually eroticising the text's viewing perspective. However, it is impossible to say which of these themes is the dominant or organising principle. As Krauss states: 'It is impossible to decide whether it is the ocular or the genital theme that is originary. What this means is that *Histoire de l'œil* succeeds in never being a profound work; it contains no hierarchy, encodes no secret' (1993: 168). It creates what Barthes calls 'une littérature à ciel ouvert, située au-delà de tout déchiffrement et que seule une critique formelle peut – de très loin – accompagner' (Barthes 2002e: 491). ['an open literature which is situated beyond any decipherment and which only a formal criticism can – at a great distance – accompany' (Barthes 1982: 123).] Formlessness seems to respond to Bernard Noël's complaint that words are governed by a socio-moral order. Bataille's text disrupts the symbolic by troubling the inner 'propre' order of language, making it both dirty with violent sex acts and dislocated from its own signifying principles.

The concept of formlessness is intriguing for it demonstrates how any kind of transgression exists in intimate relationship with the rules it sets out to undermine, an important acknowledgement for theorising the potentially revolutionary power of language. Susan Suleiman points out how, for Derrida (in his 1967 essay on Bataille), 'the transgression of rules of discourse implies the transgression of law in general, since discourse exists only by positing the norm and value of meaning, and meaning in turn is the founding element of legality' (Suleiman 1990: 74–5). Bataille's violent, sexual text provides the template for Noël's later works, since Noël's battle cry is 'Enterrez la syntaxe, comrades, elle pue!' (1990: 159). ['Bury syntax, comrades, it stinks!'] Approaching the current wave of violent, pornographic artworks we can identify an earlier twentieth-century aesthetic legacy centered upon a belief in the disruptive power of explicit sexual imagery that is split between the *informe's* ambivalence and teasing superficiality, which is to say the play of surfaces that promises but does not deliver depth, and a brutal fascination with what is visceral and abject. In both cases, however, the work is notable for its ability to resist interpretation and to make a mockery of the symbolic's powers of meaning creation.

The question that inevitably concerns us then, is: what have turn of the millennium artworks done with such a legacy? How are we to understand the twenty-first century's engagement with the power of transgression? Critical opinion over the past fifteen to twenty years has tended to emphasise the bleakest dimensions of contemporary artistic practice, arguing that, on the one hand, what was once the marginal cutting edge has been co-opted into the mainstream and, on the other, that the fascination with postmodern deconstruction has undermined the optimistic belief in art as a transgressive force. Suzi Gablik argues that: 'This pervasive need of the deconstructive mind to know what is not possible anymore would seem to represent an absolute terminus in the "disenchanted" world view; the self-checkmating of a now dysfunctional but apparently immovable dominant social structure. Deconstructive postmodernism does not ward off the truth of this reality, but tries to come to terms with its inevitability, in what are often ironic or parodic modes that do not criticize but simply declare art's pointlessness openly, and bait us with its indifference' (1991: 19).[1] Gablik goes on to cite a number of different appellations awarded to contemporary art that reinforce the conviction that art has lost all power of provocation. She speaks of 'endgame' art, which 'embodies a retrospective reading of modernism that is fully aware of its limitations and failed political ambitions', and of 'rearguardism', 'not only a rejection of revolution; it is also a deconstruction of the very idea of revolution' (1991: 18). The current critical climate surrounding art focuses almost exclusively on the melancholy abandonment of art as a weapon for political change, handling the notion of revolution with undeniable nostalgia. The aesthetic interest in pornography that began with the *nouveaux barbares* and *la trash littérature* has equally been charged with a cynical charlatanism, and as heralding a further stage in art's self-styled implosion. Yet it seems that the real disenchantment with art lies in its reception. Perhaps it is not that art or artists have truly changed in their ambitions and in the sincerity of their obsessions, but that the picture they reflect back on their society and its political realities is one that is very hard to stomach.

In her work *Sens et non-sens de la révolte*, Julia Kristeva suggests that there is potential for political engagement in contemporary art in just such acts of spectatorial discomforture. Her argument rests on the identification of a new form of liberal judicial order in contemporary society, which she proposes has dispensed with both crime and punishment unless they serve the demands of mass media spectacle. If we are no longer punished, Kristeva argues, we are now 'normalised'. The result is to diminish and render invisible the dynamic of power in society, foreclosing the pleasures of transgression. Yet for Kristeva transgression is essential: 'le bonheur n'existe qu'au prix d'une révolte. Aucun de nous ne jouit sans affronter un obstacle, un interdit, une autorité' (Kristeva 1996: 14). ['happiness exists only at the price of a revolt. None of us has pleasure without overcoming an obstacle, a prohibition, authority' (Kristeva 2000: 7).] She therefore emphasises the necessity of reintroducing a 'culture-révolte' to forestall the threat of society's own self-alienation. She goes on to describe how such an aesthetic might look; it would require us to 'dépasser la notion de *texte*' (1996: 15) in order to put in its place 'la notion *d'expérience*' (1996: 16). ['going beyond the notion of text'… 'the notion of experience' (Kristeva 2000: 8).] Kristeva does not tell us how to do this, but we may usefully recall the legacy of Bataille's and Noël's pornography that celebrates formal, structural upheaval. In the absence of a strong cultural sense of rule-driven order, it may be possible for structural play to be taken to an extreme point, a vanishing point perhaps, that in the act of exceeding its own limits becomes an experience in itself. And the art that Kristeva draws our attention towards as best suited for the purpose is 'tout particulièrement les formes artistiques insolites, "laides", que proposent les artistes' as such works are 'conscients de leur place de révoltés dans le nouvel ordre normalisateur et pervertible.' (1996: 17). ['particularly the unusual, even ugly art forms that artists ... aware of are now proposing ... aware of their place as rebels in the new normalizing and pervertible order' (Kristeva 2000: 9).] Unlike Gablik, who reads into aesthetic disenchantment a stagnation of artistic force, Kristeva hails the possibility of revolution via precisely the discomfort, the lack of understanding and the repulsion that such works engender in the viewer or reader. Perhaps, then, the so-called charlatanism of some contemporary French art, its resistance to meaning creation, its sheer ugliness, can be reread as potentially revolutionary?

One of the most startlingly 'disenchanted' pieces of contemporary art, and one that explicitly links pornography and revolution, is Bertrand Bonello's film, *Le Pornographe*. Bonello's pornographer, played by Jean-Pierre Léaud, is enticed out of retirement by a much-needed paycheque to direct another film. However, times have changed, personally, politically and aesthetically, and the film charts the pornographer's difficult passage through his relationships and his own ideology over the course of the shoot. Bonello's film is rather extraordinary in that it dispenses with any kind of narrative continuation, providing instead a series of fragmentary episodes that repeatedly, rather relentlessly in fact, fail to cohere or find development. Every plot line set up by the film grinds to a meaningless halt, the energy they are intended to generate slowly sucked into the film and denied cathartic release. The director's relationships with his family members, his wife and his prodigal son (who has refused to talk to him for years because of his job), slowly decline without this signifying anything. The scenes pertaining to the pornographic shoot become ever more infrequent and finally die out. At the heart of this gradual implosion are two key failures: the failure of revolution and the failure of the representation of sex.

Alive to the socio-historical dimension, this film stages a comparison between the generations, between the political choices made by the pornographer and those made by his son. In an interview reluctantly granted by the pornographer he remembers his beginnings in the industry, at the time of Bataille's resurrection as champion of the intellectual Left Bank, when 'faire le porno était aussi un acte politique' ['making porn films was also a political act.']. By contrast, his son, at university in Paris, becomes the instigator of a would-be student uprising, brought on by the recognition that: 'Nous vivons une époque sans fête et nous y avons contribué. Il faut réflechir longtemps et mesurément et puis prendre des décisions radicales et sans appel'. ['We live in a joyless age that we have helped to create. We need to take stock calmly and at length and then take radical, irrevocable decisions.'] These words are taken from a card printed and distributed by the students and read in a voiceover against the image of their demonstration. In contrast to the inevitably evoked memories of May '68, it is subtle to the point of non-existence. They could be students handing out flyers to a social event, yet, as one leaflet floats into the gutter and lies there, the voiceover continues to announce the appearance of 'les symptômes d'une nouvelle guerre' but one which 'ne se fera avec les armes'. ['the symptoms of a new war' ... 'will not be fought with weapons'.] Although the link between revolution and language in the French imagination holds good, long gone are the radical intentions of Tel Quel's *révolution textuelle*, as the text of the handout proclaims that: 'Nous utiliserons les mots d'une manière radicale. Nous avons décidé de rester imprenable. Seulement le silence comme ultime protestation. Taisons-nous'. ['We will use words in a radical manner. We have decided to remain impregnable. Only silence as the ultimate protest. Let us be quiet.'] There seems to be an inevitable analogy here with Gablik's evocation of a 'self-checkmating' and dysfunctional structure mirrored between art and society. Silence is indeed the ultimate weapon in an endgame that marks the death of creative political thinking, and the symbolic castration of the *intellectuel engagé*.

It is interesting to note that this scene follows on from a biting parody of the lazy and shabbily constructed sex scenes of commercial pornography. Initially we see the cast and crew walking into the middle of nowhere for an outside shoot. The female actors are dressed as eroticised cowgirls, there are no props beyond one real horse, and no attempt at creating any kind of framed backdrop. Instead, standing in the middle of a field, one woman leads a horse to where two 'cowboys' are standing and says: 'Je suis très fatiguée. J'aimerais rentrer à la prochaine ville pour me reposer'. ['I'm very tired. I'd like to get to the next town for some rest.'] The men reply 'Vous voulez vous allonger, c'est ça?' The woman agrees, the men agree that they are also tired and one suggests 'on doit tous s'allonger ici sur l'herbe' ['You want to lie down, is that it?' ... 'we should all lie down here on the grass'], simultaneously touching the woman's breast. She sketches the most perfunctory gesture of indignation then declares 'C'est-à-dire que... je vois... Après tout, pourquoi pas?'. ['Well, that's to say... I see... After all, why not?'.] The next shot is of one man taking her from behind while she manually manipulates the other. That such slovenly art is clearly being held up to ridicule is shown by Léaud's reaction of holding his head in his hands in a gesture of despair. We know that his career foundered whilst attempting to make a pornographic film that took the fox hunt as its structure, but replaced the prey with a woman. This avant-garde premise was considered too outrageous and too difficult to produce, but it serves the purpose of reinforcing his artistic credentials. Throughout the film we see his control over the shoot being undermined by his younger second-in-command, who at one point tells him he is too old for this work. Our sympathies are with Léaud, and with the desire for aesthetic sincerity that he represents, rather than the slick, superficial commercialism that drives the futile clichés of contemporary porn. The succession of the scenes suggests more profoundly that shoddy art leads to crippled politics, in other words, to silence in both domains.

Yet *Le Pornographe* is not simply a critique of the disenchanted modern world; instead it engages in that most postmodern of structures, a critique that is also a performance of some of the main aesthetic preoccupations of contemporary art, which the current interest in pornography only serves to highlight. The film critic Linda Williams, discussing the contemporary cultural scene in America, identifies a paradoxical state of representation which she calls 'on/scenity'. She defines this in the following terms: 'On/scenity is the gesture by which a culture brings on to the public scene the very organs, acts, "bodies and pleasures" that have heretofore been designated ob-off-scene, that is, needing to be kept out of view' (Williams 1999: 282). Williams is arguing that there has been a 'discursive explosion' of sexuality in contemporary culture, that is not the mark of liberation from transgression and taboo, but that is in thrall to a kind of explicitness, compelled to show and tell everything. Such representational transparency is met by a contemporary fascination with the place of the ontological subject in reception, a place that pornography, with its intention to arouse and move the spectator, ideally exemplifies. The film theorist Vivian Sobchack argues that we need to 'come to grips with the carnal foundations of cinematic intelligibility,' adding that 'Despite the relatively recent academic fetishization of "the body", theorists still don't quite know what to

do with their unruly responsive flesh and sensorium' (Williams 1999: 289–90). Sobchack's thesis acknowledges the necessary presence and responsiveness of the body in the cinematic experience, whether it be erotic or not. The moving images of cinema solicit an attraction not just of the eyes but also of the flesh. Sight, for Sobchack, then, commutes to touch. 'We do not touch the flesh that appears on the screen but our senses "make sense" of the vision of touch in our own flesh. It is in this sense that we can say we are "touched" or "moved" by the virtual bodies on the screen' (Williams 1999: 290). Historian of visual culture, Jonathan Crary puts it another way when he talks of 'the carnal density of modern vision' (1992: 149), which we can take to mean the appeal to the visceral in our viewing that forces us to recognise our own participation in visual representations. In other words, these theorists are working within a recently highlighted dimension of spectatorship; modern spectators are increasingly made aware of their vulnerability to the images they see, and increasingly involved in sensorial ways – as opposed to intellectual ones – of making sense of onscreen images. However, this puts the spectator in an unusual position in relation to film. Linda Williams describes this position as 'not "gazing" – in the sense of omnipotent mastery, but "looking" – in the sense of vulnerable fascination' (1999: 295). Such a contemporary positioning of the spectator responds well to Kristeva's demand for an aesthetics of experience in the field of reception, but can we also identify within it the seeds of a new form of revolution?

There would seem to be an intuitive link between the contemporary spectator who is vulnerable to images, and a contemporary trend in filmmaking to present the same spectator with graphic, explicit and potentially troubling images to view. *Le Pornographe*, with its discontinuous cutting between graphic sex acts and a more conventional, if exhausted, narrative structure manifests a fascination with explicit sex as a way to puncture the frame of representation, to trouble and undermine the smooth functioning of the symbolic. Rather than simply fall under the banner of disenchantment, we can read into this film an adherence to another kind of contemporary art, identified by Hal Foster in his critical work, *The Return of the Real*. Jacques Lacan defines the real as that which lies beyond representation; thus the desire to see the real in art is necessarily foreclosed. However, Foster points to a trend in contemporary American art, dating from the pop art of Andy Warhol onwards, that posits the real as a holy grail, but recognises it can only exist in momentary form as an effect 'between the perception and the consciousness of a subject *touched* by an image' (1996:132).[2] In other words, a form of art that recognises that its impact is in its experience rather than its interpretation; an art that makes the spectator conscious of their own being, rather than lost in contemplation of the aesthetic object. In just such a fashion, *Le Pornographe*'s use of troublingly explicit sexual material seeks to impose an experience on its spectators of a 'real' sex act. Kristeva's revolution, in such a context, would be brought about by the shock of the real shaking the spectator out of comfortable illusions of safety and security in the face of art. As such it would recall the positivism of earlier avant-garde attempts to disconcert and alarm spectators with 'happenings'.[3] However, times have changed, and the spectatorial relationship to representation is more sophisticated and also more alienated than it was in the early part of the century; now, the strategy of puncturing the frame of representation with troubling images that pertain to the real has a tendency to produce instead the 'hyperreal' as defined by Jean Baudrillard.

Baudrillard's concept of the hyperreal refers to an excessive form of simulation. Baudrillard argues that there are three levels of simulation, the first producing an obvious copy of reality, and the second level a copy so exact that it blurs the boundaries between reality and representation. Contemporary society goes one step further than this by generating a model of a real without origin or reality: a hyperreal. The hyperreal produces a reality not based on any real referent, in other words, a virtual reality that is a perfect and stable significatory double of the real that is free from reality's vicissitudes. The sexual act at the heart of pornography is a good example of this hyperreal, and one which Baudrillard himself often uses: 'Simulation désenchantée: le porno – plus vrai que le vrai – tel est le comble du simulacre' (1988: 86) ['Disenchanted simulation: porn, more real than the real, and the height of simulation' (Poster 2001: 157)], and he identifies in contemporary pornography's overstretched attempts to exhibit the real a paradoxical exhaustion of reality: 'Plus on avance éperdument dans la véracité du sexe, dans son opération sans voiles, plus on s'immerge dans l'accumulation des signes, plus on s'enferme dans une sursignification à l'infini, celle du réel qui n'existe déjà plus, celle d'un corps qui n'a jamais existé' (1998: 53). ['The further we advance in desperation into the veracity of sex, into its unveiled operation, the further we immerse ourselves in the accumulation of signs and the further we imprison ourselves in an infinite process of oversignification of both the real, which already exists no longer, and the body, which has never existed.'] Baudrillard is also interested in the collapse of perspectival space in porn film, which he equally links to the hyperreal. He is referring here to a paradoxical sensation of total involvement, or immersion, on the part of the spectator along with, simultaneously, alienating detachment. One of his examples for this is fly-on-the-wall television documentary, which undermines the structure of voyeurism by removing the perspectival distance of a window or the distance between the scene and the camera, but which at the same time insists the camera is 'not there', collapsing distance and bringing the spectators into the action. This is the basic premise of what we most recently have come to term 'reality' TV. Richard Lane glosses this paradox of perspective in the following terms: 'The viewers are absent and present, at a distance and up close; they enjoy the thrill of this hyperreal situation: hyperreal because they cannot say that one position is real and another false' (2000: 98). Pornography achieves the same result: 'sexe tellement proche qu'il se confond avec sa propre représentation: fin de l'espace perspectif, qui est aussi celui de l'imaginaire et du phantasme – fin de la scène, fin de l'illusion' (Baudrillard 1998: 48). ['such a close-up on sex that it merges with its representation: the end of perspectival space that is also the end of imagination and fantasy – end of the scene, end of the illusion'.] This impossible alternation between real and false, impossible because undecidable, and because fundamentally irrelevant, is the key to Baudrillard's hyperreal. The hyperreal does not exist in the realm of good and evil, it is not the place of/for ethical judgement, instead it is measured in terms of its performativity; which is to say, how well does it function? Pornography is entirely disinterested in the representational value of its images; instead its focus is exclusively on its own performativity and on the response it can elicit from the spectator.

The staging of graphic sex acts in *Le Pornographe* offers a significant exploration of the hyperreal in the tensions created between the real and representation. The first lengthy scene of the shoot provides a prime example of the aesthetic desire to puncture the impermeability of the spectator with an undeniably real sex act, yet the ambivalence of the fictional frame transports us into the dimension of the hyperreal. The film has already played with the ambiguous status of the filmmaking process, with some shots framing the camera and lighting equipment whilst others focus on actors and actresses with no explanation as to their presence. The film therefore cites the documentary while constructing a fictional representation, provoking a paradoxical collapse of the viewer's perspective. Can we say that two actors actually having sex or a film crew setting up their equipment are images that belong to the realm of the real or the not-real? This film emphasises the very undecidability of such an opposition both in the creation of film per se and in the staging of the pornographic. The camera has already lighted upon the well-known porn star Ovidie (who perhaps needs no introduction) but without entertaining any difference between her onscreen and offscreen persona. In the first and most significant sex scene, we are clearly onset. Léaud as director has quietly but authoritatively given direction to his team, asking for silence from the actors and a still, close-up framing of the sex act itself from the cameras. Initially the scene develops as planned and we are forced to watch a lengthy, unerotic, but visibly 'real' act of sexual penetration. As the scene stretches out uncomfortably, so the assistant director (who seems to assume the burden of spectatorial frustration and discontent) begins to take over, inviting the previously unseen cameras to enter the foreground of the screen, intruding upon the actors but also disrupting the awkward intimacy between them and the spectator. At the assistant director's command music begins to play, the actress is now obliged to moan and the sex becomes non-linear and discontinuous, interrupted by his demands for shots of fellatio. The disconcerting sense of viewing something 'real' in the pornographic sex act is thus itself punctured by the intrusion of the paraphernalia of film production, and what might, in the pornographer's hands, have become something avant-garde and unsettling, is transformed in his assistant's hands into something clichéd that appeals self-reflexively to its own processes of construction. Across its progression, the scene threatens an overproximity to the real that collapses into anti-climax, in all senses of the term, with the director failing to get the scene he wants, the sex act failing to culminate as it should, and the representation failing to attain the status of the real.

The ambiguity of the real and the representational in this staging of the pornographic appeals to the concept of the hyperreal, yet within this film we can also trace elements of Bataille's formlessness, or the structural play with the logic of representation that was a key feature of Bataille's own erotic texts, and which may be seen as part of the aesthetic legacy inherited by contemporary art's engagement with the erotic. The concept of the *informe* has been influencial across all artistic media and has subsequently received detailed critical theorization. In the critical text *Formless: A User's Guide* by art historians Rosalind Krauss and Yves-Alain Bois, Bataille's original concept of formlessness is separated provisionally into four subcategories, two of which are useful here. The first of these is termed 'pulse', and defined as the 'endless beat that punctures the disembodied self-closure of pure visuality and incites an irruption of the carnal' (1997: 32). In other words we are again in the area of the dense carnality of vision, the bodily response that is felt through and manifested within the throbbing pulsatile image. We can consider pulse as the material element pornography relies upon to short-circuit the intellect of the optical and attain instead the realm of the libidinal. Krauss and Bois insist that no erotic image is necessary in the experience of pulse, but the hypnotic tension displayed in the unquestionably real act of penetration in *Le Pornographe* seems to be focused upon the relentless, rhythmic thrusting of the male actor. However, in the same way that the actors are abruptly forced to stop and change position, so the viewer's engagement with the pulse is interrupted, and from this moment on, the scene, and in fact the rest of the film, is subject to the second category of formlessness, which is entropy. Entropy is defined as 'the constant and irreversible degradation of energy in every system, a degradation that leads to a continually increasing state of disorder and of nondifferentiation within matter' (1997: 34). The negativity of entropy presupposes an original order that subsequently deteriorates. In the case of this film, narrative structure is from now on subject to a process of carefully controlled attrition, and, leading out from this initial failed sexual act, it stages a controlled and gradual implosion. *Le Pornographe*, like *Histoire de l'œil* before it, certainly succeeds in never becoming a profound work, in never containing a hierarchy or encoding a secret. Instead we are subject to the endless play of surfaces that seduce our vision and amount to nothing.

Formlessness and the hyperreal are profoundly enmeshed, the difference between them being based in a different emphasis on undecidable residues. Whereas formlessness explores the ludic possibility of creating material resistance within art that is a fallout of its own systems, the hyperreal explores how the material resistance is both produced and coopted by the paradoxical system that is representation. In Bataille's concept excessive form produces an undecidable residue that resists. In Baudrillard's more recent theory, that undecidable residue is sought and placed on view only to find itself subsumed by new levels of abstraction. *Le Pornographe* presents intriguing perspectives on both concepts, subject as it is to both the implosion of form and the puncturing effect of the real. In particular, its presentation of the collapse of form into formula and cliché offers us further pause for thought. Marie Nimier in her text *La Nouvelle Pornogaphie* talks of the way that 'Rien n'est naturel dans une production porno, tout est réinventé, codé, surdimensionné. Cela dit, il y a un problème: ces codes changent moins vite que les mentalités' (2002: 32). ['Nothing is natural in a work of porn, everything is reinvented, coded, metatextual. That said, there's a problem: these codes change less quickly than people's mentalities.'] The concept of code is an important one for Baudrillard, who sees is as the foundation of the hyperreal, and Nimier's quote here indicates the hyperreal structure of an original model that has no real referent. What we see in the sex scene is a battle of coding between the directors, as Léaud's more unconventional approach is replaced by the traditional pornographic signifiers of panting, moaning, sleazy music, and so on, with the result that a kind of atrophy of coding sets in. This clash of codes generates the descent into formlessness and the hyperreal, triggering a concentric spiral of entropic ambivalence. Yet in that very clash of different codings the real appears, produced as it is lost when the film draws attention explicitly to the screening put in place over the sex act.

We can understand the concept of the screen via Lacan, who proposed that objects in the real look at us every bit as much as we look at them.[4] Lacan posits a screen that mediates and modulates between the gaze of the object coming from the real (what he terms the object-gaze) and the gaze of the spectator. Without this screen in place the spectator would see 'too much', blinded by the gaze, traumatised by the real. Hal Foster suggests that the function of the screen is 'to negotiate a *laying down* of the gaze as in a laying down of a weapon' (1996: 140). However, the fascination in contemporary art with attempts at removing the screen sets in motion a game that is dangerous, essentially because it forces representation to recognise its limits over and over again. Žižek, discussing the

Lacanian object-gaze, suggests that the pornographic, in its aim of showing something 'real' inevitably forces the spectator into a perverse relationship with the image. This is because:

> Instead of being on the side of the viewed object, the gaze falls into ourselves, the spectators, which is why the image we see on the screen contains no spot, no sublime-mysterious point from which it gazes at us. It is only we who gaze stupidly at the image that 'reveals all' [...] It is the spectator himself who occupies the position of the object. The real subjects are the actors on the screen trying to rouse us sexually, while we, the spectators, are reduced to a paralysed object-gaze. (Žižek 1992: 110)

The result of this is that by 'showing everything', the pornographic film misses the importance of the enigmatic quality of the object-gaze. The film inevitably goes too far and overtakes the spectator's desire. 'The unattainable/forbidden object approached but never reached by the "normal" love story – the sexual act – exists only as concealed, indicated, "faked". As soon as we "show it" its charm is dispelled [...] Instead of the sublime Thing, we are stuck with vulgar, groaning fornication' (1992: 110). The *mise-en-abîme* structure of *Le Pornographe* invites us to watch the screen as it is erected before the real of the sex act, working backwards, as it were, from the uncompromising, vulgar real to the representational coding that would invite a taming of the gaze and reintroduce some kind of viewing pleasure. However the ambivalence of the frame in this film ensures an uncomfortable alternation between performance and critique of the hyperreal, leaving us in the grip of Baudrillard's 'circulation aléatoire ou insensée, ou rituelle et minutieuse, de ses signes en surface' (1988: 78). ['aleatory, meaningless, or ritualistic and meticulous, circulation of signs on the surface' (Poster 2001: 153).]

This leads us to consider the particular fascination contemporary art displays with the pornographic act as a commentary upon Gablik's rather derogatively described postmodern 'need to know what is not possible', and this in relation to the fundamental disjunction between the real and representation, as well as to Kristeva's belief in a positive, revolutionary role for disquieting art. Contemporary film calls urgent attention to the limits of the visible and the viewable, with the erotic put in play not to provoke the spectator into engagement with an external world, but to plumb the depths of their own subjectivity. Instead of the empowering sexual charge invested in previous avant-garde appropriations of pornography, the contemporary erotic provokes a reception of profound discomfort and uncertainty, and instead of the hope of climactic catharsis, current art tends towards painful and anguished frustration. There is an underlying moral intent in a great deal of recent criticism, evolving from a nostalgic belief in what art 'ought' to do to its spectators. Contemporary art still produces a strong reaction in its audience, it is just that the reaction is now one of extreme anxiety or distaste. *Le Pornographe* is a clever and subtle film, but the experience of watching it is quite excruciating. This does not mean that art has abandoned its intention of delivering piercing insights into our culture, rather it indicates the profoundly troubling nature of those insights. What contemporary art like *Le Porngraphe* tells us is that reality has changed beyond all recognition, due to a fundamental uncertainty surrounding representation's ability to deliver that reality to us. The visibility of the real is nowhere more clearly in question than in graphic acts of sex and violence where mediation is both required and repudiated, intrusive and protective.

The revolution, then, of which Kristeva speaks, would appear to be conducted in the terms of a productive if painful return to the once dependable act of aesthetic experience – the interchange between spectator and representation – in order to destabilise and disrupt the fundamental nature of that experience. '[C]ar, lorsque vous êtes devant ces débris, ces flashes de sensations, ces objets disséminés, *vous ne savez plus qui vous êtes,*' Kristeva writes. 'N'est-ce pas le redoutable privilege de l'art contemporain que de nous accompagner dans ces nouvelles maladies de l'âme?' (1996: 20). ['for when faced with these fragments, these flashes of sensations, these disseminated objects, you no longer know who you are' … 'Is it not the fearsome privilege of contemporary art to accompany us in these new maladies of the soul?' (Kristeva 2000: 11).] However, this revolution of the soul remains deeply problematic for actual political engagement. The loss of self that accompanies the most intense experiences, coupled with the direct challenge to representation's ability to present authentically, often results in a worrying loss of faith at the point where representation is politically desirable. We can see this process at work in the representations of heterosexual relationships, where the ethical is displaced in favour of the sensational, and we can see it also in the representation of violence, which becomes glamorised or de-realised.

It is no surprise, then, that Baudrillard's hyperreal, whilst clearly in evidence in the pornographic, has also become somewhat notoriously linked to the contemporary experience of war, most notably in Baudrillard's provocative essay 'La Guerre du Golfe n'a pas eu lieu'. Baudrillard's argument would seem at first glance to be outrageous, denying bloodshed and violence on an unimaginable scale, yet it is precisely the unimaginable dimension of the event that Baudrillard is concerned with. 'Nous ne sommes plus dans une logique du passage du virtuel à l'actuel, mais dans une logique hyperréaliste de dissuasion du réel par le virtuel' (1991: 15) ['We are no longer in a logic of the passage from the virtual to the actual but in a hyperrealist logic of the deterrence of the real by the virtual' (Poster 2001: 233)], he claims. Baudrillard points here to the collapse of 'grand narratives' of rationalism, progress and technology, and to the dubious erection of structures of knowledge, based on models that are never innocent or free from political ideology, but he also maintains a pertinent opposition between contemporary culture's fascination with the real and its simultaneous construction of a defensive, protective screen of virtual representation:

> Il semble que cette hantise du passage à l'acte règle aujourd'hui tous nos comportements: hantise de tout réel, de tout événement réel, de toute violence réel, de toute jouissance trop réel. Contre cette hantise du réel nous avons créé un gigantesque appareil de simulation qui nous permet de passer à l'acte 'in vitro' (c'est même vrai de la procréation). A la catastrophe du réel nous préférons l'exil du virtuel, dont la télévision est le miroir universel. (1991: 16)

> [It seems that this obsession with the passage to action today governs all our behaviour: obsession with every real, with every real event, with every real violence, with every pleasure which is too real. Against this obsession with the real we have created a gigantic apparatus of simulation which allows us to pass to the act 'in vitro' (this is true even of procreation). We prefer the exile of the virtual, of which television is the universal mirror, to the catastrophe of the real. (Poster 2001: 234)]

Inevitably Baudrillard's provocative distinctions seem too clear-cut when placed in comparison with contemporary works of art, yet it is easy to identify the influence of Baudrillard's thinking on French aesthetics. This is particularly so in the case of Yann Moix's novel of sex and war, *Partouz*, analysed earlier in terms of gender relations and to which we might now make a productive return.

In *Partouz*, Moix makes the unconditional statement: 'La première hyperguerre mondiale avait commence ce 11 Septembre™' (Moix 2004: 48). ['The first world hyperwar began this 11th September™.'] This is because the terrorist event has provoked a change in public awareness: 'Aucune catastrophe ne pourrait plus jamais être lue sans, au préalable, être passée au tamis, au scanner de la possibilité d'attentat. Ben Laden avait embenladénisé le monde à vie' (2004: 47). ['It's no longer possible for any catastrophe to be understood without, in the first instance, being sifted or scanned for the possibility of a terrorist attack. Bin Laden has Binladenised the world for as long as he lives.'] The consequence of this is to undermine the binary opposition between war and peace:

> Le monde n'était plus en guerre: il était devenu guerre tout court. Guerre en non-guerre, c'était désormais la même chose. Depuis le 11 Septembre™ 2001, tout était guerre, même la paix. La paix n'était plus le contraire de la guerre, elle était son contexte, son milieu naturel [...] La paix était devenue une sorte de cas particulier de guerre. (2004: 47–8)

> [The world was no longer at war: it had quite simply become war. War and non-war were henceforth the same thing. Since September 11th ™ 2001, everything was war, even peace. Peace was no longer the opposite of war, it was its context, its natural environment [...] Peace had become a particular kind of war.]

The sense of the real invested previously in the opposing concepts of war and peace has given way to the hyperreal uncertainties of perpetual, virtual war. It is perhaps not surprising, then, in a world where opposites merge and become indistinguishable, that this narrative displays extreme confusion over the link it makes between revolution and the erotic. On the one hand, the erotic provokes a call to arms, not as in Bernard Noël's case, out of a need to use an unacceptable medium to provoke a stagnant society, but out of the proposition that the erotic itself is a cause and a symptom of cultural moral stagnation. Yet in an evocation of the critique and simultaneous performance of the hyperreal that haunts *Le Pornographe*, the narrator is himself speaking from a club *échangiste*, in search of sexual self-dissolution. The link between revolution and eros is not a question of intellectual *écriture* (although the extraordinary, excessive discourse of the narrative nevertheless appeals to disruptive and subversive forms of *écriture*) but rather a purely cultural one that finds an analogy in the battle between the sexes: 'La drague est guerre' (2004: 168). ['Going on the pull was war'.]

But what is most noticeable in this 400–page novel on the hyperre-
alities of war and sex, is the narrative's inability to make progress. In
a world where cause and effect have come to resemble one another,
where 'La réalité n'était qu'un cas particulier du rêve', (2004: 117)
['reality was only a particular instance of dreaming'], the fundamental
drive of narrative towards meaning creation, towards a conclusive
overview is entirely abandoned. Ronald Jones talks about a 'hover'
culture in art, where the idea of innovation crumbles, leaving in its
place an uncomfortable stasis (Gablik 1991: 16). Moix's novel is
remarkable for its outright provocativeness, to the point of being at
times dangerously insulting towards women and religious beliefs.
Yet for all Moix's invocation of the most powerful appeals to anger
and action, his narrator cannot get out of the swingers' club, or find
the woman he loves, and there is no way of integrating 9/11 into the
web of history, literature and the erotic.

If, as these artworks seem to suggest, revolution is no longer
imaginable, precisely because it would only be a product of the
imagination, one way or another, the real drive behind the representation of graphic sexual acts focuses not on provoking spectators
into action in the external world, but into plumbing the depths of
their own subjective responses. The next section will consider how,
in the absence of forward-motion in art, the 'hovering' effect of art
takes us into the darkest recesses of the body and the soul.

The revolution within: abjection

The citation of pornographic images in contemporary art works no
longer seems to fulfil its original function of provoking spectators
and readers into revolutionary zeal, either out of moral disgust or
out of reckless exposure to deconstructed systems of meaning and,
in consequence, power. One way to understand this sea change is
through Baudrillard's concept of the hyperreal, the current cultural
confusion over the relationship between images and the real. But
we need to add to this picture another highly influential factor in
western art, which is the contemporary fascination with the experience and representation of trauma. It is clear to see in the recent
wave of intellectual sexual art that the impermeable, tireless protagonists in Sade or even Bataille and Noël, have been replaced by
the suffering, damaged individuals of Houellebecq and Despentes.
It is interesting, for example, just how many of these pornographic

films and narratives concern individuals who cannot get sex, or who experience it as rape or aggression when they finally do. This would seem to be a significant dimension of the late twentieth-century aesthetic climate; as Hal Foster proposes, 'for many in contemporary culture, truth resides in the traumatic or abject subject, in the diseased or damaged body' (1996: 166). Whereas the old school shock of pornography lay in the individual's blatant transgression of society's order, recent pornography has focused on a new kind of contemporary subject who is the victim of a dislocated, indifferent, loveless world, where terrorist attacks, random street violence and debilitating illness undermine any sense of corporeal security. What makes these works of art so very difficult to read and, in many ways, so lacking in aesthetic pleasure, is the queasy combination of graphic sexuality with physical and psychical damage. Eroticism has become desperate, a last-ditch attempt to dredge up ontological certainties, rather than the powerful, transgressive, fearless weapon of political attack it once used to be. Furthermore the internal contradictions of narratives that include erotically stimulating material within a context of trauma create very unstable conditions for their own reception. The reader or spectator is both invited and repelled by the work, intrigued and horrified, offered pleasure and threatened with dissolution. Inevitably such artistic material finds the pathway to revolution foreclosed, as all forward motion is suspended in favour of an undecidable oscillation between dubious sexual stimulation and the traumatic threat of the real. Rather than revolution we find instead the pattern of *revolvere*, which as Kristeva points out, equally signifies the endless repetition and return that evokes the Lacanian missed encounter with the real.[5] The whole emphasis of pornographic citation has shifted, then, from being directed towards engagement with the external world, to the troubling invocation of horror, disgust, discomfort and pity within the subject.

One of the most recent critical texts to reflect on this new pornographic movement in France is Michela Marzano's *La Pornographie ou l'épuisement du désir*. In this text, Marzano's premise is that: 'la pornographie contemporaine, qui naît autour des années 1990, propose, elle, une "surexposition" de l'acte sexuel, afin d'éliminer toute barrière entre l'intérieur et l'extérieur du corps' (Marzano 2003: 184) ['contemporary pornography, beginning in the 1990s, offers an "overexposure" of the sexual act in order to eliminate any barriers between the interior and exterior of the body'], and in consequence, 'on assiste au passage de *l'hyperréalisme* à la *transpar-ence* et à la *surexposition sexuelle*' (2003: 189). ['we move from *hyperrealism* to *transparency* to *sexual overexposure*'.] Marza-no's thesis is a disapproving one that celebrates eroticism, which she understands as holding intact a certain private interiority (the 'noyau dur' or 'pudeur' of the subject), and condemns pornography as being inhuman in its exposure of that same interiority. While such an approach may indeed express the processes underlying, and some of the consequences resulting from, the pornographic exposi-tion of the body in contemporary French aesthetics, we must ask whether the artworks that result can be interpreted as simplistically as Marzano suggests. The desire to see the truth of the body, to look unflinchingly at the real (however fantastic such an aim might be) has undoubtedly resulted in works of a black and bitter negativity. But the inner contradictions of these works ask us to reassess the abject or traumatised body in society, to reconsider the link between sexuality and representation, and to readdress the anxieties and desires of postmodern culture. One text which responds in perplexing ways to Marzano's critique is *La Jeune Femme et la pornographie* (1991) by the Quebecois poet Roger des Roches. Republished in 2005 by La Musardine, itself founded in 1995 to produce exclusively erotic titles, the text tells the story of Hélène B., a woman in love with a man she has never met who decides 'de se livrer entière' (2005: 13) ['give herself entirely'] to him via an extensive pornographic documentation of herself. What might be a romantic proposition is given a disquieting twist, as Hélène B. is a victim of terminal cancer with only a few weeks to live.

In this text, then, there is a fundamental opposition put in place over the question of whether pornography represents all or nothing. Marzano's declaration that: 'La représentation obscène efface même la possibilité d'un spectacle, car, lorsque tout est à voir, il n'y a tout simplement plus de scène' (2003: 106) ['obscene representation erases even the possibility of spectacle, for when everything can be seen, there is simply no scene left to view'] is directly opposed by the narrative's insistence that 'La pornographie ne promet pas: elle donne, livre, exécute' (des Roches 2005: 85). ['Pornography doesn't promise: it gives, delivers, acts out.'] Pornography becomes the young female protagonist's chosen medium because it offers her clarity and a completeness that more conventional representations eschew. However, this perspective on pornography is complicated by the presence of two different modes of reception within the text. The representation of her body illuminated by 'la lumière crue, pure et fine, la lumière royale de la pornographie' (2005: 20) ['the harsh, pure, keen light, the royal light, of pornography'] is destined for the young man Robert Y., the unknowing object of the woman's desire. At the same time the reader is turned into a voyeur, not just of the photographic and filmic images she creates, but also of the very process of creation she is engaged upon. The reader's perspective is a profoundly uncomfortable one, torn between response to the erotically stimulating textual images evoked, and the acknowledgement of what lies behind them; a sick, diseased, dying body. Marzano's argument that in contemporary pornography the body is pierced 'par le regard obscène qui le dévoile jusqu'à sa disparition' (2003: 162) ['by the obscene gaze which reveals the body to the point where it disappears'] is complicated by the hallucinatory play of contradictory images of the body in *La Jeune Femme et la pornographie*. Rather than effect its own disappearance, the obscene body in this text appeals to two levels of reality that co-exist but cannot be reconciled: the body as fantasy image of abundant sexuality and the body as mortal, sick and abject. What Marzano's text ultimately fails to acknowledge is that contemporary pornography is fascinated by the way that erotic intentions can result in startlingly different outcomes. Or we can look at this a different way by recalling Žižek's postmodern proposition that: 'the same object can function successively as a disgusting reject and as a sublime, charismatic apparition: the difference, strictly structural, does not pertain to the "effective properties" of the object, but only to its place in the symbolic order' (1992: 143). Hence the female protagonist's tragic reliance on the pornographic not just to promise but to deliver a body in images that is clearly, transparently desirable.

Similarly to *Le Pornographe*, this text explores the hyperreal through a self-reflexive attention to the process of image creation, but at the same time, the reader is made attentive to the way the hyperreal, so carefully maintained in its ambivalence in Bonello's film, here collapses into the horrifying brutality of the real. Having exhausted the possibilities of photography, Hélène B. buys a video camera and attempts to create herself in film. The task turns out to be far harder than she initially suspected, requiring a spontaneity and presence that are more difficult to inhabit than the carefully prepared photographic images. Attempting to masturbate for the camera, Hélène B. becomes conscious of Robert Y.'s absence and her own isolation. Imagination proves insufficient and the painful solitude of pornographic pleasure is momentarily glimpsed. Fighting a sense of the ridiculous and a fantasy of Robert Y. with another woman, Hélène B. suddenly loses her self-control and screaming out 'no', rips off her wig and throws it away. 'La caméra continuait de tourner. Crâne chauve. À peine quelques poils follets ourlés sur le dessus de la tête. Les yeux tout à coup si cernés, les traits si défaits, le corps si parfaitement trahi par le corps. *Coupez!*' (2005: 60). ['The camera continued to roll. Bald skull. Just a little soft down rimming the back of the head. Eyes suddenly dark-ringed, features haggard, the body so perfectly betrayed by the body. *Cut!*'] It is possible that the camera records the real at this point, but we are no longer on the side of the image, rather we are uncomfortably, queasily close to the abject body that lies beneath. The pornographic image is explored in highly contradictory ways in this text, as something 'trop vrai', something revelatory, that shows despite itself the disarray inside the human body, and yet it is equally invested by those who use it (Hélène in this case) with the belief that 'La pornographie offre la vie heureuse, la terre solide sous nos pieds … afin que l'on puisse aimer, manger, prier, manger, espérer d'une façon insensée que tout se termine bien' (2005: 85). ['Pornography offers a happy life, firm ground beneath our feet… so that we can love, ear, pray, eat, hope in a crazy way, that everything will turn out all right.'] Pornography becomes useful, then, to the contemporary aesthetic perspective as the heterogeneous union of fantasy and reality, of hope and fear, of the possibility that the real might turn out to be reassuring, and the acknowledgement that the reality of the body is one of limitation and decay.

Attempting to reconcile the contradictory images of pornography over her own body, it is no surprise that Hélène B. is soon 'partout à la fois'. 'Je suis hors de moi' she writes in her diary (another form of representation for Robert Y.), 'A la fois ici et là […] Transparente et confuse'(2005: 94). ['everywhere at once. I am outside myself' … 'At once here and there […] Transparent and confused'.] Impending mortality, the sense of the body's alterity, the loss of self experienced in the documentary project and of the self given to the other in hopeless, unrequited desire compound the physical pain of Hélène B. Yet the discontinuity of the body allows the extraordinary fantasy ending of the text. After her suicide, Hélène B.'s executor arrives at Robert Y.'s house with her documentary remains. The female executor then sets about satisfying Hélène's final demand, which is that she should perform in Hélène's place the sexual seduction of Robert. This is represented in the text in the form of a posthumous letter detailing their encounter, so that Hélène's voice should haunt the narrative's conclusion, as well as participate fantastically in the sexual act. Given that the text has stated Hélène's suicidal inclinations from the start, and given the testimonial nature of her multi-media project of autofiction, it would seem that her voice has always already originated from a fold within time, an impossible crack in the continuum between life and death, just as her body has inhabited an impossible realm belonging to both the real and representation, displaying simultaneously both mortal sickness and vital health.

The image of the subject that is created by this text is one of extreme abjection, *à la* Kristeva. For Kristeva, the abject self is a permanent exile who asks '"Où suis-je?" plutôt que "Qui suis-je?". Car l'espace qui préoccupe le jeté, l'exclu, n'est jamais *un*, ni *homogène*, ni *totalisable*, mais essentiellement divisible, pliable, catastrophique' (1980: 15–16). ['"Where am I?" instead of "Who am I?" For the space that engrosses the deject, the excluded, is never one, nor *homogeneous*, nor *totalizable*, but essentially divisible, foldable and catastrophic' (Kristeva 1982: 8).] The abject self is troubled at the level of borderlines and boundaries, uncertain where the self ends and the other begins. The term refers to a radical undecidability in the body's self-possession and finds immediate expression in liminal corporeal matter, such as blood, sweat, tears, vomit, shit. Its genesis is in the earliest stages of the child's development, before object relations, the distinction between self and other, are fully apprehended, when the child has the premonition that the presence of the mother in the self threatens unified subjectivity and must be expelled. What is here theorised as confined to a developmental stage of childhood has increasingly become a significant dimension of postmodern art, capturing the aesthetic imagination in ever more pervasive ways. Kristeva herself predicts this in 1980 when *Pouvoirs de l'horreur* was published, proposing that: 'Dans un monde où l'Autre s'est effondré, l'effort esthétique – descente dans les foundations de l'édifice symbolique – consiste à retracer les frontières fragiles de l'être parlant, au plus près de son aube, de cette "origine" sans fond qu'est le refoulement dit originaire' (1980: 25). ['In a world in which the Other has collapsed, the aesthetic task – a descent into the foundations of the symbolic construct – amounts to retracing the fragile limits of the speaking being, closest to its dawn, to the bottomless "primacy" constituted by primal repression' (Kristeva 1982: 18).] The collapse of the Other can be understood as the failure of authority invested in the symbolic, in the paternally invested systems of meaning creation, and in this context, the concept of the hyperreal must represent an extreme manifestation of radical symbolic uncertainty.

The image, both in Bonello's cinematic work, and more problematically in *La Jeune Femme et la pornographie*, offers itself most readily as the site/sight of the hyperreal. The textual exploration of photography as agent of the hyperreal and source of radical abjection is again the focal point of Valérie Tordjman's sickly tale of pornography, murder and hysteria, *La Pornographie de l'âme*. Magnus Mayeul is a pioneer of photography, working alongside Charcot in La Salpêtrière, documenting the sexually licentious images of hysteria. He also has a sideline borrowing the dead bodies he photographs at the morgue and turning them into pornographic images. The character of Mayeul is remarkable for his indifference to crucial borderlines, between life and death, for instance, with the result that his responses are often misplaced and disquieting. Looking at the 'nature morte' (still life) he has just arranged of the decapitated head of a young man crowed with thorns, against the breast of a woman, tastefully finished off with an arrangement of fruit and seafood: 'Il est assailli de tendresse: une douleur inavouable. Mayeul ne comprend pas pourquoi l'épaisseur de son corps n'est pas un rempart' (Tordjman 2004: 23). ['He is overcome by tenderness: a shameful pain. Mayeul doesn't understand why the thickness of his body is not a defence.'] His ability to be easily moved, easily 'touched' by extreme emotions that are themselves overwhelming composites of pleasure and pain, results in a fear of his own porosity, his openness to contamination. Yet this sense of contamination comes from his incapacity to make distinctions, or perhaps more accurately, his fascination with the paradoxical transcendence of oppositions of which photography becomes the symbolic epitome. In a life founded on paradox, Mayeul's internal contradictions are both his pride and his downfall, and photography provides a means to experience, to document and to conceptualise his inner conflictedness.

Mayeul finds himself attracted to one of the hysterics, Charlotte, who disappears from La Salpêtrière dressed as a man but turns up again in the brothel Mayeul frequents. Keen to see her again, Mayeul finds no difficulty in making the transition to photographing prostitutes as, in any case, 'l'observation clinique transpire la promiscuité populaire d'un hotel garni' (2004: 50–1). ['clinical observation is sweaty with the common promiscuity of the brothel'.] However, Mayeul does run into difficulties when mixing business with pleasure. He takes a transgressive image of Charlotte dressed as a hermaphrodite Christ on the cross, has sex with her, kills her, has sex with her again, and takes more pictures for his clients, the collectors of pornography. Charlotte has become too close to the porous Mayeul through erotic contact, making him miss his still lives and the safety of the corpse. The experience of photographing her and of having sex with her both make him vomit, a reaction he repeatedly has to extreme emotion, and a physical manifestation of his inability to police his borders sufficiently. His murderous response is an excessive one that seems not to trouble him in the least; far more important is his own self-preservation, his battle to transcend the abject uncertainty of his limits. Recalling Kristeva's description of the corporeal experience of abjection: 'Ces déchets chutent pour que je vive, jusqu'à ce que, de perte en perte, il ne m'en reste rien, et que mon corps tombe tout entier au-delà de la limite, *cadere*, cadavre' (1980: 11) ['Such wastes drop so that I might live until, from loss to loss, nothing remains of me and my entire body falls beyond the limit – cadere, cadaver' (Kristeva 1982: 3)], we find Mayeul's anxious description of his vomiting attack: 'j'ai eu peur de mourir. Chaque fois que je verse des larmes, que l'urine chaude, la merde et le sperme me quittent, j'ai peur en secret; aussi je m'économise' (2004: 73). ['I was afraid of dying. Every time I spill tears, or lose hot urine, shit and sperm, I am secretly afraid; and so I conserve myself'.] However, the experience with Charlotte quickly coheres into a routine, and any number of 'charlottes' appear across Paris, victims of an unknown attacker.

Kristeva argues that 'L'abject est pervers car il n'abandonne ni n'assume un interdit, une règle ou une loi; mais les détourne, fourvoie, corrompt; s'en sert, en use, pour mieux les dénier' (1980: 23). ['The abject is perverse because it neither gives up nor assumes a prohibition or rule or a law, but turns them aside, misleads, corrupts, uses them, takes advantage of them, the better to deny them' (Kristeva 1982: 15).] This is true at the level of Mayeul's criminal activities but it is also identifiable at the level of narrative discourse, where, in a move reminiscent of Bataillean formlessness, signifying chains intersect and echo one another across the text. The lexicon of photography, the 'trou' of the camera and the light which 'pénètre' reveals its proximity to the erotic, but equally its relationship to murder; the possession of the image is analogous to sexual possession, and also to possession in death: 'Je ne compte plus, je photographie. Je prends une vie, puis une autre et une autre encore' (2004: 79) ['I'm no longer counting, I'm photographing. I take one life, then another, then one more'], Mayeul declares. And the aggression of his actions is subsumed into an amorous and self-denying gesture: 'On peut aimer les morts plus que tout, plus que sa propre vie, au point de se perdre' (2004: 79). ['You can love the dead more than anything, more than your own life, to the point of losing yourself.'] Mayeul's inescapable chains of paradox are nowhere more evident than in his response to extreme erotic or murderous emotion. The acts intended to designate the limits of his body and locate the center of his subjectivity result, in their excessiveness, in the *jouissance* that causes radical loss of self-possession. But then, this is a text that strives to undermine all oppositions to an outrageous degree, denying distinctions between image and reality, life and death, inside and outside, madness and reason. Photography and the pornographic provide the crossover points, where all distinctions merge into 'l'instant suprême' (2004: 78).

Mayeul reaches the climax of his own narrative with another series of binary transgressions that will transform him into the model as well as the photographer, both partners in the sexual act and a man as well as a woman. This is achieved by having a waxwork copy of himself made, and will result in a number of photographs, one of which, the image of a court card, features opposing portraits of Mayeul as man and woman in a dizzying hall of mirrors. The outcome is as internally conflicted as we might expect: 'Il n'a jamais été aussi seul et aussi plein de lui-même' (2004: 113–14) ['He had never been so alone, nor so full of himself'], the narrative tells us, while Mayeul recognises 'le chaos bruyant de mon désir d'être tout à la fois' (2004: 136). ['the resounding chaos of my desire to be everything at once'.] The intention of Mayeul's final excesses seems to be to incorporate all contradictions within himself, to transcend his boundary difficulties by locating all boundaries internally. But the satisfaction of all desires, the incorporation of all possible oppositions can only have one outcome; Mayeul's triumph is also his tragedy and the final pornographic photograph of himself with his waxwork double is intended also to be the image he takes of his death; the ultimate 'nature morte'.

In this text the experience of the abject is linked to multiplication; the absence of self-unification reflected in an endless procession of images, doubles, uncertain bodies hovering between the medical and the erotic, the sexual and the murderous, the pornographic and the mystical. The collapse of all distinctions between self and other, as well as between preservation and destruction, make this the most amoral of texts. In this respect it would seem to be profoundly apolitical, and yet it could be argued that, like those of Houellebecq's characters, especially in *Extension du domaine de la lutte*, Mayeul's neurotic and murderous attempts at self-mastery are distant cousins to those isolated and loveless sufferers, the Existentialists. Camus' Meursault, in his delight in sensual pleasures and his unmotivated murder of the Arab, would not be alarmed by Mayeul's unreflexive excesses. However, the case for Existentialism's projection into the contemporary pornographic is made elsewhere in this book (notably in Chapter 3, pp. 93–7). For the moment we can trace a line of genealogy from existential alienation in the wastelands of uncertainty surrounding the nature of subjective experience, to the radical individual dislocation explored in these texts of abject pornography. This dynamic relates also to the development in Kristeva's texts, from her 1980 work on abjection, with its prediction that the fragile foundations of subjectivity would become the primary basis for works of art, to her recent *Sens et non-sens de la révolte* with its assertion that abject art can be understood as potentially revolutionary. How are we to understand this progression? Perhaps if we recall that French political engagement from the 1950s onwards stressed the absolute necessity of exploring the foundations of language before effective social change could be achieved, so the contemporary climate finds itself instinctually driven to explore the basis of subjectivity before the individual – in terms of the political subject of engagement – can entertain a proper revolutionary stance. Just as earlier French avant-garde politics demanded an exploration of mental structures, so current avant-garde art demands an exploration of corporeal ones. Yet now, as then, the texts and films that inhabit this perspective remain bound up in aesthetic conceits so far removed from the everyday and the recognisably political that we must question the real potential of their message. When they do include overt references to the political, as in the case of *Partouz* and *Le Pornographe*, the collapse of reliable structures of engagement is so absolute that it becomes difficult to envisage a way out of the impasse. Kristeva places her hopes in the spectator, whose aesthetic experience will somehow prove transformative, but it seems a lot to ask of the spectator whose internal limits have been confronted and undermined, to subsequently marshal sufficient subjective resources to construct a political response. Ultimately we have to read these artworks with the ambivalence they so playfully and desperately conjure up, as both expressions of a need for original revolutionary action and a collapse into deathly inertia.

Notes

1 Gablik is discussing visual and plastic arts here but it is intriguing to see just how closely her account corresponds to the prevailing *Weltanschauung* in literature and film as well. This corresponds to the notable similarities we draw from differing forms of pornographic representation in this analysis. The shared concern of different media, in contemporary works that cite pornographic tropes, to promote an experience in the spectator was discussed in more detail in the Introduction, above.

2 Foster argues that, while it may express a recognition of its own instability, it is a form of art that wants 'the real to exist, in all the glory (or the horror) of its pulsatile desire, or at least to evoke this sublime condition' (1996: 140).

3 The performances of Dadaist poets such as Tristan Tzara and the theatre of Antonin Artaud provide pertinent examples of such 'happenings'.

4 The Lacanian theory here is taken from his 1964 seminar on the real and the 'objet petit a' (see Lacan 1973).

5 See the opening chapter of Kristeva's *Sens et non-sens de la révolte* (1996) for her detailed and comprehensive exploration of the evolution of the word 'révolution'.

5

Critical distance: Catherine Millet, Virginie Despentes

As we have seen throughout the previous three chapters, one of the things at stake in the contemporary fascination of western culture with the pornographic is the question of the kinds of contact that might be possible between the artwork and its recipient. This question is also an organising principle in the work of two female figures central to the recent prominence of sexually explicit material within French intellectual culture, and who have gained international prominence largely on this basis: namely, Catherine Millet and Virginie Despentes. Millet's international bestseller, *La Vie sexuelle de Catherine M.*, brought this cultural penchant for explicit sex together with a favourite recent genre, that of life-writing, replacing this genre's usual accounts of illness or family trauma with unstinting descriptions of her unusually promiscuous sexual activity. The stakes of aesthetic contact are here raised, as the work confronts readers with the question of the extent to which the individual whose intimate experiences we are following is the Catherine Millet whose name appears on its cover. Rather than salacious confession or self-seeking exhibitionism, the book has as a driving concern the question of the kinds of distance it is or is not possible to maintain between the author Catherine Millet, her stand-in 'Catherine M.' and her reader. Despentes, for her part, broke through with the uncompromising, trashy, debatably feminist and pornographically fixated thriller *Baise-moi*, and has since produced a body of work whose characteristic bluntness is often achieved by its author's use of or reference to the codes and practices of pornography and the sex industry more generally. This serves two purposes: it is part of Despentes' forceful if ambiguous confrontation of the violence of misogyny; and it is one of the manifestations of her interest (shared with Dustan and Rémès; see pp. 105–7) in a form of writing which would minimise its aesthetic elevation, in order to get as close as possible to the world it represents. The pornographic has a double role in this respect: omnipresent in the culture Despentes describes, its ubiquity in her work signifies this work's proximity to this culture; and the supposed lack of aesthetic distance which in part characterises the pornographic is precisely what Despentes is seeking to achieve. Both Millet and Despentes are, then, essentially concerned with the distance between their work and the world around it; as this chapter will seek to show that the work of both is defined by the difficulties entailed in regulating this distance.

Catherine Millet, almost intact

He that toucheth pitch shall be defiled therewith.

(Ecclesiasticus/Sirach XIII, 1)

Very few discussions of *La Vie sexuelle de Catherine M.* fail to refer to its author's status as editor of the respected magazine *Art Press*. The success of this work undoubtedly has much to do with its status as the erotic confession of a notably intellectual woman; but this does not by itself account for the book's popularity. For Millet's text also owes its success to the highly contemporary aesthetic drama it plays out – a drama all about contact and distance. An erotic memoir can hardly fail to promise a kind of affective, effective contact with its reader; a contact which is destined to remain an impossibility. But, as Laura Marks has argued (2002, discussed earlier in relation to Breillat; see p. 76), the fantasy of our culture is precisely that it would be possible to be in contact with that which is by definition mediated. And it is this dance between separation and proximity which characterises the aesthetic of Millet's text, making it, like Breillat's films, timely beyond its expectations.

Having briefly established the obscenity which constitutes its unavoidable promise of contact, we will now explore the strategies by which Millet's text refuses this very contact, before considering the interruption and frustration of these strategies by other aspects of the work, as well as the photographic accompaniment proposed by Millet's partner, Jacques Henric. While the 'official' aesthetic of Millet's text – an aesthetic of distinction – will be confronted with its failures, our argument will be that it is precisely the *intermittences* of this official aesthetic that give her text its exemplary status. Millet, her text, and her readers end up in an odd state of distanced proximity; and in this state, they enact the structure of feeling that defines their culture.

It is necessary to this argument that *La Vie sexuelle de Catherine M.* be recognised as containing a significant amount of material which could reasonably be regarded as obscene (in the broad, not the legal, sense of the word). It may appear curious, even otiose, to provide examples of obscenity from what is after all a notoriously explicit sexual memoir, but this is in fact useful for two connected reasons. First, as we will see, Millet is at pains to distance her work from the crude efficacy of the simply pornographic: the transitivity of pornography, and the code of literality by which this is assured, are consequently aspects of the work she seeks to minimise. Second, Millet's efforts in this direction are largely successful. There is, in fact, surprisingly little in the book which may be easily character-ised as unvarnished, explicit obscenity; surprisingly little that is not articulated through the intellectual and aesthetic frames which for Millet seek to maintain the work's integrity. It is accordingly worth acknowledging from the start that the intermittence of these frames is far from inevitable, is not the result of an insubstantial intellectual scaffolding collapsing under the weight of massive obscenity. But obscene material there undoubtedly is, as in the following example, chosen more or less at random:

> La tête à la hauteur des parties qui se présentaient, je pouvais sucer et pomper pendant que, les bras sur les accoudoirs, je branlais deux sexes en même temps. Mes jambes étaient très relevées et, l'un après l'autre, ceux qui avaient été suffisamment excités venaient poursuivre dans le con.
>
> Je transpire très peu mais j'étais parfois inondée de la sueur de mes partenaires. Par ailleurs, il y a toujours des filets de sperme qui sèchent en haut des cuisses, quelquefois sur les seins ou le visage, voire dans les cheveux, et les hommes qui partouzent aiment bien décharger dans un con déjà tapissé de foutre. (Millet 2002a: 22–3)
>
> [With my head on a level with the dicks that made themselves available, I could suck at one while, with my hands on the armrests, I jerked off two more at the same time. My legs were lifted up very high and, one after another, those who had become sufficiently aroused, followed through in my cunt.
>
> I sweat very little but sometimes I was drenched in my partners' sweat. There would also be threads of sperm that dried along the tops of my thighs, sometimes on my breasts or my face, even in my hair, and men who are into orgies really like shooting their load in a cunt that's already plastered with cum. (2002b: 14, modified)]

If this kind of literality appears obscene, this is largely thanks to the effectivity it threatens to unleash: in a way all too well metonymised by the bodily fluids of the second example, the writing is perceived as contagious, threatening to touch its reader in a manner as unwelcome as it is, in any meaningful sense, impossible. Advising others to avoid the work, one reader (Mary Ann Krupa, of Pittsburgh) wrote: 'I had to put this book down after the first chapter because I felt like my hands were covered in semen'.[1] This apparent immediacy renders the work suspect, either morally or aesthetically: as we discussed in our Introduction, it is the aim of effectivity through literality that consigns the pornographic for the most part to the status of the sub-aesthetic (see Dyer 1992 and Clover 1993). In its obscenity, the pornographic is like pitch: immediately, without negotiation, contact is defilement. The work becomes *tacky*: experienced as somehow sticking to its reader, it is for this reason relegated to the merely generic. Which is exactly what Millet wants to avoid. Hence the strategies referred to above: this kind of contagious obscenity is not greatly present in the work, whose sexual material is instead filtered through an extensive series of intellectual and aesthetic frames – to which we will now turn.

Throughout her memoir, Millet consistently valorises *distinction*: her concern is to maintain a kind of separation, hierarchical and exclusive, both within the worlds of sexual exchange she describes, and between herself as author and her fleshly reader. The paradox is evident: the documentary of promiscuity whose aesthetic refuses precisely this. But the affirmation of distinction, however surprising, is the most prominent characteristic of Millet as narrator. It would of course be absurdly naive, not to mention vulgar, to imagine that the world of sexual promiscuity is necessarily any less socially regulated than that of any other pastime. And Millet certainly makes it clear that her world of swinging is a world of strict etiquette. A vital element of this world is, accordingly, what she calls the 'distance de transition' (2002a: 31) ['transitional space' (2002b: 14, modified)], a separation that ensures the safe operation of the confusion that follows. With its social distinctions duly maintained, this world is free to become one of easy circulation, which in turn serves to reinforce its distinction from the wider world. Like the *maison close*, this 'monde clos' (56) ['closed world' (2002b: 40)] becomes a social microcosm distinct from the world around it, but whose distinction is maintained by its replication of the social structures of this world.

The importance Millet attaches to this idea of distinction goes beyond the social regulation of her sexual activity, however. It is also essential to social dealings in general, where she prefers to remain apart from the sentimental concerns of friends (77). What she refers to as her disdain is above all for the tackiness of these concerns: their sentimentality, yes, but also a vulgarity that Millet represents as somehow *sticky*:

> J'ai fui ces conversations d'abord parce qu'elles sont le plus souvent enrobées de considérations sentimentales qui les rendent immédiatement poisseuses, ensuite parce que, quelle que soit l'intimité que l'on partage avec l'interlocuteur ou l'interlocutrice, les mots auxquels on a recours sont toujours mauvais, approximatifs ou vulgaires. (iv)

> [I avoided these conversations, first because they are usually dressed up with sentimental considerations which make them immediately tacky, second, because, however close one might be to one's interlocutor, the words one uses are always bad, vague or vulgar.]

This avoidance of sentimental contact is accompanied by a strict division between the promiscuity of her swinging activity, and a dislike of any contact which is not contained within this world of sticky exchange:

> Qu'en l'absence de la personne, on touche un objet qui la touche, c'est la personne qui est atteinte par contiguïté. Ma langue pouvait bien, dans une partouze, nettoyer une chatte où venait de décharger quelqu'un qui s'était d'abord excité sur moi, mais la pensée de m'essuyer avec une serviette qu'une femme, venue clandestinement chez moi, aurait passée entre ses cuisses, ou que Jacques utilise la même qu'un invité dont il ignorerait la visite m'horrifie comme si nous avions à redouter une épidémie de lèpre. (169)

> [If, while someone is away, you touch something that they are close to, the person in question is involved by contiguity. During an orgy, my tongue could easily lick round a pussy which had just been stuffed by a man who had first got off on me, but the thought of drying myself on a towel that some woman who came clandestinely to my home may have used to wipe between her thighs, or the thought that Jacques might use the same one as some guest of mine whose visit he knew nothing about, horrifies me as much as a bout of leprosy. (2000b: 133, modified)]

There is an interesting dynamic at work here, as Millet maintains a sharp separation between her sexual activity within the swinging world (in which, if the appropriate etiquette is respected, promiscuous contact is the norm) and the rest of her life, including other instances of sexual activity (in which such contact, whether physical or emotional, direct or by proxy, is to be avoided). And the distinction which is the organizing concept here is especially celebrated when it comes to the image that Millet has of herself as promiscuous. Her refusal of the usual hypocritical misogynistic condemnation of the sexually active woman is understandable, but its habitual expression via the reaffirmation of her ethos of distinction ironically risks repeating this condemnation. When she describes street-walking prostitutes, for example (see 140), ostensibly in a spirit of solidarity (she too has climbed into the cabs of articulated lorries for sex), her description of their mismatching outfits marks a subtle social distance. For what interest is it to anyone whether the prostitutes' clothing and accessories match? It is of interest to Millet because this observation allows her to maintain her position as not one of them, despite the limited similarity in their behaviour. Equally, recalling her adolescent sexuality, Millet insists:

> Je n'étais pas une 'collectionneuse', et ceux que je voyais dans les surprises-parties, garçons ou filles, flirter [...] avec le maximum de gens pour s'en vanter le lendemain au lycée, m'offusquaient. Je me contentais de découvrir que cette défaillance voluptueuse que j'éprouvais au contact de l'ineffable douceur de toutes lèvres étrangères, ou lorsqu'une main s'appliquait sur mon pubis, pouvait se renouveler à l'infini puisqu'il s'avérait que le monde était plein d'hommes disposés à cela. Le reste m'était indifférent. (15)

> [I was not a 'collector', and I thought that the boys and girls that I saw at parties [flirting] with as many people as possible so that they could boast about it the next day at school, were somehow offensive. I was simply happy to discover that the delicious giddiness I felt at the ineffably soft touch of a stranger's lips, or when a hand fitted itself over my pubis, could be experienced an infinite number of times because the world was full of men predisposed to do just that. Nothing else really mattered. (2002b: 7–8, modified)]

Offended by competitive, exhibitionistic promiscuity, indifferent to its tawdry world which knows nothing of the ineffable and the infinite, Millet keeps her distance.[2]

It is essential to Millet that her choice of a promiscuous lifestyle should not see her confused with those for whose promiscuity she expresses her scorn or her subtle social distaste. Hence, she claims that her sexual activity represents a quasi-religious vocation, whose freedom is that of the self-determination which follows from an absolute existential commitment (64). This is, in one sense, the familiar idea of the freedom that comes from abandoning moral scruple or prejudice – but characteristically, Millet expresses this in terms of her elevation: 'Baiser par-delà toute répugnance, ce n'était pas que se ravaler, c'était, dans le renversement de ce mouvement, s'élever au-dessus des préjugés' (161). ['To fuck above and beyond any sense of disgust was not just a way of lowering oneself, it was, in a diametrically opposite move, to raise oneself above all prejudice' (2002b: 126).] For all the intertwinings of her chosen lifetsyle, then, Millet remains resolutely independent:

> j'ai dû alors confusément comprendre que si les relations avec les amis pouvaient s'étendre et croître sur le mode d'une plante grimpante, vriller et se nouer dans une totale et réciproque liberté, et qu'il suffisait de se laisser porter par cette sève, je n'en devais pas moins décider, moi-même, résolument et solitairement, de ma conduite. J'aime cette solitude paradoxale. (48)

> [I now feel that it was then that I first hazily grasped the fact that, if relationships with friends could spread and grow like a climbing plant, twisting knotting together in perfect and reciprocal freedom, and that all you had to do was to let yourself go with the flow of its sap, it was nonetheless up to me to decide on my own behaviour for myself, resolutely and solitarily. I like this paradoxical solitude. (2002b: 34, modified)]

The book is, accordingly, an affirmation of what is repeatedly referred to as the *singularity* of its heroine. In the essay appended as a preface to the paperback edition of the work, its author even expresses her incredulity at the idea of a discrepancy between this emphasis on distinction and the sweaty, tangled subject matter of the book:

> Est-ce parce qu'il s'agit de sexe qu'on se serait attendu à ce que je renonce à ma conscience comme on y renonce dans l'extase? Mais en admettant qu'on puisse écrire dans ces conditions, l'effet ne serait-il pas de susciter l'empathie du lecteur? Or, le projet n'était que d'exposer une sexualité singulière, celle de Catherine M. (ii)

> [Did people expect me to abandon all self-awareness, as in moments of ecstasy, just because it's a matter of sex? But – even supposing it is possible to write in such conditions – would this not have the effect of arousing the empathy of the reader? And my project was simply to set out a singular form of sexuality, that of Catherine M.]

This is writing, Millet stresses, and writing with a particular aim. Nothing could be further from her intention than to arouse the reader's empathy: this is precisely what she explicitly shuns. Rather, this writing seeks to confirm and further the distinction of its singular heroine. The sexuality in question is, accordingly, that of 'Catherine M.', carefully and protectively suspended in the elegant universe of 'Fiction et Cie' (the collection in which the text was originally published), behind whom the author can take cover if necessary: 'Lorsqu'on s'inquiète de savoir si je suis affectée par les attaques contre le livre ou contre moi, je réponds mollement parce que mon impression dominante est que les adversaires enfoncent leurs épingles dans un fétiche qu'ils ont confectionné eux-mêmes' (ii). ['Whenever people are concerned to know whether I am affected by the attacks on the book or on myself, I feebly reply that my overriding impression is that my opponents are sticking their pins in a fetish they have made themselves.'] This fetish is not just the creation of such critics, however: she is also the singular creature of Catherine Millet, who can contemplate her, and her success, from a relative distance: 'Maintenant, je regarde l'auteur de *Catherine M.* comme celui-ci a pu regarder son sujet, et je ne m'identifie plus complètement ni avec l'un ni avec l'autre' (ii). ['Now, I look upon the author of *Catherine M.* as she looked upon her subject, and I no longer identify completely with either of them.'] There is a constant distancing at work here, in which the author of the preface is not quite the author of the book, who is not quite its heroine. And so, for Millet, her writing must be anything but the messy contact it describes, lest it become, like the shared towel or her friends' confidences, horribly vulgar:

> A cela s'ajoute que la vulgarité, par définition est ce par quoi les gens se mélangent. J'ai beau avoir pratiqué ce qu'on appelle 'la sexualité de groupe', si je me situe dans l'ordre de l'échange verbal – sans intention d'établir un rapport érotique –, je ne tiens pas à *toucher* l'interlocuteur ou l'interlocutrice dans le tréfonds de son instinct sexuel, ce qui se produit presque toujours lorsqu'on use abruptement du vocabulaire obscène. Manié sans précaution, ce vocabulaire affecte les sens presque aussi directement qu'un contact physique. Dans leur vulgarité, certains, hostiles à mon livre, ont eu dans leurs déclarations des *gestes* à mon égard. Mon souci est qu'ils pouvaient faire croire à leurs lecteurs que j'avais adopté un même style vulgaire. Non, à l'encontre de leur désir, je ne me *mélange* pas à eux. Le choix de mots justes se rapportant au sexe

est un travail exigeant qui, à l'exception de la parole perpétuellement remise en cause en présence d'un analyste, relève donc plutôt de l'écrit que de l'oralité. (iv–v)

[To this must be added the fact that vulgarity is by definition that element within which people mix. For all that I may have engaged in what is referred to as 'group sex', if I find myself in a verbal encounter – with no intention of establishing an erotic connection – I have no desire to *touch* my interlocutor in the depths of his or her sexual instincts, which is what invariably happens when one suddenly uses obscene vocabulary. Deployed indiscriminately, this vocabulary can affect the senses almost as directly as physical contact. Being vulgar, some people, who were hostile to my book, made declarations which featured *gestures* in relation to me. My worry is that they could make their readers believe that I had adopted the same vulgar style. No, contrary to what they desire, I will not *mix* with them. The choice of the right word when it is a matter of sex is a demanding form of work which, with the exception of the way in which the spoken word is constantly placed in question in the psychoanalytic encounter, has more to do with writing than with speech.]

But Millet's work cannot solely be accounted for in terms of this distinction, this refusal of contact. Not merely because of the difficulty of sustaining this refusal in a book which can hardly avoid – somewhere, eventually – affecting the bodies of at least some of its readers. Rather, and more interestingly, because Millet on occasion also allows herself to deploy images of exactly the kind of sticky promiscuity she generally attempts to contain within her sexual adventures, in the context of describing either her fantasy life, other accounts of her sexual activities or the status of her book. These images serve to interrupt or snag her general insistence on distinction, in ways which ensure that the overall aesthetic of her work remains stuck to complexities which, though it might rather ignore them, are central to its success.

At one point, Millet relents from her hard-line insistence on the rigour of the swinging ethos. With a wry detachment from her younger self, she recalls her shock on learning of the busy sexual activity apparently to be found around academic conferences, and her dismissal of such opportunistic sleaziness as mere 'carnival', unlike the rigour of an existential commitment. In order, as she puts it, to temper the severity of this judgement, Millet then relates a fantasy which, as she acknowledges, shows her fantasy life overturning the principles of her lifestyle:

en dépit de la morale que je viens d'exprimer, je me suis beaucoup excitée en m'imaginant être le sac à foutre d'une bande de congressistes énervés qui me fourraient en cachette les uns des autres [...] C'est là un de mes scénarios les plus sûrs pour m'amener à jouir d'un état d'avilissement maximum. (125)

[despite the moral stance I have just expressed, I have often been aroused by imagining myself as a spunk bag for a group of stressed executives at a meeting, they would each dump their load in me secretly [...] That's a surefire stellar scenario for me to get off on in a state of complete degradation. (2002b: 96)]

The pleasure derived from 'avilissement' is no longer sublimated into a kind of self-elevation: rather, the point of this fantasy is its banality, its abandon of the formality and etiquette of the swinging world, its collapse of multiple couplings into a clichéd scenario which is quite simply and avowedly tacky. And this enjoyment of a kind of contamination which Millet's text generally seeks to circum-scribe is also evident in her account of the pleasure she once took – really, now, not at the level of fantasy – in describing an encounter marked by its lack of hygiene: 'Je me complais dans l'évocation de cette malpropreté et de cette laideur contagieuses, en même temps que je savoure le léger dégoût de mon interlocuteur' (74). ['I take pleasure in evoking this dirtiness and this contagious ugliness, at the same time savouring the disgust of the man questioning me' (2002b: 55).] Here Millet's affirmation of contagion at the level of the recalled encounter becomes a *mise-en-abîme* of the oral narra-tion of this encounter, in which the power of the vulgar word (of which she is elsewhere so wary) is, in a lexical choice which seems deliberately to evoke sensory contact, 'savoured', and Millet shows a delight in the effective capacity of narrative which she elsewhere seeks to restrict to the realm of the actual sexual encounter.

On a couple of occasions, a similar overspill is discernible in Millet's description of her own book. Whereas she generally presents the book as an elevated labour of symbolisation, Millet elsewhere allows the murk of its subject matter to scandalise her usual aesthetic. Recalling the origin of the idea for the book, she uses an image which anticipates that which she will later give to represent her horror of unregulated promiscuous contact: 'Et je crois bien que c'est ainsi, occupée à passer une serviette de toilette sur mon sexe, que pour la première fois j'ai pensé qu'il faudrait dire la vérité sur tout ça.' (92; cf. 169, quoted on p. 153) ['And I think it was in that position, as I ran a towel between my legs, that I first thought I ought to tell all about it' (2002b: 70).] This writing, here, telling this truth, is brought into a proximity with bodily fluids which it is otherwise supposed to shun. And similarly, contemplating the success of her book, Millet sees its circulation as akin to the free flow of bodies it represents:

> Comment ne pas voir, dans la circulation du livre et dans la circulation de la parole autour, ce qui, dans l'ordre du possible, est envisageable comme réalisation de ce lissage des relations humaines, lissage qui se ferait au travers de la libre reconnaissance du désir sexuel, au travers de sa tolérance, et dont quelques-unes de mes pages donnent une représentation évidemment utopique, fantasmatique? Et comment ne pas se réjouir de cette vision? (xiv)

> [Who could fail to see, in the circulation of the book and of all the talk about it, something which might be thought of as the actualisation, in the realm of the possible, of the kind of well-oiled human relationships – well-oiled thanks to the free recognition and the acceptance of sexual desire – of which some of my pages give an obviously utopian, fantasmatic representation? And who could fail to rejoice at this vision?]

A spectrum is here established, from the fantasmatic free circulation of desire, through its relatively free circulation in the real sexual activity Millet recounts, to the circulation of the book as image of this fantasy – tying the book by analogy to the world of real, bodily exchange.

There thus emerges a sense of Millet's book as not so much distinct from the tacky world of vulgar circulation, as poised on its edge, elevated beyond it when expressing its 'official' aesthetic, but dipping into it from time to time, including – and this is intriguing – when it considers its own status. This structure of *relative* separation is thematised at one moment in terms of semi-clandestine sexual activity, deliciously guaranteed only by what Millet calls an 'écran trop mince ou imparfait' (135). ['a thin or flawed screen' (2002b: 104).] This imperfect screen is also that separating the text from the world of unregulated exchange, a separation which is desired in its ethos of distinction, but compromised by its invocations of a promiscuous contact (including imaginary, fantasmatic contact) beyond the boundaries of the swinging world. When the text concludes with an imagistic synthesis of Millet's real body and its representations, then, this slippage from its aesthetics of distinction is safeguarded by being internalised, but is also the model which – in its externalised, contagious form – she has been resisting. In this conclusion, Millet narrates a particular sexual encounter with her partner, Jacques Henric. Delighting in the seamless transition on this occasion from being photographed to being penetrated, Millet surprisingly describes herself as 'déjà pleine de la coïncidence de mon corps vrai et de ses multiples images volatiles' (234). ['already filled by the coincidence of my real body and these multiple, volatile images' (2002b: 186).] Now this is also, of course, an oddly conventional use of conjugal union as narrative climax (see Roger 2001: 922). But it is remarkable that this text, which so emphasises its attachment to an ethos and an aesthetics of distinction, working to separate its author's body from the risk of affective contact which its symbolisation paradoxically entails, should end by betraying this distinction in an image of the fusion of the real body and its representations. Striving to elevate itself beyond the affective contact which its explicit subject matter can hardly avoid, the text topples back over into an affirmation of this very contact, the momentum of its climactic rhetoric joining the real and its images in a moment of unsurpassed intensity. And it is precisely because her images are *volatile* that they will make contact in ways Millet would generally rather avoid, but on which, as we have seen, her writing seems irreducibly caught.

These volatile images also promote the successful circulation and reception of Millet's text. When Millet celebrates the circulation of her book as a template for the movement of desire within her fanta-sised libidinal economy (xiv, quoted above), the edition of her book prefaced by this text demonstrates the implication of her body and its images in this circulation: from the austerity of the 'Fiction et Cie' edition, the text now features on its cover the naked image of its author, appealing explicitly to the titillation of the reader the text is so keen to disavow. And there was no need to wait for this edition for such an implication to be apparent: the publication of the original edition of *La Vie sexuelle de Catherine M.* was accom-panied by that of the volume from which this cover image is taken, namely *Légendes de Catherine M.*, a collection of photographs of Millet in varying states of undress, and reflections on the aesthetic status of these images, by Henric. In its accompaniment by this volume, Millet's text sees its 'official' aesthetic further compromised, its interest further enhanced; it is, accordingly, by means of a brief account of the significance of this accompaniment that our discus-sion of the aesthetic entanglements of Millet's text will conclude.

As we have seen, Millet's writing teeters on the edge between the distinction to which it lays claim, and the vulgarity which it cannot quite avoid, both insisting on and risking what Henric calls the 'cordon protecteur de l'écrit' (2001: 149). ['the protective cordon of writing'.] His publication of these photographs of her body exacerbates this situation, producing, as he recognises, an unavoidable *vulgarity* (see 182).[3] This is to say that Henric acknowledges what Millet cannot quite embrace: that explicit material – however finely wrought – is to some extent irreducibly vulgar; that, in Millet's words but contrary to her dominant aesthetic, in its reception, 'c'est la personne qui est atteinte par contiguïté' (Millet 2001: 169). ['the person in question is involved by contiguity' (2002b: 133, modified).] Citing the phenomenological discussions of the relationship between vision and touch evoked above in our discussion of Breillat, referring specifically to Merleau-Ponty, along with Descartes and Levinas, Henric engages the heart of the aesthetic debate at work here, making great play of the notion that the images he is presenting of Millet might constitute a kind of contact: in mock alarm, he exclaims, 'Nous voilà mal partis, Catherine, avec ces photos. Tous ces yeux à mains, sur toi!' (60–1). ['It's not looking good for us, Catherine, with these photos! All these eyes with their hands all over you!'] Henric is playful where Millet is ambivalent; what he thereby knowingly foregrounds is that the distinction which Millet prizes is haunted by the possible effective contact to which her aesthetic remains stuck. The photographic supplement of Henric's text uses the ineradicable indexical literality of film photography (again as discussed above in relation to Breillat) to dramatise this bind with especial clarity. Thanks to this indexicality, a photograph of Millet's body serves also as evidence of its (sometime) real presence, forming the ontological bond which for Barthes constitutes (as it had for Bazin) the referential pathos of all photography, keeping the image stuck to its referent, while opening the possibility of another contact, that with an unknowable future spectator.[4] Which is to say that Henric's book returns us insistently to the impossible notion that the inevitable mediation of representation might also act as the medium of effective contact. And in so doing, he delineates to perfection the drama of 'Catherine M.'

For what Henric suggests, and what Millet suspects, is that the stakes of their enterprise entail the effectivity that is the business of every disreputable, vulgar genre from soap opera to cheap horror movie and, pre-eminently, the pornographic: namely, the fantasised collapse of the insulating distance proper to the aesthetic, and the conversion of this insulation into a channel for the communication of real contact between the more or less aesthetic object and its recipient. It would be naive to imagine that in such genres, the distance of the aesthetic is actually abolished; but it is impossible to ignore the constitutive role played by the idea of this abolition in the establishment of these genres as such. Moreover, as Millet's text shows, the aesthetic per se cannot rule out the possibility that it might be having an effect, really, somewhere, despite and across its inevitable distance. The 'cordon protecteur de l'écrit' might always just be 'un écran trop mince ou imparfait'. This possibility represents the dream or the guilt of today's cultural production; its figure is what Benjamin (a major reference in Henric's text), in the *Arcades Project*, calls the trace, namely 'the appearance of a nearness, however far removed the thing that left it behind may be'. The inversion of his more familiar notion of the aura ('the appearance of a distance, however close the thing that calls it forth'), the trace seems to effect contact regardless of distance: 'In the trace, we gain possession of the thing', writes Benjamin; 'in the aura, it takes possession of us' (1999: 447).[5] In 'The work of art in the age of mechanical reproduction', Benjamin famously describes the waning of the aura of the authentic artwork or cultic object, caused by 'the desire of contemporary masses to bring things "closer" spatially and humanly', which leads dialectically to 'the urge [...] to get hold of an object at very close range by way of its likeness, its reproduction' (1992: 216–17). And those cultural forms which define contemporary production – the webcam, say, or reality television or the memoir, erotic or otherwise – are haunted by the defining notion that their reproductions might operate in the mode of the trace, might indeed effect actual contact.

But this association might also move in the opposite direction, reinscribing the aura dialectically within its destruction. Just as the aesthetic, as Millet shows, might always be betraying its defining distance, so too is the contact effected by the artwork inseparable from its constitutive impossibility. It is true that after a century of artistic production characterised by the spectacle of its defining frame being placed in jeopardy, we can no longer take refuge in the prophylactic virtues of the aesthetic: for all our protestations about the constructedness of any representation, it is impossible to avoid at least the fantasy that effective contact might nonetheless be taking place. But equally, this remains ineradicably a contact in which no-one is touched – in which, while we might think to 'gain possession of the thing', as Benjamin puts it, the vacancy of its fascinating non-presence also 'takes possession of us'. And so it is that, poised between the realisation and the impossibility of actual contact, the volatile image of 'Catherine M.' becomes symptomatic of the tacky culture she strives to rise above: displaying the intermittent, articulated rhythms of distance and proximity which form the truth of its dream of real contact.

A comparison might perhaps serve as a way to bring out in conclusion what has here been presented as a key part of the contemporary interest of Millet's text; and the necessary comparison here is with another recent erotic *succès de scandale*: Natacha Merritt's *Digital Diaries* (2000). Presenting more or less explicit digital photographs of herself and various companions in and around a range of sexual activity (condensing, as it were, Millet's text and Henric's photographic supplements), Merritt aims for precisely the kind of self-revelation, and fusion between her aesthetic and sexual activity, that Millet mostly rejects; she also thereby takes ownership of these images, and hence of her own effective, vulgar presence, in a way that Millet refuses. But this is exactly what makes Millet interesting: rather than instantiating like Merritt the impossible dream of actual contact, her work (by itself, and a fortiori with Henric's photographs) dramatises both its gravitational pull and its inevitable aporia. What Millet shows in exemplary fashion is the structure of our defining fascination: not the thing itself (as if this were possible), but the drama of its distant immediacy.

Virginie Despentes: keeping it real

Comment se fait-il qu'il ne se trouve guère d'écrivain féminin qui cherche à venger ses sœurs des traitements assez rudes parfois auxquels les soumettent les auteurs masculins correspondants?

(Boris Vian)

[Why is it that hardly any female writers seek to avenge their sisters for the sometimes rather rough treatment they receive at the hands of the equivalent male authors?]

If there is one French work which has contributed more than any other to recent debates about the presence of pornography in mainstream or arthouse culture, that work is the film, released in 2000 and directed by Virginie Despentes and Coralie Trinh Thi, of Despentes' 1994 novel, *Baise-moi*. While Breillat's *Romance* or Millet's *La Vie sexuelle de Catherine M.* offered irrefutable evidence of the confrontation between intellectual culture and explicit sexual material, *Baise-moi* took matters further, initiating a scandal which led to a shift in the legal definition of the boundaries between pornography and legitimate art.[6] The film was initially given a 16 certificate, accompanied by an warning stating: 'Ce film, qui enchaîne sans interruption des scènes de sexe d'une crudité appuyée et des images d'une particulière violence, peut profondément perturber certains spectateurs' (Camy and Montagne 2002: 219). ['Some viewers may find this film, in which insistently crude sex scenes and strikingly violent images follow one another without interruption, profoundly disturbing.'] It was released as scheduled on 28 June 2000. On 22 June, the Conseil d'Etat had received two requests for the film to be given an X certificate, respectively from the pressure group Promouvoir and from three parents of 16–18–year-olds. On 30 June, the Conseil d'Etat decided that the film should be placed on a list of films forbidden to under-18s: as the 18 certificate had been abolished in 1990, the only way to do this was to give the film an X certificate. The basis given for this decision was the view that 'le film *Baise-moi* est composé pour l'essentiel d'une succession de scènes de grande violence et de scènes de sexe non simulées [...]qu'il constitue ainsi un message pornographique et d'incitation à la violence susceptible d'être vu ou perçu par des mineurs' (in Camy and Montagne 2002: 219). ['*Baise-moi* is essentially composed of a succession of highly violent scenes and scenes of unsimulated sex [...] it thereby constitutes a message which is both pornographic and an incitement to violence, and which is liable to be seen by minors.'] For a would-be mainstream film, the consequences of an X certificate are financially disastrous: the film receives no state or financial aid, is taxed at 33 per cent instead of 18.6 per cent, cannot be freely advertised, and can of course only be shown in licensed outlets. After a considerable amount of heated debate, including support for the film from Breillat among others, a 'décret' was eventually issued reintroducing the 18 certificate: since the film could no longer legally be seen by minors, it was free to be rereleased on 29 August 2001.[7]

Baise-moi is thus really bound up with the question of pornography to a greater extent than any of the contemporary works which share its preoccupation with the explicit representation of sex. Both *Romance* and Bonello's *Le Pornographe* have had their run-ins with the censors; neither gave rise to such an extended or significant affair.[8] And the Conseil d'Etat were not simply wrong in their judgment: co-written and co-directed by sometime porn actress Coralie Trinh Thi, and starring two others – Raffaëla Anderson and Karen Bach – chosen on this basis, the film does indeed feature plenty of non-simulated sex.[9] The factors driving this are not limited to a desire to shock or to produce the kind of 'trash aesthetic' for which the film was widely attacked, however. Seen in the context of Despentes' work in general, the rawness of the film version of *Baise-moi* has to be considered in the light of this work's defining vectors: the twin desires to produce a form of representation which would minimise its distance from the world represented, and to use this form of representation to confront the misogyny and alienation of this world. This section will accordingly explore these features of Despentes' work, beginning with some suggestion of the presence of pornography, and references to the sex industry more broadly, in this work, before considering her aesthetic and socio-political aims, and concluding with a discussion of the problematic relation between these aims and the means deployed to achieve them, with specific reference to the questions of misogyny and pornography. It will, again, necessarily be a question of distances: between Despentes' work and its world, and, crucially, between this work and the pornography with which it repeatedly engages.

Entering Despentes' world, we enter a world suffused with pornography. The written version of *Baise-moi* opens with Nadine watching an extreme hard-core video, whose various scenes and standard tropes are described in unblinking detail. Nadine is a prostitute; Manu, her future comrade, has made porn videos, and it is over porn that they bond, when Nadine realises she recognises Manu from one of them. (Which leads to a nice moment of self-consciousness in the film version, as Nadine – porn performer Karen Bach – says to Manu – porn performer Raffaëlla Anderson: 'T'aurais pas fait des films pornos?'.) ['I don't suppose you've ever made any porn films?'.] The pornography they subsequently consume is described with the seasoned eye of a connoisseur, in terms of a repertoire of tropes; it is in terms of these tropes that their various sexual encounters are generally described. *Les Chiennes savantes* (1996) is set in the sex industry (in which Despentes has famously worked): its first-person narrator, Louise, is a performer in a peep show, and her text continues to view the world through a pornographic lens, consistently describing its female characters with the brutal materialism of its milieu. In *Les Jolies Choses* (1998), Pauline discovers that her now-dead twin Claudine has made a porn film; the apogee of Pauline's musical career sees her performing with this film as a backdrop. The collection *Mordre au travers* (1999) features a sexually available housewife who has made a sex video, a lonely adulterer whose need for consolation passes entirely by way of the tropes of pornography, a woman who masturbates for the benefit of her voyeuristic neighbour (who, along with his twin sister, eventually tortures and kills her), and another whose poverty forces her to become a dominatrix (once only, as her righteous anger leads her to assault her wealthy client while he is tied up). *Teen Spirit* (2002) is less imbued with this atmosphere, although while its narrator, Bruno, is living his agoraphobic bachelor lifestyle before discovering he has a teenage daughter, his descriptions of women and sexual activity (as well as those offered by his friend Sandra) are enthusiastically reductive and pornographically formulaic. But the novel gradually becomes increasingly sentimental: its trajectory shows that Despentes has more recently chosen to move away from concentration on the pornographic as such. This is confirmed by her most recent work, *Bye Bye Blondie* (2004), which explicitly situates the earlier part of its narrative in a time before the mass availability of hard-core pornography, and pays no particular attention to the genre in its contemporary narrative, which allows Despentes to depart significantly from this aspect of her previous work, and indeed to introduce a notably romantic, indeed sentimental tone into her sex scenes. Taking Despentes' work as a whole, however, it is difficult not to acknowledge the preponderance of pornographic references it contains. The examples just given are far from summarizing the entirety of Despentes' world, therefore; but they are equally far from constituting an exhaustive list of all the ways in which her work cites, or even aligns itself with the pornographic, by whose presence this work is therefore persistently characterised. And for all that her two most recent texts seem to have distanced themselves somewhat from this, at the time of writing (September 2005), Despentes is reported to be writing and directing a porn film to be produced by the major French producer Marc Dorcel.[10]

As Shirley Jordan notes (2002), and as Nicole Fayard has

eloquently argued (2005 and 2006), Despentes' work borrows heavily from the codes of popular culture, particularly from those of hard-core pornography, which she appropriates for subversive ends. This extensive appropriation also, often, allows Despentes to use a recognisably pornographic aesthetic as shorthand for the alienating materialism she wishes to denounce. In order to do this, however, she first seeks to produce a form of representation that can get as close as possible to the world defined by this alienation: a form of representation that would approximate as far as possible to the transcription of this world and its textures. Again, the pornographic, with its mythic promise of immediacy, is of use to Despentes in this quest. Repeated reference to this aesthetic thus functions as a *mise-en-abîme* of Despentes' formal goals: in this respect, her work could be defined as aspiring to the condition of pornography. What she has developed is what Barthes, in *Le Degré zéro de l'écriture* (2002a), called an *écriture*: a way of writing that encodes a social or cultural situation. Accordingly, the opening of the written version of *Baise-moi*, with its extensive description of hard-core pornography, may be read as a statement of intent: the pornographic detail has some meaning in terms of characterisation (Nadine's consumption of pornography) and milieu (in which pornography is omnipresent), but mostly serves to announce the kind of writing to come. A kind of writing which, like the pornography it has just folded into its texture, will seek to minimise the distance between itself as representation and the world it purports to represent.

Despentes' writing is thus the very opposite of Millet's, which seeks – with uneven success, as we have seen – to maintain this aesthetic distance securely in place. There are various ways in which Despentes' *écriture* makes a claim to be considered as in some sense the fresh imprint of the world it presents: its extensive use of slang, defiantly unexplained references to popular musical culture, and persistent presentation of mostly soft drugs as a part of everyday life, are among the most prominent, and all make use of the nineteenth-century association between realism as a mode of representation, and urban decadence or low culture as its object. The figure by which this relation is produced in Despentes' work is, moreover, the classic realist figure of metonymy.[11] Repeatedly, the reader is called upon to recognise some textual detail as an authentic part of the contemporary cultural landscape, and so to reconstitute this landscape as the whole of which the text is a part. A typical example from *Les Chiennes savantes*: 'La voisine était brune, portait souvent un anorak bleu comme ceux que les gosses de pauvres récupèrent au Secours Populaire' (2002a: 32). ['The girl who lived next door was a brunette, and often wore the kind of blue anorak poor kids get from the Secours Populaire.'] The structure of this last example is straight out of nineteenth-century realism ('he was sporting the kind of waistcoat worn by those men who …') and, as in its archetypal use by Balzac, the cultural detail – here, the humanitarian organisation Secours Populaire – asks to be accepted as situating the diegesis in a world recognisably that of the contemporary reader.[12] As Dustan suggests in *Premier essai* (as quoted in Chapter 3, pp. 111–12), perhaps the 'trash literature' of the 1990s would indeed best be seen as a realism for its time.

In its purest form in Despentes, this kind of metonymy involves the use of the proper name or the brand name. The opening words of *Teen Spirit* are exemplary in this regard (another opening which makes a clear statement about the *écriture* to come): 'Je tirais sur un gros joint en étudiant les fesses de J. Lo sur MTV' (11). ['I was smoking a fat spliff while studying J. Lo's ass on MTV.'] Soft drugs, pop music, reductive misogynistic materialism, cable TV. But more than this: the body and proper name as brand (J. Lo), in the era of the capitalist globalisation of culture (MTV). Despentes here again recalls our discussion of Dustan in Chapter 3, in this case by deploying the same referential technique: confronted by a world in which consumerism has attained hegemonic status, she presents the brand as if it were simply the name of the thing. Although they are often, interestingly, those of prescription drugs, these names function most intensely when they invoke the brands most typical of contemporary western capitalism, from BMW (shortened to 'BM', of course (2001a: 160)), to KFC (2001b: 28), to the highly nuanced world of fashion, especially sneaker culture: 'Une femme plutôt grasse en survêt informe, grisâtre, Stan Smith pourries et le crâne rasé' (2002a: 191–2); 'Converses noires, montantes, jean Diesel, veste Levi's' (2004: 227). ['Quite a fat woman in a shapeless tracksuit, sort of greyish, with rancid Stan Smiths and a shaven head'; 'black high-top Converse, Diesel jeans, Levi's jacket'.] Don't know your Stan Smiths from your Converse? Sorry, says the text: my world is the world of those who do. Speaking the language of the commodity fetish, Despentes' texts seem to dissolve the novelistic boundaries which inevitably separate them from this context, by means of the very novelistic trick of importing its key consumerist or low-life features as so many everyday metonymies.

'Ici le fétide n'a aucune connotation romanesque' (2001: 28) ['These fetid details are not trying to create some kind of "novelistic" atmosphere'.]: the job of these metonymies, for Despentes, is not to give the bourgeois reader an exciting glimpse into a seedy under-world (see her comments in Grangeray 2004). The point, rather, is to write on a level with the world described. Unlike Dustan, however, Despentes is not seeking to celebrate this world: rather, she wants to denounce its injustices. Not the least of which would be the reduc-tive materialism in which capitalism and misogyny find a shared logic. *Teen Spirit* is eloquent in this cause, and makes explicit this implicit link between consumerism and pornography:

> Pub Dior, d'une beauté inquiétante, femme étriquée dans un cadre, les fesses en l'air, attendant qu'on la prenne, la violente, la surbaise. En guise de propagande, ils exhibaient leurs propres filles. Voilà notre attitude correcte: toujours prêts à se faire prendre, toujours prêts à se faire défoncer. (2002c: 153)

> [Dior ad, disturbingly beautiful, a woman crammed into a frame, ass in the air, waiting to be taken, assaulted, screwed good and proper. They displayed their own daughters by way of propaganda. This is the pose we're supposed to adopt: always ready to be taken, always ready to be broken into.]

Just as for Houellebecq, the pornographic aesthetic expresses the extension of the logic of the market to the bedroom (see Chapter 6, pp. 188–9), so for Despentes, the objectification of the female body in this advertisement condenses the alienation effected by late capitalism, the individual's worth reduced to his or her economic effectivity. A similar point is made by Pauline in *Les Jolies Choses*, as, after her first experience of women's magazines, she decides to reinterpret sexual alienation in economic terms. Noting the new cultural obligation for women to display their properly cultivated and fetishistically itemised body, she concludes that this is driven not by male desire, but by the profit motive: (2001b: 83). And rich or poor, we are all victims, says *Teen Spirit*:

> Il suffisait d'aller faire un tour dans les quartiers riches pour s'en convaincre une fois pour toutes: personne ne profitait de cette merde. Femmes déformées de honte, corps culpabilisés, jamais assez minces, jamais assez

jeunes, jamais assez bien habillés. Les journaux, toujours complaisants, s'inquiétaient de ce que l'émancipation des femmes avait dévalorisé, fragilisé les bonshommes. Sans jamais signaler que la castration se faisait au travail, pour le bien-être de plus personne. (2002c: 153)

[If you wanted to convince yourself once and for all, you just had to go and walk round the rich areas: nobody was getting anything good out of all this crap. Women, twisted with shame, their bodies filled with guilt, never thin enough, never young enough, never well enough dressed. The papers – merrily going along with it all as ever – were worried that women's liberation had undermined our poor menfolk, turned them all into fragile wrecks. But they never pointed out that the real castration happened at work, and was no longer to anyone's benefit.]

The violent objectification of the female body would on this account be representative of a broader drive to treat human beings as objects. But Despentes' suggestion of the 'backlash' agenda of the press also qualifies this argument, her references to this contemporary western female body showing both that 'emancipation' can be recuperated as new forms of alienation, and that this body still occupies a pre-eminent place when it comes to objectification. Despentes' denunciation of late-capitalist alienation does not, therefore, obscure her specific, sustained denunciation of misogyny. In Despentes' world, men mostly refer to women as 'putes', 'salopes', 'pouffiasses', and so on, and treat them accordingly. ['tarts', 'bitches', 'sluts'.] The language of male sexual excitement – however gentle and polite the man may otherwise be – is the language of the sexual insult (2001b: 123; 2002a: 109). When, in *Les Jolies Choses*, Pauline ventures out in the clothes of her dead twin sister (whom she has previously dismissed as a bimbo), she discovers the harassment this generates. Dressed as she is, this is considered inevitable, as demonstrated by Despentes' use of free indirect discourse to speak the language of the world and its judgements: 'Elle est tout à fait publique, abordable, tout à fait faite pour que tout le monde s'occupe d'elle. Elle est sapée pour ça'. As this is still role-play, however, Despentes can critically decode the masquerade: 'Et personne ne se rend compte qu'elle n'est pas du tout comme ça. C'est la première fois qu'elle comprend, qu'en fait aucune fille n'est comme ça' (2001: 91). ['She's completely public, accessible, completely designed to be everyone's business. Dressed for it'; 'And nobody realises that she's not like that at all. She understands now, for the first time: no girl is really like that.']

By the time she makes it on to the metro, Pauline has been groped, sexually insulted by two young girls (who dismiss her assertion of female solidarity), and twice rescued by more or less dubiously motivated male interventions (92–5). Her role as 'Claudine' does not simply involve enduring this kind of attention, however. It also involves the kind of performance designed to sustain its salacious interest, which Pauline initially reads as impossibly humiliating. In her efforts to make a career for herself in the music business, Claudine has made a video, in which, notably, she crawls on all fours. The continuity between this performance and Claudine's porn video is evident, as is the text's alignment with Pauline's disenchanted response. When Pauline watches her sister's pornographic performance, this critical tone continues: the two women (Claudine and a redhead named Claire) are described as in a dreadful state:

> Elles ont l'air crevées, l'une comme l'autre, elles cherchent à donner le change, à rester bien pimpantes. Elles sont exténuées, ça se voit, ça fait drôle. Et les keums continuent de défiler, s'enfiler dans leur bouche, la plupart bandent très mal, ça les empêche pas d'y aller. (219)

> [They look all in, both of them, they're trying to give each other a breather, to stay nice and sexy. They're exhausted, you can see it, it looks funny. And still there's hundreds of guys, sticking it into their mouths, most of them can hardly get it up, but that doesn't stop them having a go.]

A critical perspective on performance in the sex industry also runs through *Les Chiennes savantes*, whose setting it forms, and whose narrator repeatedly demystifies the mechanical strategies used by the performers for the predictable, feeble excitement of their male customers. And if we move from the tawdry world of the peep show to that of the swingers' club, we find, far from an assembly of happy *libertins*, rooms full of sagging middle-aged male flesh, mostly limp penises being ineffectively pleasured by disproportionately attractive women (when they are not nervous wives, reluctantly there to keep their husband company), a grim physicality: 'Corps malades, souffrant en gémissant, misère de la mort proche, corps blancs, difformes, cherchant un soulagement[…] C'est pas que ça baise ou que ça s'éclate. Mais il est question de parties génitales. En contact. Exhibées' (2001b: 158). ['Sick bodies, suffering, moaning, the misery of death just around the corner, white, misshapen bodies, looking for some kind of relief […] It's not about screwing or having a good time. But it is about genitals. Touching each other. On show.']

(This morbid corporeality is made dramatically clear in the film of *Baise-moi*, as Nadine and Manu massacre the members of a 'Cercle libertin', and the usual trappings of a staid, male-oriented eroticism come to adorn the flaccid white flesh of the dead bodies.)[13] And if Despentes is so often concerned in such contexts with male erectile or ejaculatory dysfunction – it features in *Baise-moi*, *Les Chiennes savantes*, *Les Jolies choses* and *Teen Spirit* – it would seem to be in order to denounce, like Breillat, the lengths to which men force women to go in order to reassure themselves about the functioning of their generally dismal, tired member. It is this that underpins the world of misogyny whose various aspects she thus describes: the conscription of women into the miserable or violent service of male weakness.

Of course, this spectrum of exploitation, objectification, humiliation and abuse runs to the rape suffered by Manu and Karla in *Baise-moi*, establishing the novel and its filmic version in the 'rape-revenge' genre.[14] Manu's defiant response to this experience captures what is repeatedly at stake for Despentes in the misogyny she challenges: like Breillat in *Romance* and *Anatomie de l'enfer*, she is targeting the male obsession with a mythical female interiority, supposedly identified with the female sexual organs, which leads to the fascinated stigmatisation and violation of these organs. Immediately after their rape, Manu explains to a horrified Karla how she was able to remain apparently unmoved by the experience – which had the effect of disgusting and to some extent dissuading their attackers, as she refused to react as they wanted her to:

> c'est jamais qu'un coup de queue [...] Je peux dire ça parce que j'en ai rien à foutre de leurs pauvres bites de branleurs et que j'en ai pris d'autres dans le ventre et que je les emmerde. C'est comme une voiture que tu gares dans une cité, tu laisses pas des trucs de valeur à l'intérieur parce que tu peux pas empêcher qu'elle soit forcée. Ma chatte, je peux pas empêcher les connards d'y rentrer et j'y ai rien laissé de précieux... (2001a: 56–7)

> [all they did was fuck us [...] I can say it because I don't give a fuck about their poor jerk-off cocks and because these aren't the first and because they can go shit on themselves. It's like a car that you park in the projects [i.e. estate], you don't leave anything valuable in it 'cause you can't keep it from being broken into. I can't keep assholes from getting into my pussy, so I haven't left anything valuable there ... (2003: 52)]

Manu displaces her interiority, refuses to locate her identity in her sex. But men will, throughout Despentes, insist on trying to find it there, like those customers described by Baudrillard at a Japanese peep show, staring into the performers' exhibited vaginas (1988: 51–2). As Baudrillard points out, this fascination with what has been designated obscene is a matter less of sex than of representation, and leads ultimately – as in Marie's 'desire' to meet Jack the Ripper in Breillat's *Romance* – to butchery and evisceration, in the futile attempt to find whatever it is men think is hidden in the female sexual body (as in the fantasies of Zagdanski and Bataille, discussed in Chapter 1). As Nadine puts it in *Baise-moi*: 'Elle se demande combien il mettrait pour lui voir les entrailles, qu'est-ce que les garçons peuvent bien s'imaginer que les filles cachent pour toujours vouloir les voir de partout?' (2001a: 59). ['She wonders how much he'd pay to see her innards, what it is guys think girls are hiding so that they always want to see them in every place' (2003: 54).] When Stef and Lola, two employees at the peep show in *Les Chiennes savantes*, are butchered in their apartment, Roberta (another performer) complains: 'On passe notre vie à transpirer pour que des connards se branlent [...] Et ça leur suffit pas, de nous réduire à ça, il faut qu'en plus ils viennent chez toi pour te regarder dessous la peau comment ça fait tes os... Il faut qu'ils nous aient jusqu'au bout...' (2002a: 75). ['We spend our life sweating so that these tossers can jerk off [...] And it's not enough for them, reducing us to doing that, they still have to come round to your place, to have a look under your skin, see what your bones look like ... They have to have every last bit of us.'] The imagery of butchery is insistent: in Louise's words, the victims 'se sont fait charcuter chez elles [...] sur les photos c'était des gros tas de viande' (59). ['got butchered at home [...] on the photos they were just big piles of meat'.] For Roberta, accordingly: 'Tu sais ce qu'on est? Des tapins, des putains, du trou à paillettes, de la viande à foutre...' (75). ['You know what we are? Tarts, whores, just some gash in a sequined dress, meat to be fucked ...'] The continuum of the male abuse of women in Despentes extends from verbal violence via lechery and molestation to exploitation, objectification, rape, and murder, and she will not let her readers forget this.

Except that the murders in *Les Chiennes savantes* are committed not by a predatory male but, somewhat ridiculously, by a dog. And if they have a sexual dimension, it is not as the final manifestation of misogyny, but as the expression of the sorry jealousy of the dog's owner, the unstable Laure. The thesis of male violence is established in order to be undone, which suggests that Despentes' position in relation to the seamless misogynistic continuum she evokes needs a little nuancing. It is clear that male violence, including sexual violence, is mostly denounced – with the possible exception of the rape in *Les Chiennes savantes* of Louise (who until then has throughout her life refused all physical intimacy) by Victor. Victor's standard assertion that rape was the only way he could get her to do what she really wanted, seems worryingly confirmed by Louise's subsequent enthusiastic conversion to the extreme joys of the rough sex she has with him (2002a: 182). Similarly, in *Les Jolies Choses*, Pauline, having played the role of the sister she thought of as a bimbo, and prostituted herself with the record-company boss to get an advance, discovers that this – along with her subsequent new promiscuity – excites her as if she had discovered a previously hidden second nature (2001b: 179, 198). Even Gloria, in *Bye Bye Blondie*, who in the earlier part of the novel's time-frame has never seen a porn film – with a wry nod to the more recent explosion of pornographic material in the media, Despentes mentions that 'à l'époque c'était réservé aux obsédés et aux abonnés de Canal, encore guère nombreux' – finds that, nonetheless, 'elle prenait spontanément toutes les attitudes du genre' (2004: 139). ['Back then it was reserved for perverts and Canal Plus subscribers (still few and far between)'; 'she spontaneously adopted all the genre's typical poses'.] At such moments, a kind of interiority seems to return to Despentes' female characters, in which the only available frame for the interpretation of sexual pleasure is the misogynistic structure of female abasement, a structure they enthusiastically internalise (but without any of the destabilising effects we saw above in Escalle, for example). Mocking her male peep-show customers, Louise nonetheless enjoys her work, just as their pathetic fantasies imagine (2002a: 77). And when her friend Saïd appears in her booth, she is particularly excited by his orgasm: in contrast to all the feeble penises elsewhere in Despentes, with their dribbling climaxes, here at last is a proper, solid one, inspiring 'respect' (82). All of which might query the distance between Despentes and the pornographic world of fantastical phallic power she also critiques.

What, for example, is the outcome of the second 'good sex' sequence in the film of *Baise-moi* (the first being that in which they have sex side by side in their hotel room), in which Manu and

Nadine separate to have fulfilling sex with men they have picked up (a man in a bar for Manu, the hotel receptionist for Nadine)? In both cases, it is the standard pornographic narrative climax, the spectacle of male ejaculation (onto Manu's backside; in front of Nadine's face following fellatio). The film's syntax structures this section around the desire to see the definitive marker of pornographic pleasure: positioning male ejaculation as its own climax by the rhythm of its editing, the film betrays its own investment in the phallocentric tropes that Despentes elsewhere mocks. The ambivalence in question is exemplified by Pauline in *Les Jolies Choses*, who mocks but is also complicit with the tropes of pornography (2001b: 189–90). Just as male ejaculation is embraced as narrative punctuation in *Baise-moi*, so does pornography become an inevitable end point to the trajectory of Pauline's musical career in *Les Jolies Choses*, her triumphant showcase celebrating her late sister's magnificent performance: 'Quand elle jouit elle est belle. Même si ce qu'ils disent est moche, même s'ils la prennent pas bien, même s'ils ont des sales gueules. Quand elle jouit, et c'est dur de croire qu'elle simule, elle est super-belle' (215). ['When she comes, she's beautiful. Even if what they're saying is awful, even if they don't know how to take her properly, even if they are an ugly lot. When she comes – and it's hard to believe she's faking – she's dead beautiful.']

Despentes' work often, then, appears complicit with the misogynistic structures it denounces, of which the conventional pornographic representation of female sexuality might be thought to form an integral part. The test, indeed, of how effectively Despentes confronts misogyny might well be the relationship this work entertains with pornographic tropes and techniques. Throughout *Les Chiennes savantes*, for example, female characters are insistently introduced via a sexually objectifying description, which expresses the gaze of the narrator Louise. The film of *Baise-moi* features sequences which do little or nothing to disrupt the position of the spectator of conventional pornography, from the way the camera lingers over and cuts up the bodies of Manu and Nadine as they dance in their underwear in their hotel room, to the framing and editing of shots during the first 'good sex' sequence (not to mention the techno soundtrack with its female voice moaning 'ecstasy' and 'aah, sex'); or from the swift cross-cutting during the second 'good sex' sequence, to the delineation of the bodies of the swingers as Nadine has an initial look around their club. The film has been criticised for its appropriation of the style of the most brutal of thrillers (evident especially in its use of repeated, fetishistically brief slow-motion replays); as these examples indicate, it is also the case that it often seems to deploy – with precious little defamiliarisation – standard pornographic tropes which effect precisely the kind of objectification whose violent rejection it celebrates. But it would be naive to lament Despentes' supposed failure to keep a safe distance from these tropes. For Despentes' work is not simply opposed to pornography. It does indeed seek to oppose misogyny – but it seeks to do so without thereby rejecting the pornographic. The debatable success of its opposition to misogyny – the extent to which it seems to have embraced the positions it also critiques – may be thought to indicate the unlikeliness of this attempt; but this is nonetheless what Despentes appears to be doing. Accordingly, Shirley Jordan's convincing argument that Despentes does maintain a distance in her use of pornographic material (for example by means of the self-consciousness introduced by featuring the making and consumption of pornography as part of the diegesis), and that she therefore produces a kind of 'anti-pornography', still situates Despentes' work paradoxically, and rightly, within the pornographic genre (2002: 137).[15]

The stakes of this attempt to occupy the pornographic as a kind of internal opposition are clearly high, and are in fact co-extensive with Despentes' attempt to critique the materialism of the world she represents. For Despentes' production of an *écriture* which would be as one with the world it represents might be accused of forsaking all critical distance: her metonymic citation of this world's commodity fetishes might just be extending their domain, creating novels whose texture is indistinguishable from that of the world they want to critique. Dustan, who, as we have seen, also uses this technique, has no such problem: he is happy to celebrate consumerism while maintaining an oppositional identitarian politics. And Rémès, who does want to effect such a critique, does so via witty, energetic, confrontational *détournement* of the mechanisms of advertising, as we saw in Chapter 3. Out here in the exhausted mainstream, however, surrounded by the collapse of revolutionary narratives we considered in Chapter 4, Despentes' denunciation of the shared reductive materialism of capitalism and misogyny seems repeatedly tainted by complicity, her mimicry of their metonymies more faithful than parodic. Her desire to denounce the objectification of women, for example, would perhaps be more convincing if she did not produce work in which this also seems to be embraced, including as a source of sexual pleasure. With specific reference to the pornographic, Despentes would seem *both* to effect displacements which make her explicit representations incompatible with its conventions (largely, as Jordan shows (2002), by means of thematising its production and consumption, and giving her female protagonists both effective agency and some psychological depth), *and* to produce work within which these conventions continue to function unperturbed, alongside these very displacements. Unlike Breillat, Despentes offers no extensive theoretical consideration of the relationship between her work and the pornography it so often features, quotes or resembles. But she does say: 'J'ai le sentiment d'avoir une mission à remplir, j'allais dire une mission de vengeance, mais ce n'est pas tout à fait ça. Il faut faire éclater les choses. Rendre de la dignité, de l'humanité' (Vallaeys and Armanet 2000). ['I do feel like I'm on a mission, I was about to say a mission of vengeance, but it's not quite that. We need to shake things up. Bring some dignity back, some humanity.'] Sexual violence is to be confronted by a heightened, perhaps self-conscious or parodic sexual violence, in order that it might be exploded. (On this, see Jordan 2002, especially 136–8; and Fayard 2005 and 2006.) 'Il est temps pour les femmes de devenir les bourreaux', says Despentes, 'y compris pour la plus extrême violence et tout ça ...' (in Jordan 2002: 132). ['It's time for women to start dishing it out, including really extreme violence and all that stuff...'.]

However unsatisfactory this might be, perhaps we should see Despentes as both displacing and embracing the pornographic, partly in the interests of an emancipatory ideal that this uneven approach can only imperfectly serve. It might be that her work does indeed offer a 'new pornography', both critical of the old and promising alternative possibilities; *and* that it is not pornographic at all; *and* that it is just more of the same old pornographic fare. Take, for example, the following moment from the first 'good sex' sequence of the film of *Baise-moi*. As Nadine and Manu are having sex side by side on their hotel beds, Nadine looks across at Manu. But the shot is framed so that she looks straight into the camera. The viewer is invited to acknowledge Nadine's subjectivity and agency within this situation, and hence the irreducibility of this scene to a putative pornographic aesthetic from which these would be absent. (This is subsequently confirmed when one of the men they have picked up is kicked out of their room for attempting to run the encounter as a male-focused pornographic fantasy.) In addition, there is a kind of defamiliarisation, as the actress Karen Bach confronts the viewer's gaze (this is only strengthened, now, by the pathos of her death), and we are invited to recognise the mediated intersubjective, aesthetic and economic encounter in which we are situated. But equally, this is the porn performer Karen Bach, engaged in a scene of non-simulated sex, looking into the camera to affirm to the pornographically inclined viewer the reality of her presence, and so to validate this viewer's pleasure. And it is also, again, Nadine, but this time as enthusiastic consumer of pornography and a powerful locus of focalisation throughout the film. Her subjectivity, and this moment as a whole, are in fact both irreducible to and inseparable from the pornographic. Awkwardly, what this moment condenses is the realisation that, in Despentes, criticism goes hand in hand with complicity. Just as Millet cannot quite regulate as she wishes the distance between her work and the world, so in Despentes is the question of critical distance never quite satisfactorily settled.

Notes

1 Reader's comment at www.amazon.com, accessed 19 December 2003.
2 On this, see Diski 2002. Roger (2001: 917) argues that Millet's refusal of prostitution derives from a refusal of *temporal* separation.
3 As Roger observes, Henric's photographs are thus 'disastrous' for Millet's image (2001: 924–6).
4 See Barthes 2002d, especially 851–2. Henric quotes Barthes on the risk entailed by this literality (2001: 133).
5 On trace and aura in Benjamin, see Vasseleu 1998: 93–7 (this passage quoted on 96); and Marks 2000: 80–1.
6 For an account of the affair, on which the following description draws, see Camy and Montagne 2002.
7 The full text of the relevant legal judgments is reproduced as an appendix to Ogien 2003: 164–72.
8 On the fate of *Romance* at the hands of the Australian censors, see Martin 2005. *Le Pornographe* was cut by 11 seconds for UK release with an 18 certificate, the offending section showing the standard straight pornographic 'money shot' of male ejaculation.
9 Despentes says Anderson and Bach were chosen on the basis of their performances in John B. Root's *Exhibition 99* (Vallaeys and Armanet 2000). Anderson recounts her experiences in the pornography industry in *Hard*, in which she confirms this (2001: 261, n. 1). Bach committed

suicide in January 2005. Their reflections on *Baise-moi*, and on pornography, may be found in Garcin 2000.

10 *Les Inrockuptibles*, 504, 505, 506 (triple edition, 27 July–16 August 2005), 9.

11 This point – metonymy as laying claim to a kind of aesthetic proximity – is derived from work by Ingrid Wassenaar, acknowledged with gratitude.

12 On this technique in Balzac, see Prendergast 1978: 154–5. Despentes repeats the Secours Populaire reference, almost verbatim, in *Bye Bye Blondie* (2004: 160).

13 For Despentes' comments on the misery of swingers' clubs, see Vallaeys and Armanet 2000.

14 On the genre, see Read 2000. Martinek (2005) establishes a significant context for *Baise-moi* by means of a comparison – *mutatis mutandis* – between the response to rape it presents and that narrated in Samira Bellil's important *Dans l'enfer des tournantes* (2002). This connection is also made in Spoiden 2004.

15 As Linda Ruth Williams points out, the self-consciousness of *Baise-moi* also extends to the art-house encounter with hard core: as Nadine has sex with a client, the film playing on the television is Noé's *Seul contre tous* (2001: 20).

6

Michel Houellebecq: misery, pornography, utopia

'I am the star of French literature', said Michel Houellebecq to Emily Eakin. 'The most radical one of all.' Eakin continues: 'He reached over and petted my knee. "What's your name again?" he mumbled. "How would you like to be in my erotic film?"'

(Eakin 2000)[1]

Houellebecq's emergence at the end of the twentieth century as the latest, and possibly the most convincing recent holder of the post of *enfant terrible* of French letters is well documented; not the least significant role in this rise to prominence has been played by the kind of deadpan, melancholic *provocation* described in this scene.[2] Moreover, the reference to the erotic is essential: Houellebecq's work has consistently confronted, with his characteristic ambiguous provocation, questions of sexuality and sexual liberation, and it has invariably done so by invoking the phenomena in which contemporary western culture has tended to see the stakes and contradictions of such questions as being paradigmatically played out: the renewed fashionability of group sex, for example, or the sex industry or sex tourism; most centrally, of course, the hegemonic presence of pornography as this culture's preferred sexual reference point. In the early novels, *Extension du domaine de la lutte* (1994) and *Les Particules élémentaires* (1998), the references are mostly to pornography and to group sex, and are often violently misogynistic, mediated more or less through the troubled consciousness of male characters, accompanied by predictions of the extinction of the useless male sex and a sentimental attachment to the historic sufferings of womankind. With *Lanzarote* (2000), the tone becomes less aggressive (although the misogyny remains), sex tourism emerges, and the focus is less on pornography, more on paedophilia. *Plateforme* (2001) engages extensively with sex tourism; again, the criticisms of women remain, although their tone is less vitriolic (and they are in part smuggled in through the voice of a sympathetic female character). In *La Possibilité d'une île* (2005), there is a consideration of the cultural status of pornography, and the portrayal of women is more schematic than hostile, if not without its reductive aspects. The provocative engagement with key contemporary debates and practices concerning sexuality and its representations which runs through this trajectory has allowed Houellebecq to maintain one important dimension of his satirical timeliness: he confronts his culture's widespread sexual dilemmas and anxieties via reference to the forms this culture habitually uses to represent these areas to itself.

But Houellebecq is not just seeking to provide a chronicle of contemporary sexual mores. Rather, he has installed himself, for the moment at least, as a significant writer because his work, and the now louche, now earnest persona which accompanies it, both diagnose and reproduce to perfection the gaudy miseries of current western culture. He is not a realist, he insists: realism is pointless and unbearable, as we have all already had more than enough of the misery of reality (1999: 5). For some, however, including a number of major allies such as Dominique Noguez (2003), Julian Barnes (2005) and J. G. Ballard (2005), Houellebecq has nonetheless produced texts which offer an all too rare attempt to engage with the contemporary world at an important metaphysical level; and this would also appear to be Houellebecq's sense of the stakes of his enterprise. Houellebecq would seem to be essaying a complete picture of his contemporary world (though more in the mode of satire than of realism), in which he is principally concerned to explore the crisis created by the development of the technologies of cloning, to lament the reductive effects of free-market economics and the violently hierarchical sexual liberalisation he sees as its libidinal corollary, and, perhaps oddly, to maintain a sentimental attachment to the redemptive possibility of love. Oddly, that is, because the irony and self-consciousness in which so much of Houellebecq's writing is bathed would seem to rule out such an attachment, just as they would seem to render ineffective any social or political criticism. His texts intermittently juxtapose irony and sincerity in a manner which makes it impossible to know which tone we should be taking seriously, if any. And it is no less impossible to know what to make of this first difficulty: it might be an inconsistency, or it might be a comment on the limits of the kind of communication possible in the contemporary novel. (For Houellebecq's thoughts on this, see 1998a: 72–5.) It is, perhaps, reasonably easy to know what Houellebecq is against; it is extremely tricky to work out whether he thinks there is any alternative.

Indeed, Houellebecq may be read as starting – like the works discussed in Chapter 4, perhaps – from the exhausted, depressing premise that there is in fact no alternative. The existential despair expressed in the opening pages of *Extension* might have to be taken seriously: what if *all* the narratives we use to reconcile ourselves to the world were, in fact, bankrupt? For Houellebecq, this would take in narratives of individual self-fulfilment, of political liberation and of artistic innovation. The redemptive teleology underpinning all of these might, he suggests, now have to be seen as a self-serving delusion, in which we kid ourselves that our activities are gradually leading us towards some happier tomorrow. In Houellebecq's analysis, political and artistic resistance to the onward march of consumer capitalism has failed. The affirmation of individualism by movements of sexual liberation has allowed them to be conscripted into the logic of the market; political protest, mass demonstrations and avant-garde artistic production are equally easily absorbed by the generalised spectacle by which this market propagates its ideology. Literature *might* offer an alternative: it is still just about possible to occupy what he terms an 'aesthetic position', to step aside, disconnect from the spectacle, possibly via the resistant, slow, anti-commercial rhythm of literary writing (see 1998a: 72–80).[3] But this can at best represent an interruption: it cannot constitute a programme of collective resistance. This is the very definition of the position we have here been calling the 'exhausted mainstream', whose despairing denunciations contrast with the affirmatively oppositional identitarian politics of Dustan and Rémès, for example (see Chapter 3). Houellebecq might be exaggerating the situation, of course. But we ought perhaps to take seriously for a while the notion that, equally, he might not be.

What if there were, in fact, no oppositional narratives left to the triumph of consumer capitalism, as its advocates would have us believe? How then would it be possible to – for example – write a novel (destined to become a commodity) to affirm one's horror at this universal commodification, and one's persisting (and thoroughly commodified) faith in a kind of sentimental goodness which might transcend the commercial? Without, that is, simply falling into the convenient bad faith of pretending that one's literary activity were per se certain to offer a valid form of resistance? Houellebecq's despairing answer to this dilemma might, perhaps, be to produce texts in which sentimentality – like the aesthetic – appears no longer as a transcendent goal towards which one might work, but as a brief interruption of the degraded world around it. The dreadful irony of his work, on this reading, would be that it is necessary to embrace the degraded world in order to attain these brief moments of respite. Once again: Houellebecq might be wrong. But if he is not, his work may at least have the singular merit of confronting honestly the appalling cultural cul-de-sac in which we have been abandoned by the collapse of progressive narratives.

But this curious, and potentially noble feature depends on another to be apparent. The signature tone of Houellebecq the novelist is only really striking inasmuch as it is juxtaposed with material which cannot but outrage. Principally, this means the Islamophobia, racism and misogyny which ring through Houellebecq's prose fictions; but also, depending on the particular constituency, it might take in the occasional homophobia; the explicit descriptions of group sex; or the repeated suggestion that the supposed liberations sought in western countries over the last four decades have resulted in little more than new, more virulent, and hypocritically pro-capitalist forms of individualism. Now it is doubtless important to avoid naivety here: these attitudes are not (or not all, and not all at once) ascribable to Michel Houellebecq, balding 40–something French novelist/poet/ recording artist. Of course, they are mediated variously through his writings, generally by the framing presence of a narratorial structure which renders undecidable their status in relation to the texts of which they form such a striking part. They may, indeed, be there to reproduce to perfection the misery of the contemporary world. But still: there they are.

The claim that his presentation of offensive material is securely mediated through his novels' fictional apparatus was sometimes used in Houellebecq's defence at the time of his trial in 2002 for incitement to racial and religious hatred, following the appearance in the magazine *Lire* in September 2001 of an interview in which Houellebecq expressed, dismissively, criticisms of Islam which seemed to tally with the derogatory opinions of the narrator of his novel *Plateforme*. Having received the support of witnesses including Noguez, Fernando Arrabal, Josyane Savigneau and Philippe Sollers, Houellebecq was acquitted on the grounds that his criticisms concerned Islam and not Muslims or Arabs more generally, and that in this case criticism of a religion could not be equated with racism or construed as an incitement to the hatred of its adherents. The verdict was hailed as a great victory for the principles of *laïcité* and freedom of expression.

If the argument that to insult a religion expresses no animosity towards its believers may perhaps seem to rest on a rather nice distinction, Houellebecq subsequently appeared enthusiastically to embrace the freedom it gave him: in *La Possibilité d'une île* (2005), his contemporary narrator, a comedian called Daniel, creates shows, sketches and short films which insult Arabs, Jews and Christians, and give rise to complaints, death threats, and so on (59). This all-round offensiveness seemed not to be the main concern of those for whom Houellebecq's prominence formed the talking point of the 2005 *rentrée littéraire*, however. Rather, the question was a literary one: as a novelist, was Houellebecq any good? Or was he just an able self-publicist whose mediocre books provided ample proof of the decadence and venality of French publishing? It must be said that by 2005, this was hardly a particularly new question. But it was posed with renewed vigour, and a host of articles, books and pamphlets about Houellebecq piggy-backed on the publication of his novel (thereby of course forming an indispensable part of the spectacle some of them wanted to lament).[4] The question then formed the focus of the obligatory media fuss around the 2005 Prix Goncourt, for which Houellebecq's principal rival was François Weyergans, with his much more respectably literary novel, *Trois jours chez ma mère*. Weyergans was successful in the second round (by 6 votes to 4), some of the jury having apparently refused point blank to contemplate the award of the prize to Houellebecq, determined to affirm their supposed independence from the publicity machines of the publishing industry.[5] (Although *La Possibilité d'une île* did win the Prix Interallié.) It is not our aim here to judge the relative merits of *La Possibilité d'une île* and *Trois jours chez ma mère*, but rather to note that at stake in this highly predictable debate was the question of literary value; and that the Goncourt committee's decision affirmed a belief in a kind of literary value supposedly untainted by the relentless commercialism of the surrounding culture, with Houellebecq cast as the squalid representative of this tacky culture.

Houellebecq's writing is in fact carefully constructed to pose the following question, while making any answer extremely difficult: does he offer a diagnosis of the various ills of the contemporary western world – or should his work be considered a symptom of these ills? Critical of this world, he also negotiates it with great success, giving us – if his sales are anything to go by – what we want. There is thus an ironic, implosive dimension to Houellebecq's critique of the global marketplace he finds around him. Exhausted denunciation of the hegemonic victory of commodity fetishism has no option: if its thesis is true, then – as we have just seen in the case of Despentes – it must also itself be saturated by the presence of the inane trinkets it describes, and which it is, thanks in part precisely to this saturation, destined to become.[6]

And Houellebecq knows this. One of the features of his writing is its capacity to fold critical dialogue into its own fabric, dangling the reader's thoughts before her as a kind of limp *déjà dit*, closing down in advance the space of dispute or discussion. In Houellebecq's melancholy universe, we all know everything already (including, of course, the fact that we all know everything already...) – but far from making us wise, say, or kind, this weary sense of omniscience simply closes us in within our stupid modernity. We can disagree with this presentation; we cannot deny that this disagreement is already staged within the work. We can dismiss Houellebecq, but we cannot catch him out. His work is, unavoidably, *both* the ultimate symptom *and* the critical diagnosis of the mediated, self-conscious, lost world it describes. And this is nowhere clearer than in its use of pornography.

For Houellebecq – more straightforwardly, perhaps, than for Despentes – pornography demonstrates the reductive materialism of contemporary sexual relations. The paradigm of the measurable, marketable body to which western men and women are now to aspire, is the pornographic body, reduced to a few fetishised parts, attributes and acts. Pornography, throughout his work, is, accordingly, stupid and bad. Against this, he sets for example the possibility of love, a potential buffer zone before the expansion of the market into interpersonal relations. Thus far, his work diagnoses what it critiques. But – again like Despentes' – Houellebecq's texts are stuffed full of scenes and descriptions whose terms are precisely those of this reductive, materialistic pornography. Moreover, the love he appears to celebrate is often embedded in relations which are inseparable from the logic or practices of pornography, the sex industry, sex tourism, and so on. At which point, his work is also a symptom of what it critiques. Relations between the sexes, notions of masculinity and femininity, the history of western feminism in the late twentieth century – these and similar issues are unavoidable throughout Houellebecq's work, and are invariably addressed via the use of explicit sexual material, often with specific reference to the codes or the consumption of pornography. This chapter will, accordingly, begin with Houellebecq's treatment of questions of gender, most especially the portrayal of women, including the discourses of misogyny and anti-feminism by which this work is marked. It will subsequently specifically explore his use of the tropes of pornography, before going on to suggest something of the ambivalent status of the pornographic in his work. Finally, an account of his representations of group sex, swinging and sex tourism will serve to bring this ambivalence into focus. The aim here will be to take seriously the stakes attaching to the pornographic in Houellebecq's writing. For it is through his use of such material that he most insistently presents his singular, and highly demoralising, imbrication of degradation and idealism.

Misogyny and anti-feminism

It is – to say the least – not difficult to find misogynistic images, *topoi*, and vocabulary throughout Houellebecq's writings. (Indeed, his success probably has something to do with a cultural moment of backlash in which, after a short period of relative unacceptability, such material has returned – but knowingly, and as supposedly transgressive – into circulation.) Houellebecq's main characters tend to be rather lonely heterosexual men, whose leisure pursuits may include sex tourism, visiting peep shows, adult cinemas or prostitutes, masturbating over home-shopping catalogues or rap videos, or spending much of their disposable income seeking contacts on the *Minitel rose*. Since we spend a lot of our time in their slightly seedy company, it is hardly surprising that its casual misogyny is present in the texts they inhabit.

In general, this entails the relentless objectification of female characters, reduced to so much sexual meat, to be evaluated with a classic mixture of disdain and desire. (Just as Despentes's sex workers complain, in fact, as seen in Chapter 5, pp. 171–2.) The most brutal example of this is the presentation of the character Catherine Lechardoy, in *Extension du domaine de la lutte*, which culminates in the following comment: 'Ce trou qu'elle avait au bas du ventre devait lui apparaître tellement inutile. Une bite, on peut toujours la sectionner; mais comment oublier la vacuité d'un vagin?' (2000a: 47). ['That hole she had at the base of her belly must appear so useless to her; a prick can always be cut off, but how do you forget the emptiness of a vagina?' (1998b: 44).] As this suggests, Houellebecq's female characters are often described in the baldest, most reductively sexual terms. Whether in fantasy or reality, they feature principally as the objective correlatives of male desire (however tired); in keeping with this position, women are regularly designated – especially in the earlier texts – by the dismissive terms of a casually misogynistic vocabulary. And as is conventional, the scorn which motivates such terms is most powerfully inscribed in the figure of the woman as sexual being. Houellebecq's women find their sexual bodies scrutinised; the cool detachment of the description is set against the heightened intensity of the scene, to the greater exposure of the flesh detailed. The defamiliarising materialism of such descriptions reaches its high point in *Extension du domaine de la lutte*, with a reference to 'les femmes qui m'ouvraient leurs organes' (2000a: 15) ['those women who were opening their organs to me' (1998b: 13)]: the sexual woman is reduced to her anatomy. (Which also, elsewhere, is her destiny: *Les Particules élémentaires*, in particular, features authoritative statements about the inevitable fate of the physically beautiful or ugly young girl, seduced by old *roués* or left on the shelf: see especially 2000b: 57–8.) Even when this reductiveness appears mutual, it is clear where the agency lies: Daniel, in *La Possibilité d'une île*, declares: 'les occasions de disposer mon organe dans un des orifices adéquats ne m'ont pas manqué' (2005: 24). ['opportunities for placing my organ in one of the appropriate orifices were never lacking' (2006: 15).] This reduction seems to articulate a particular loathing: not only does the more or less constantly insulting lexis build up a kind of misogynistic momentum, the texts house an especial disgust at the spectacle of female flesh – specifically, female flesh which is ageing or, especially, fat. From the miserably named Brigitte Bardot in *Extension du domaine de la lutte*, to Annick in *Les Particules élémentaires*, to Isabelle in *La Possibilité d'une île*, fat women are presented with characteristic Houellebecquian objectification, horrified at the treatment to which they appear doomed, but also, often, complicit in this treatment.

To criticise Houellebecq for the insistent presence of such material in his texts is already to situate oneself in a position which these texts themselves criticise, however. That is to say, it entails an alignment with feminist critical discourses which have emerged over the past hundred years or so as part of the very liberation movements Houellebecq is setting out to critique. And it seems reasonable to suppose that the misogyny found in his texts represents a challenge (to put it mildly) to just the kind of liberal feminism likely to subtend this critical position. For Houellebecq situates feminism within the context of a narcissistic, self-deluding, pseudo-liberalism which has served simply to facilitate the encroachment of the logic of the free market into the private life of all westerners. Having established the largely misogynistic atmosphere of his texts, we will now focus on their specifically anti-feminist moments, which provide the skeleton for their more visceral provocation.

The context of the challenge to feminism to be found in much of Houellebecq's writing is that of a general critique of the ethos of self-fulfilment which he sees as having characterised the west roughly since the 1950s. This ethos is principally attacked in *Les Particules élémentaires*, where it is presented as corrosive in a variety of ways. First, it justifies the parental neglect which leads to the virtual abandonment of first Bruno, and then Michel (2000b: 27–30); second, it is characterised by a deep-seated hypocrisy, in which its supposedly liberal attitude to difference is in fact just a more rigid conformism (60, 177). Moreover, its adherents are motivated less by lofty ideals than by lust, and are as opportunistic as they are pretentious (97–8). More seriously, what one might generally characterise as the 'anti-establishment' groupings of the period are presented as guilty of a profound historical naivety, in which what they think of as liberation in fact simply extends the individualistic ethos of the market into private life. In emphasising individual self-fulfilment, these groupings have unwittingly espoused the logic of consumerism; their rebellions have done little more than break down the few remaining social structures to offer any resistance to this logic. (See for example 2000b: 116.) Unchecked, this logic determines that sexual relations henceforth become a realm of unregulated competition – with the inevitable creation of a sexual *lumpenproletariat*: 'Tout comme le libéralisme économique sans frein, et pour des raisons analogues, le libéralisme sexuel produit des phénomènes de *paupérisation absolue*' (2000a: 100; see also Abecassis 2000: 811). ['Just like unrestrained economic liberalism, and for similar reasons, sexual liberalism produces phenomena of *absolute pauperisation*' (1998b: 99).]

Complicit with the individualistic ethos of consumerism, demands for self-fulfilment (among which this perspective numbers feminism) ensure their own inevitable defeat: for the market will move on, no product can dominate indefinitely. The women who had liberated themselves from oppressive social structures thus, supposedly, find themselves adrift, bereft of the support these very structures might have provided (see for example 2000b: 107). Houellebecq often has such sentiments reinforced by putting them into the mouths of sympathetic female characters: Bruno's lover Christiane, for example, who says of such women, 'Elles vendent un corps affaibli, enlaidi; elles le savent et elles en souffrent' (2000b: 140–1). ['They try to trade on their looks, even when they know their bodies are sad and ugly. They get hurt, but they do it anyway' (2000d: 166).] Or Valérie, in *Plateforme*, who acts as a validating foil for the theses on the collapse of sexual relation in the west elaborated by the narrator, Michel, confirming them with the words, 'je crois que tu as raison. La libération sexuelle, en Occident, c'est vraiment fini' (2001a: 253). ['I think you're right. Sexual liberation in the West is over' (2003: 243).]

This, then, would be the bankruptcy of feminism as it appears in Houellebecq's texts: its proponents have shot themselves in the foot, and have ended up regretting, or even espousing precisely the models they purported to reject. By the end of the century, feminism seems to have withered away to a caricature of self-assertion, as presented at the start of *Extension du domaine de la lutte*, and termed, 'Les ultimes résidus, consternants, du féminisme' (2000a: 6). ['the last dismaying dregs of the collapse of feminism' (1998b: 4).] The positively coded female characters in Houellebecq's more recent fiction do, in fact, tend to be both assertive and profession- ally successful: but they tend to be those, such as Valérie in *Plate- forme* or Isabelle in *La Possibilité d'une île*, who share the disabused and anti-feminist view of recent sexual relations expressed by the male characters, and who are happy to pleasure these characters in standard ways (dressing up in sexy outfits, for example) without seeing the politics of their relationship as problematic. In Houelle- becq, anti-feminism is in part articulated by the kind of misogynistic objectification encountered above; alternatively, the objectification may become corrosively laconic, reducing a complex politics to a metonymic banality. 'Elle ressemblait à une féministe, du reste elle portait un pull-over de féministe', writes Houellebecq in 1997; later, this woman is named, belittlingly, as 'pull-over' (1998a: 142). ['She looked like a feminist, and anyway, she was wearing a feminist jumper'.] Banal, drenched in bad faith, reducible to a superficial predictability – as Houellebecq remarked at the conference devoted to his work in Edinburgh in October 2005, in his writings, 'le féminisme est mort'. ['feminism is dead'.]

Critical frames

The objections to Houellebecq's presentations of women and feminism are easy to generate; and it is, as we will argue later, entirely right that they should be made. As mentioned above, however, the real problem is that this offensive material is not simply being espoused by Houellebecq. It is, in fact, framed. Unfortunately, this framing is notable for its instability; and so it is not even possible to make a standard move whereby Houellebecq would be redeemed from the charge of misogyny by the relieved realisation that this is all just in some sense being quoted. It *is* being quoted, as we will now see; but the quotation marks are at times all but erased. And this, perhaps, is why Houellebecq has known such a *succès de scandale*: because his texts scandalise, but, scandalously, do so evasively, moving the goalposts (see Abecassis 2000: 803). We will now, therefore, examine how Houellebecq's texts work to situate the kind of discourses quoted above as framed by the viewpoint of a particular character, or reproducing the tropes of bankrupt genres. Once it has become apparent that his framing techniques make it impossible to accuse Houellebecq of embracing the offensive material he presents, it will then be necessary to demonstrate the slipperiness of these techniques, and the return, beyond its supposed neutralisation, of this troubling material. First, though, the insulating frame.

In the case of *Extension du domaine de la lutte*, matters are pretty straightforward: the text is clearly narrated by a misogynistic (if at times wittily so) narrator: 'Il se peut, sympathique ami lecteur, que vous soyez vous-même une femme. Ne vous en faites pas, ce sont des choses qui arrivent' (2000a: 15–16). ['It may be, dear reader and friend, that you are a woman yourself. Don't be alarmed, these things happen' (1998b: 13).] The misogyny and anti-feminism to be found here, then, are easily ascribable to the personal agenda of this angry, ineffectual individual, let down by his former lover. The clinical tone in which the women he encounters are described is, moreover, in part symptomatic of an isolation which becomes a severe depression, bordering on psychosis, and including a period of voluntary institutionalisation. The murderous adventure into which he leads the miserable Tisserand not only fails; it is also a continuation of the violence he has already, with blank pleasure, inflicted on himself, or about which he fantasises: smashing a mirror, for example, or punching through a window-pane (128, 141); castrating himself, or gouging out an eye with a pair of scissors (143). It is hard, in this case, not to see the misogyny woven through this text as itself implicitly disowned, displaced by its articulation through this desperate frame.

As for *Les Particules élémentaires*: here things are more complicated, but there are certain similarities with the earlier novel. The vast majority of the misogynistic vocabulary and objectification to be found here is clearly ascribable to the viewpoint of Bruno Clément, another desperate case, which again features a moment of institutionalisation. Indeed, the text explicitly links Bruno's voyeuristic sexualisation of every woman he sees to his mental instability. Explicitly the 'animal oméga' in the jungle of sexual competition (2000b: 43) ['omega male' (2000d: 48)], Bruno is deprived even of the mercy shown by most animals to their most miserable peer, and destined to a life of brutalisation (46). Generally, then, this is the source of the reductive vision of women in the text; again, it is hardly valorised as authoritative or even level-headed. When it is backed up, this is usually by other characters, who may themselves be mocked. (The exception to this would perhaps be Christiane, to whom we will return below.) Moreover, Bruno even at one point discusses the surprising misogyny of Aristotle, for whom a short woman was not human, belonged to another species (135), indicating the cultural framing of the supposed naturalisations of misogyny, and thereby foregrounding his own perspective as open to similar criticism. All of which makes it impossible to take the misogyny of the text as endorsed by the text: rather, it would appear that it is itself being held up as a discourse to be critiqued. In these early texts at least, then, where the misogyny is most extreme, some sort of prophylactic distance is suggested to insulate the text from the material it presents.

If this is the case, the reason may be found in Houellebecq's critique of individualism, as discussed above. For the misogyny and anti-feminism to be found in his texts mobilise just the reductive, materialistic anthropology he sees as responsible for the hegemony of the free market, both economically and sexually. Thus, a frequent strain of this critique is an attack on the very genre which might be thought to underpin the objectifying *topoi* multiplied by Houellebecq throughout his texts: pornography.

Whereas one might have thought it possible to align Houellebecq's writings, with their relentless reduction of women to sexualised bodies, with the formulaic habits of pornography, in fact this genre is frequently denounced in these writings, which gives further support to the notion that this reduction is itself also the object of such denunciation. Quite often, Houellebecq uses the classic tropes of hard-core pornography, particularly when it is a matter of male ejaculation.[7] In *Particules*, Bruno ejaculates over Christiane's face or breasts (2000b: 149, 241); in *Lanzarote*, Pam licks the narrator's sperm from Barbara's breasts (2000c: 58); in *Plateforme*, Michel ejaculates onto Valérie's face (2001a: 188); in *La Possibilité d'une île*, Daniel ejaculates onto Isabelle's breasts (2005: 38), or onto Esther's face, or into her mouth, in a style which explicitly follows a pornographic model (200). But such scenes are invariably debunked or transcended, often by the introduction of a brief, unstable emotional element. In Bruno's case, this is premature ejaculation, or a weak erection brought on by an excess of emotion; in *Plateforme*, the emotional disturbance is Valérie's: 'Elle ferma les yeux; j'éjaculai sur son visage. A ce moment, je crus qu'elle allait avoir une crise de larmes; mais finalement non, elle se contenter de lécher le sperme qui coulait le long de ses joues' (2001a: 188). ['She closed her eyes; I ejaculated over her face. At that moment I thought she was going to burst into tears; but she didn't, she simply licked at the semen trickling down her cheeks' (2003: 180).] The emotional response is resolved into a pornographic cliché, of course, effectively repressed: but it remains there as a momentary, irreducible and potentially critical interference with the code.

While it may offer a kind of comfort to many of his lonely protagonists, the world of pornography is also presented by Houellebecq as cruel and exclusive. Masturbating over his copy of *Swing Magazine*, Bruno is aware primarily of his inadequacy in the face of its contact advertisements (again presented in terms of reductive pornographic *topoi*): 'il ne se sentait pas à la hauteur pour un *gang bang* ou une douche de sperme [...] Numéro après numéro, il devait s'y résigner: pour réellement parvenir à s'infiltrer dans le réseau porno, il avait une trop petite queue' (2000b: 101). ['he did not feel up to a *gang bang* or a *sperm fest* [...] Issue after issue, he came to the conclusion that his cock was too small for the porn circuit' (2000d: 118).] This is generalised by Michel in *Plateforme*, according to whom westerners are ashamed of their body for not being up to the standards set by pornography (2001a: 254). The reductive materialism of these new standards is just that critiqued by Houellebecq in the colonisation by market forces of what used to be private life; this is no accident. For pornography, according to Houellebecq, played the key role (and was seconded by women's magazines) in the reduction of romantic or sexual relations to a simple, violent realm of competition, based on 'des critères simples et objectivement vérifiables (âge – taille – poids – mensurations hanches – taille – poitrine pour les femmes; âge – taille – poids – mensurations du sexe en érection pour les hommes)' (1998a: 66). ['simple and objectively verifiable criteria (for women: age, height, weight, bust, waist and hip measurements; for men: age, height, weight, size of erect penis)'.] Satirising this in a text from 1998, Houellebecq (or the anonymous narrator of his piece) finds himself connected to 'Sandra W.' by Minitel. He asks her to describe herself: she replies with her height, weight and bust size. 'Il est vrai', he continues wryly, 'que les ratiocinations sociologiques à la Proust sont aujourd'hui avantageusement remplacées par des notations sobres et lumineuses, du style: 300 kilofrancs. Certes, il paraît anormal que les paramètres de l'échange sexuel restent tributaires d'une description lyrique, impressionniste, pour tout dire peu fiable' (2001b: 33). ['It is true that nice sociological distinctions of the Proustian kind have today been replaced, to the great benefit of all, by sober, limpid ratings along the lines of: 300K. It seems therefore all the more aberrant that the parameters of social exchange should still remain in hock to a mode of description that is lyrical, impressionistic, and ultimately highly unreliable'.]

In this redefinition of sexuality as a brutal hierarchy in which competition takes place on the basis of such physical attributes, it is, for Houellebecq, pornography that sets the tone. The originator of this relentless materialism was, apparently, Sade: within 'le système *sadien* [...] les bites sont uniformément rigides et démesurées, les seins

silicones, les chattes épilées et baveuses' (2000b: 244). ['the *Sadean*
system [...] cocks are invariably enormous and rock hard, breasts
are enhanced, cunts wet and shaven' (2000d: 293).] Entry into this
system seems inevitably to corrode, and predictably to lead to an
endless search for new, more extreme stimulation: from swinging
to sadomasochism, in *Particules* (2000b: 244); from swinging to
paedophilia in *Lanzarote* (2000c: 68–9, 79–81). Imitation of pornographic tropes is stupid and counterproductive: the women who
masturbate Bruno in the couples' clubs he visits with Christiane
do so in a way devoid of pleasure: 'Obsédées par le rythme fréné-
tique des actrices du porno institutionnel, elles branlaient sa bite
avec brutalité, comme une tige de chair insensible, avec un ridicule
mouvement de piston' (2000b: 245). ['Imitating the frenetic rhythm
of porn actresses, they brutally jerked his cock in a ridiculous piston
motion as though it were a piece of dead meat' (2000d: 294).]

What is more, the fashionable intellectualisation of pornography
is ridiculed: when Bruno's father takes up with a former porn actress
named Julie Lamour, we are told that 'Lors d'un dîner chez Bénazéraf
sa maîtresse avait rencontré Deleuze, et depuis elle se lançait
régulièrement dans des justifications intellectuelles du porno, ce
n'était plus supportable' (2000b: 78). ['Since meeting Deleuze at one
of Bénazéraf's dinner parties, she had taken to giving lengthy intellectual justifications of porn – it had become unbearable (2000d: 91,
modified).] When Daniel, principal narrator of *La Possibilité d'une
île*, reflects on his work as a screenwriter, he realises that pornography is the only fashionable genre he has yet to exploit. Recalling
the repeated failures of attempts to produce 'quality pornography',
he concludes that the field, although lucrative, is irredeemably resistant to aesthetic or intellectual improvement. This is illustrated by his
memory of visiting the shooting of a porn movie, where the reductiveness of the genre is signalled not only by the miserable dialogue
('Je t'excite, hein, ma salope. – Tu m'excites, oui, mon salaud'), but
by the brutal materialism with which the director treats his actors.
'Si vous bandez pas, les mecs, vous serez pas payés!', he yells; 'les
acteurs', concludes Daniel, 'étaient simplement traités comme
des bites sur pattes' (2005: 159–61). ['"I excite you, eh, my little
slut" – "Yes, you excite me, my little bastard"'; '"If you don't get a
hard-on, guys, you won't be paid!"'; 'as for the actors, they were just
treated like cocks on legs' (2006: 135).] Later, Daniel reflects deject-
edly on what he calls 'le projet millénaire masculin, parfaitement

exprimé de nos jours par les films pornographiques, consistant à ôter à la sexualité toute connotation affective pour la ramener dans le champ du divertissement pur' (341). ['The centuries-old male project, perfectly expressed nowadays by pornographic films, that consisted of ridding sexuality of any emotional connotation in order to bring it back into the realm of pure entertainment' (2006: 294).] Houellebecq is very clearly treating pornography – including its recent intellectual, literary or aesthetic modishness – as a cultural trend which both exemplifies and shapes the cruelty and alienation of this culture.

If the objectifying gaze through which Houellebecq's women are habitually presented resembles that of the pornographic, then, it may well be that it is this gaze, and not the women it takes in, that forms the object of Houellebecq's attack. And it is indeed the case that the position from which this gaze habitually emanates comes in for plenty of criticism from Houellebecq. 'Dans l'histoire de l'humanité', he said in 1996, 'il est en effet possible que la masculinité soit une parenthèse – une parenthèse malheureuse' (1998a: 117). ['It may in fact be that, in the history of humanity, masculinity will turn out to be just an interlude – and an unhappy one, at that'.] Contemplating a catalogue of hard-core pornographic videos which features the most reductive, misogynistic descriptions imaginable, he remarks, 'Pour la première fois de ma vie, je commence à éprouver une vague sympathie pour les féministes américaines', concluding that, if women are also beginning to demonstrate the need evident in many of these videos to humiliate their partners in order to feel sexually adequate (as his biologist friend Angèle claims), 'nous sommes foutus' (1998a: 125). ['For the first time in my life, I am beginning to feel vaguely sympathetic towards American feminists'; 'we are screwed'.] *Particules* features more than one claim (generally focalised through either Bruno or Michel) that women are nobler, kinder, just *better* than men. It has generally been women who have devoted their life to loving and caring for others (2000b: 90–1); they are gentle and understanding, where men are aggressive and cynical (134); all of which leads Michel to the same question as that posed by Houellebecq in the very article which opened with his metonymic reduction of a supposed feminist to her pullover: 'A quoi servent les hommes?' (1998a: 142–4; see also 2000b: 165). ['What are men for?']

Things seem to be evening out: perhaps the tendency to reduce women to objects is the kind of moral or emotional vacuity that

Houellebecq seems generally keen to denounce, and which he finds, pre-eminently, in pornography. It might be that Houellebecq is less the champion of one sex or the other, than a generally misanthropic satirist, deploying a reductive materialism where necessary in order to debunk the hypocrisies of his targets, or to bemoan, sentimentally, a world devoid of human warmth. Thus, Bruno's penis can just as easily become a piece of Baudelairean meat – 'un bout de viande suintant et putréfié' (2000b: 154) ['a piece of sweaty, putrefying meat' (2000d: 184)] – as can the bodies of the women he ogles. Michel's, in *Plateforme*, at times appears to him as 'un petit appendice exigeant, inutile, qui sentait le fromage' (2001a: 25). ['a useless, demanding little appendage that smelled like cheese' (2003: 17).] And what, in any case, is the advantage of having a penis in the first place? 'Une bite, on peut toujours la sectionner' (2000a: 47). ['a prick can always be cut off' (1998b: 44).] Houellebecq may perhaps be less the premier apologist for a pornographically inspired misogyny, than its enthusiastic critic.[8]

Pornography, happiness, utopia

This is not really sufficient as an account of Houellebecq's relation to pornography, however. Pornography is, plainly, denounced throughout his work. Of this there can be no question. But it is also espoused. One way to make this point is simply to indicate the considerable amount of material in his books that looks an awful lot like pornography (for such lists, see Deleu 2002 and Clément 2003). This will hardly do, however, as it pays little or no attention to the fact that this material is bound up with the critical context sketched above. Context cannot necessarily redeem such material, of course – this is what we are about to see. But we cannot seriously proceed as if it did not exist. What we have to do, rather, is consider just how the codes of pornography persist, even as they are being critiqued.[9]

Two examples will serve for the purpose of this consideration: the presence of pornography in *La Possibilité d'une île*; and further consideration of the relation between the emotional and the pornographic in Houellebecq's writing more generally. In both cases, we will be revisiting examples already presented above, since this will allow us to see how the extensive critique of pornography in Houellebecq sits, oddly, alongside its embrace.

As far as *La Possibilité d'une île* is concerned, there is no way to

qualify the obviously negative presentation of the world of pornography in Daniel's description of the making of a porn movie. But it
is nonetheless juxtaposed with other material in which this negative
presentation is only implicitly discernable. Having just recalled his
visit to the gruesome porn set, for example, Daniel begins to work
on a screenplay he provisionally entitles 'Les Echangistes de l'autoroute', 'qui devait me permettre de combiner astucieusement les
avantages commerciaux de la pornographie et de l'ultraviolence'
(2005: 161). ['Motorway Swingers'; 'which would allow me to
cleverly combine the advantages of pornography and ultra-violence'
(2006: 136).] This self-consciousness is woven into the project: after
an initial description of the pornographic scenario, Daniel reveals
that his film will frame this scenario, revealing that it is itself the
object of a porn film whose making is being represented within 'Les
Echangistes de l'autoroute'. Those making this film are then massacred, as are other young couples; it subsequently becomes apparent
'que les tueurs étaient eux-mêmes filmés par une seconde équipe,
et que le véritable but de l'affaire était la commercialisation non
de films pornos, mais d'images d'ultraviolence. Récit dans le récit,
film dans le film, etc. Un projet béton' (163). ['that the killers had
themselves been filmed by a second crew, and that the true aim of the
whole business was the commercialisation not of porn films, but of
ultra-violence. Plot within a plot, film within a film, etc. A watertight
project' (2006: 138).] Something very tricky, and very characteristic
of Houellebecq, is going on in this accumulation of irony. On the
one hand, the pornographic material is so embedded in layers of
citation that it cannot be taken at face value: Houellebecq's critique
is safe. On the other hand, this embedding is itself ironised ('Récit
dans le récit, film dans le film, etc.'): at which point, these layers of
citation are relativised, and the possibility returns of the text being
aligned with the pornographic cliché it has just so knowingly represented. Compare the first chapter of the third part of *Extension du
domaine de la lutte*, which features as its epigraph: 'Ah, oui, c'était
au second degré! On respire...' (2000a: 123). ['Ah yes, that was
unconscious irony! One breathes freely...' (1998b: 123).] Far from
calming troubled readers by assuring them that this is all just safely
ironic, this phrase in fact ironises precisely this suggestion, indicating
the vacuity of the relief supposedly offered by ironic citation, and
suggesting that the affects conjured up by difficult material might
in fact remain, beyond this supposed qualification.[10] This residual

structure can be awkward, as grasping it requires the suspension of an Aristotelian principle of non-contradiction; reading Houelle-becq, however, it is in fact both possible and necessary to think the following: his texts are full of offensive material; this material is qualified by intricate framing effects; this framing is both incom-plete and irreducible.[11]

This would imply, here, that *La Possibilité d'une île* is not simply seeking a critical distance from the pornography that it thema-tises. To be sure, this thematisation introduces a self-consciousness which definitively rules out the idea that Houellebecq is just naively reproducing this pornographic material; equally, that a scenario is sketched by Daniel does not necessarily mean that it is espoused by the text or its author, of course. But this is not quite the point. Rather, the point is that Houellebecq constructs his text so that the status of this pornographic material is, properly speaking, undecid-able: it may be being ironised, and so critiqued; or it may not. Later (when receiving oral sex from Esther), Daniel muses:

> La fellation est depuis toujours la figure reine des films pornos, la seule qui puisse servir de modèle utile aux jeunes filles; c'est aussi la seule où l'on retrouve parfois quelque chose de l'émotion réelle de l'acte, parce que c'est la seule où le gros plan soit, également, un gros plan du visage de la femme, où l'on puisse lire sur ses traits cette fierté joyeuse, ce ravisse-ment enfantin qu'elle éprouve à donner du plaisir. (200)

> [Since their beginnings, fellatio has always been the jewel in the crown of porn films, the only thing that can serve as a useful model for young girls; it was also the only incidence in which you could find a bit of real emotion in the act, because it is the only incidence in which the close-up is, also, a close-up of the face of the woman, where you can read in her features that joyful pride, that childlike delight she feels when giving pleasure. (2006: 170)]

Oddly, this very point is also made by Jean-Pierre Léaud's porno-grapher, in Bonello's *Le Pornographe*, to the journalist who inter-views him towards the end of the film. The self-consciousness here is evident. Pornography is discussed in terms of its constituent tropes, and in terms of its reception: Esther has, indeed, gone from an initial refusal to a real expertise in fellatio by virtue of having seen a fair number of porn films. But the self-consciousness tells us nothing about how we ourselves might receive this passage. The text is not necessarily adopting Daniel's point of view, of course. But equally, there is nothing here to tell us that it is not. In *La Possibilité d'une île*, criticism of pornography sits alongside what might, or might not, be an espousal of pornographic material, and what might, or might not, be a celebration of its pedagogic potential.

Typically, Houellebecq threads into his consideration of pornographic fellatio a positive reference to real emotion. As we saw above, it is often the case that Houellebecq's presentation of pornographic tropes – especially male ejaculation – is interrupted by such a reference, which thereby works to relativise these tropes, perhaps critically. But this relativisation is almost always a fragile affair. Let us revisit a couple of the examples cited above. Bruno's ejaculation onto Christiane's face and breasts, for example, is indeed preceded by a reference to his inability to penetrate her because of his emotional state; and this may be read as disqualifying the pornographic code from which this trope is drawn. Alternatively, however, the love that he feels may also be affirmed by this trope, which concludes their agreement to establish a relationship (2000a: 149). When Pam licks the narrator's sperm from Barbara's breasts in *Lanzarote*, this is not just qualified by a moment of intense narratorial emotion: it leads to it, meaning that if the emotion is not being ironised, then nor is the trope (2000c: 58). This might just be the narrator's skewed vision (he is described throughout this scene as not seeing clearly, as is often the case in Houellebecq's narration of such moments); on the other hand, there are few more consistently positive terms in Houellebecq's universe than the 'bonheur' on which the scene closes, apparently brought about by the realisation of a pornographic trope. Emotion interrupts the pornographic, indeed; but the pornographic also produces emotion, happiness, even love, and thus appears to be making a contribution to things Houellebecq's texts – for all that they see them as disappearing ideals – generally hold dear.

In Houellebecq's universe, then, love and pornography are diametrically opposed; but, with what reads like the remnants of a ruined dialectic, he folds the two halves of the opposition into each other, producing a strange relationship of imbrication. Why does he do this? In *Rester vivant*, he remarks that love remains as an ideal, even though contemporary life has rendered it virtually impossible: 'D'où une discordance idéal–réel particulièrement criante, source de souffrances particulièrement riche' (2001b: 10). ['From which there results a particularly striking disparity between the ideal and the real, a particularly rich source of suffering'.] Perhaps, then, the point is to suggest that we still want love, but that these are the only miserable, materialistic means we have at our disposal to realise it? In which case, love is irredeemably compromised by the ways of the world it continues to haunt; but these ways at least lead to some kind of love, however sullied – even, some kind of redemption. At the height of his encounter with the Thai prostitute Sin, in *Plateforme*, Michel declares: 'je me sentais réconcilié' (2001a: 125). ['I felt reconciled' (2003: 118).]

It is, then, this combination of denunciation and espousal that appears to characterise Houellebecq's relationship to the pornographic material which pervades his work. In this, he resembles both Breillat and Despentes; in each case, however, there are slight but significant differences. As we saw in Chapter 2, Breillat knows she has to court the pornographic in order to transcend it; the interest of her work lies in the tangled relation of materiality and its sublimation this produces. For her part, Despentes wants to denounce the reductive, misogynistic violence of the pornographic; to do so, however, she speaks its language so well that she becomes complicit with it, and seems oddly content with this, as seen in Chapter 5. In Houellebecq's case, the complication of the relationship derives from his suggestion that any transcendence of the miserable materialism of our pornographic world is available only *by way of* this materialism: the two are, as we have seen, in a relation of imbrication. By way of a closing condensation of the principal features of this relationship, we will now consider one of the dimensions in which it engages most immediately with its times: namely, Houellebecq's repeated interest in the phenomenon of group sex, including its manifestations in sadomasochism and sex tourism.

What the French call *échangisme* has recently experienced an extraordinary rise in its cultural visibility. Yann Moix's *Partouz* and Catherine Millet's *La Vie sexuelle de Catherine M.* (discussed in Chapters 4 and 5 respectively) have contributed to this phenomenon within literary culture; but the trend is much more widespread, of course. *Swing Magazine* (over which poor old Bruno masturbates in *Les Particules élémentaires*), not to mention a host of competitor titles, is available from mainstream French newsagents. Films and television programmes have been devoted to the subject. The Internet is, unsurprisingly, buzzing with possible encounters. In France, the first serious academic study of the phenomenon has just been published (Welzer-Lang 2005), shortly after another volume, this latter consecrated by a witty preface from Frédéric Beigbeder (Ley

2003); both refer to Houellebecq – along with Millet – as providing more or less documentary evidence of the world of *échangisme*. And Houellebecq has indeed repeatedly addressed the topic in his writings, from the naturists at the campsite in *Les Particules élémentaires*, to the sex tourists of *Plateforme* and the bright young things of *La Possibilité d'une île*. In many of its occurrences, Houellebecq seems content to deploy the trope of group sex to create moments of idyllic happiness. Thus, for example, in *Plateforme*, when Michel and Valérie have sex with a chambermaid (whom they pay) or with an unknown *bourgeoise excitante*, or with a couple called Jérôme and Nicole whom they meet in a swingers' club (2001a: 221–2, 290–2, 266–9) or when the narrator of *Lanzarote* has sex with Pam and Barbara (2000c: 56–8, 64–5), the experiences are what mostly counts as 'good sex' in Houellebecq: the narration and the basic fantasy are more or less straightforwardly pornographic, and the male character is overwhelmed by joy. These instances feature the characteristic combination of emotion and materialism we have just explored; beyond this complication, however, there is nothing by way of explicit criticism. When swinging as such is thematised, it is often as an island of gentle, considerate sociability amidst the hostility and alienation of the world at large (and thus the very opposite of the morbid environment described by Despentes, as seen in Chapter 5). Michel, in *Plateforme*, claims that swingers' clubs are doomed, since nowadays, sharing anything at all has become anathema (2001a: 251). Precisely for this reason, however, he admires the practice where it survives: 'Dans un monde où le plus grand luxe consiste à se donner les moyens d'éviter les autres, la sociabilité bon enfant des bourgeois échangistes allemands constituait une forme de subversion particulièrement subtile' (321). ['In a world where the greatest of luxuries is acquiring the wherewithal to avoid other people, the good-natured sociability of middle-class German wife-swappers constitutes a form of particularly subtle subversion' (2003: 312).] Bruno, in *Les Particules élémentaires*, develops this notion with reference to the naturist resort of Le Cap d'Agde, in an article entitled 'Les Dunes de Marseillan-Plage: pour une esthétique de la bonne volonté' (2000b: 215). ['The Dunes of Marseillan Beach: towards an aesthetic of goodwill' (2000d: 258).] The article sets out what is called the 'sociology' of the resort; Bruno's thesis is that this location offers a reconfiguration of the norms of social interaction dominant in the world outside, in favour of what he calls 'un principe de *bonne volonté*' (2000b: 221): it is 'le lieu adéquat d'une proposition humaniste, visant à maximiser le plaisir de chacun sans créer de souffrance morale insoutenable chez personne' (220). ['the notion of *goodwill*' (2000d: 263); 'a defining example of the humanist proposition: striving to maximise individual pleasure without causing suffering to another' (2000d: 262).] Among the participants, no contact is made without prior consent, and undesired attentions are easily refused: 'Lorsqu'une femme souhaite se soustraire à une caresse non désirée elle l'indique très simplement, d'un simple signe de tête – provoquant aussitôt, chez l'homme, des excuses cérémonieuses et presque comiques' (221). ['If a woman wishes to decline an unwanted caress, she indicates this with a simple shake of the head, and the man makes a formal – almost comic – apology' (2000d: 263).] Bruno insists that he is not idealising his subject: as elsewhere, he notes, the young and beautiful are particularly celebrated (although the old and ugly are more indulgently tolerated than in the world at large). But it is nevertheless remarkable, he claims; and it is notable that he chooses to make this point by means of a favourable comparison with pornography: 'Ce qui surprend malgré tout c'est que des activités sexuelles aussi diversifiées, largement plus excitantes que ce qui est représentée dans n'importe film pornographique, puissent se dérouler sans engendrer la moindre violence, ni même le plus léger manquement à la courtoisie' (222). ['What is most surprising is that so many diverse sexual practices – far more arousing than those one might witness in a pornographic film – can take place with such exemplary courtesy and not so much as an undertone of violence' (2000d: 264, modified).] Perhaps Bruno has at last made it, not into the miserable, materialistic world of porn, but into its superior cousin, a world of explicit sex and exemplary, humane sociability. A week of this environment provokes the most unexpected declaration on his part (not at all the kind of thing one expects to find in a novel by Houellebecq): 'Je crois que je suis heureux' (223). ['I think I'm happy' (2000d: 265).]

When Bruno and Christiane extend their activity to swingers' clubs in Paris, however, it becomes apparent that this paradise is, of course, tainted. On their first visit, Bruno is unusually sexually excited; but characteristically, his ejaculation is as premature as its orchestration is pornographic: 'La femme commença à le branler, cependant que Christiane approchait à nouveau sa langue. En quelques secondes, pris par un soubresaut de plaisir incontrôlable, il éjacula sur son visage' (241). ['The woman began to masturbate him, while Christiane continued to lick the glans. In a matter of seconds he shuddered with a spasm of pleasure and came all over her face' (2000d: 289).] Bruno is devastated; Christiane, typically, tender and understanding. Subsequently, Bruno's small penis continues to cause him embarrassment, but their trips to these clubs nonetheless represent 'des soirées merveilleuses, comme il n'aurait jamais espéré pouvoir en vivre' (243). ['wonderful nights, of the sort that he had hardly dreamed of before' (2000d: 291).] The worm is in the fruit, however: their fellow swingers turn out to be mostly pornographically inspired materialists unconcerned with pleasure or happiness, and Christiane slips towards the death which awaits all Houellebecq's redemptive women (on which, see Canto-Sperber 2001). These two developments are woven together in such a way that Bruno's disappointment as swinging turns into another dead end, sets the tone for Christiane's demise: the mechanics of *échangisme* appear as literally deathly. Again, pornography is to blame, the narrator tells us, its tropes proving as fashionable as they are infectious:

> Les hommes et les femmes qui fréquentent les boîtes pour couples renoncent rapidement à la recherche du plaisir (qui demande finesse, sensibilité, lenteur) au profit d'une activité sexuelle fantasmatique, assez insincère dans son principe, de fait directement calquée les scènes de *gang bang* des pornos 'mode' diffusés par Canal +. (243)

> [The men and women who frequented clubs for couples quickly abandoned their search for pleasure (which required time, finesse, and sensitivity) in favour of prodigal sexual abandon – an empty experience based directly on the gang bang scenes in the fashionable porn movies shown on Canal Plus. (2000d: 292)]

A world away from the supposed inventiveness of the Cap d'Agde, this is the universe of the 'Sadean system', sustained by its contemporary cultural apparatus: 'Souvent lectrices de *Connexion* ou *Hot Video*, les habituées des boîtes pour couples fixaient à leurs soirées un objectif simple: se faire empaler par une multiplicité de grosses bites' (244). ['Female regulars, often readers of *Connexion* and *Hot Video*, go out with the sole aim of being impaled on as many pricks as possible' (2000d: 293).] Their fixation with pornography makes them unable to give real pleasure; this mechanistic sex is contrasted with Bruno and Christiane's lovemaking the mornings after these sorties, described positively as 'des moments d'une tendresse extraordinaire' (245). ['moments of extraordinary tenderness' (2000d: 294).] When Christiane's decisive collapse arrives, one evening, as she is being penetrated by the sixth stranger in rapid succession, the irruption of paramedics into the sex club cannot but imply a kind of condemnation: 'L'équipe du SAMU arriva dix minutes plus tard. Tous les participants s'étaient rhabillés; dans un silence total ils regardèrent les infirmiers qui soulevaient Christiane, qui la déposaient sur une civière' (246). ['The ambulance arrived ten minutes later. Everyone in the club had dressed and in complete silence watched the paramedics lift Christiane onto a stretcher' (2000d: 295–6).]

The predictability of this narrative trajectory is somewhat redeemed by Houellebecq's determination to maintain his difficult imbrication of the sordid and the tender: just as these disappointingly brutal evenings nevertheless give Bruno moments of unhoped-for happiness, so do Bruno's sweetened memories of these evenings give rise to the very tenderness between Bruno and Christiane with which they are unfavourably contrasted. Elsewhere, however, his criticism of various forms of group sex is less nuanced. In a text from 1998, for example, he recounts his adventures (or those of a narratorial avatar) in the world of sex contacts by Minitel. This text largely serves as a vehicle for Houellebecq's parodic considerations on the pornographic reduction of sexuality to bodily attributes, as previously discussed; but it also allows him to trace the misery of this virtual milieu, accentuated by the longing for intimacy it cannot but disclose. Most of those logged on are, apparently, 'des prostituées télématiques et des hommes' (2001b: 31); the prevalent form of communication, in addition to abbreviated physical descriptions, is limited to clichés such as the derisory 'CV' Houellebecq invents for his female persona 'Supersalope': 'J'aime me promener sans culotte' (33). ['men and online prostitutes'; 'I like to go out with no knickers on'.] Various men reply. When he changes identity to 'Sandrine', he finds the fictional attributes of this new character provoke considerable interest: 'chacun veut faire la connaissance de mes 22 ans et de mon slip brésilien' (34). ['they all want to get to know me, with my "22–years-old" and my "tanga briefs"'.] Beyond the small comedy produced by this virtual role-play, there is the sadness of the alienation declared by these attempts at contact: when Houellebecq logs on again as 'Sandrine', 'beaucoup de pauvres types m'envoient des messages pleins d'espoir: "Sandrine, tu es revenue? C'est toi, Sandrine?"' (36). ['lots of sad characters send me messages full of hope: "Sandrine, are you back online? Is that you, Sandrine?".]

Were they ever to make contact, these 'pauvres types' would doubtless be disappointed: the young, in Houellebecq's universe of brutal sexual competition, have so internalised the values of the market – and of its accomplice, pornography – that their consumerist embrace of serial pleasures without consequence renders any notion of more lasting or more tender emotional bonds utterly out of date. This is the unhappy discovery of Daniel, at the end of his period as the 47–year-old boyfriend of the gorgeous 20–something Esther in *La Possibilité d'une île*: Esther, and the whole of her generation, have no interest in love (2005: 340–1). As Daniel staggers past various instances of collective sexual activity at Esther's leaving party, the participants – including Esther – either reject him or ignore him. He ends up masturbating, quickly, by the swimming pool, near a woman who may or may not be aware of his presence. Group sex has now become just another form of amusement for enthusiastic consumers, complicit with the mechanisms of sexual selection and exclusion in the modern world, where 'on pouvait être échangiste, bi, trans, zoophile, SM, mais il était interdit d'être *vieux*' (213). ['you could be a swinger, bi, trans, zoo, into S&M, but it was forbidden to be *old*' (2006: 182).]

In Houellebecq's universe, the regulation of sexual relations on the model of the so-called free market has resulted in this world of sexual consumers, as brutally uncaring as they are happy-go-lucky. In terms of his presentation of group sex, this has two extreme but logical outcomes: the subculture of sadomasochism, and sex tourism, both of which are explored in *Plateforme*. When Michel and Valérie find themselves, in the company of a fashionable modern-art set, in an S&M club (called, with layers of self-consciousness, the *Bar-bar*), Valérie is horrified by the practices they find there. Their companions use two arguments to justify these activities: that the participants are consenting adults, and that human sexuality is essentially cruel. The first of these, advanced by a character named Géraldine, is clearly presented as the *doxa* of liberal capitalist democracy (and coincides, in fact, with Breillat's defence of the right to sexual humiliation, as quoted in Chapter 2, pp. 72–4, and Dustan's assertion of the autonomy of the sexual agent, as seen in Chapter 3): 'Si je suis un majeur consentant, reprit-elle, et que mon fantasme c'est de souffrir, d'explorer la dimension masochiste de ma sexualité, je ne vois pas au nom de quoi on pourrait m'en empêcher. On est en démocratie...' (2001a: 196). ['If I'm a consenting adult [...] and my fantasy is to suffer, to explore the masochistic part of my sexuality, I don't see any reason why anyone should try and stop me. We are living in a democracy...' (2003: 187–8).] The participants have freely consented to their humiliation, and among the rational actors of the marketplace, freedom of choice is all. Valérie – to whose arguments the narrative invariably gives its rhetorical support – rejects this argument: 'Je ne crois pas qu'on puisse *librement consentir* à l'humiliation et à la souffrance. Et même si c'est le cas, ça ne me paraît pas une raison suffisante' (195). ['I don't believe you can *freely consent* to humiliation and suffering. And even if you can, I don't think it's reason enough' (2003: 187).] In what appears to be an attempt to parody Bataille, the notion of the essential violence of human sexuality is put forward by the artist Betrand Bredane; it is denied (silently) by Michel, for whom such violence, while it may be a permanent part of human experience, has nothing to do with sexual pleasure (197). As Michel and Valérie take a taxi home, she expresses her incomprehension: 'Ce qui me fait peur là-dedans [...] c'est qu'il n'y a aucun contact physique. Tout le monde porte des gants, utilise des ustensiles. Jamais les peaux ne se touchent, jamais il n'y a un baiser, un frôlement ni une caresse. Pour moi, c'est exactement le contraire de la sexualité' (199). ['What scares me about it all [...] is that there's no physical contact. Everyone wears gloves, uses equipment. Skin never touches skin, there's never a kiss, a touch or a caress. For me, it's the very antithesis of sexuality' (2003: 191).] Michel agrees, and his commentary broadens the implications of this critique, suggesting that 'les adeptes du SM auraient vu dans leurs pratiques l'apothéose de la sexualité, sa forme ultime. Chacun y restait enfermé dans sa peau, pleinement livré à ses sensations d'être unique' (199). ['S&M enthusiasts would have seen their practices as the apotheosis of sexuality, its ultimate form. Each person remains trapped in his skin, completely given over to his feelings of individuality' (2003: 191).] But sexuality, in Houellebecq, has the remarkable virtue of offering moments of contact which rupture our late capitalist isolation (and the fact that they are never sustained only increases their pathos); and so sadomasochistic practice becomes, here, the ultimate expression of the alienation which has supposedly shattered western sexual relations, the lack of contact Valérie describes perfectly emblematic of the lonely, disjointed world of individualistic consumers.

It is hard to see here an adequate account of the world of sadomasochism, any full consideration of which would at least have to take in the thoughts of such as Foucault, Dustan, and Rémès as discussed in Chapter 3. But this is not Houellebecq's point. Sadomasochism is there partly to be briefly debated, but mostly for its allegorical function. The target is not just sexual mores, but sexual mores as *mise-en-abîme* of bigger social trends, in this case alienation. And the same is true of the much more extensive treatment provided by Houellebecq in *Plateforme* of the question of sex tourism. Again, the focus is really elsewhere: sex tourism is of interest because it allows Houellebecq to make points about the nature of a global economy organised according to the principles of consumer choice, supply and demand. But in this case, his usual ambivalence is more in evidence.[12]

Michel, narrator of *Plateforme*, is both a consumer and, later, a provider of sex tourism. His point of view is hardly neutral, therefore. Arguments concerning the economics and morality of sex tourism are set out as the text develops. It is denounced by a furious Josiane as a form of slavery, praised by Robert, an *habitué* (2001a: 78, 117–22). The moral framework on the basis of which it might be possible to construct a critique such as Josiane's is almost entirely absent; consideration is overwhelmingly given to the economic and sexual factors which make the trade possible. When Valérie asks Michel what makes Thai women more attractive than western women, he shows her the sales pitch of an agency arranging marriages between western men and Thai women, which celebrates what it presents as the traditional preferences of the latter over the excessive demands of western women (132–3). This is the first half of the market, as presented in *Plateforme*: the second half is provided by the economic factors. As Michel puts it, pitching the idea of officially organised sex tourism to Jean-Yves:

> d'un côté tu as plusieurs centaines de millions d'Occidentaux qui ont tout ce qu'ils veulent, sauf qu'ils n'arrivent plus à trouver de satisfaction sexuelle [...] De l'autre côté tu as plusieurs milliards d'individus qui n'ont rien, qui crèvent de faim [...] et qui n'ont plus rien à vendre que leur corps, et leur sexualité intacte. C'est simple, vraiment simple à comprendre: c'est une situation d'échange idéale. (252)

[you have several hundred million Westerners who have everything they could want but no longer manage to obtain sexual satisfaction [...] On the other hand, you have several billion people who have nothing, who are starving [...] and who have nothing left to sell except their bodies and their unspoiled sexuality. It's simple really simple to understand: it's an ideal trading opportunity. (2003: 242)]

The Thai economy is discussed (see for example 88), leaving the reader in no doubt that sex tourism is being presented as the response of a global market to an obvious potential relation of supply and demand.

Of course, this western demand has, ironically, been created in the first place by the extension of the consumerist values of the market to the field of sexuality. At which point, it is difficult to see the opinions of Michel the narrator as being simply those of his author, who barely misses an opportunity to lament this extension. But two difficulties remain. First, nothing in *Plateforme* provides any kind of adequate argument against those Michel is advancing. Given that no author is bound to espouse the positions of her narrator, however, this is a relatively insubstantial point. More awkward is that, just as in his use of the pornographic material he also condemns, Houellebecq inserts into his scenes of sex tourism moments of apparently genuine tenderness and happiness, which as ever are positively valorised. Twice, Michel enjoys wonderful encounters with Thai prostitutes (Oôn and Sin, respectively); in each case, he experiences both tremendous sexual pleasure and a warm, friendly exchange, in which he learns a little about the background and situation of the woman (see 52–4 and 123–6). His generous payment is met with enthusiastic thanks, reminding the reader of the economic underpinnings of the relation; but the tenderness remains. When Michel decides to treat the unhappy Lionel to such pleasure, there is no reason to suppose the text finds this idea particularly objectionable.

Houellebecq's approach to the sexual practices and representations with which his work engages is everywhere characterised by this ambivalence. And this ambivalence is ultimately programmed by his sentimentality. How miserable we are, he says, only able to find the love and happiness we seek through commercialised activities such as pornography and sex tourism. But at least we can find them there, he continues: and so they demand to be celebrated, in part because they temporarily interrupt the logic of these activities. But this celebration is, therefore, doomed to embrace exactly what it opposes. Houellebecq is a materialist who is infinitely depressed by materialism. Desperately clinging to the few shreds of genuine sentiment he can find, he finds himself – along with the rest of us, quite possibly – caught up in the machine responsible for the damage in the first place.

In Houellebecq's 'erotic film', *La Rivière*, beautiful young women pleasure each other in an idyllic environment, while phrases appear declaring that this generous, sensuous activity is recreating the species. These portentous snippets and the languorous pace create a distinctively contemporary tone, in which unavoidable irony is combined with what might be utter sincerity. This might just be soft porn with ambitions; it might be a kitsch reframing of these soft-porn images; it might be a genuine portrayal of a gynocentric utopia. In *La Possibilité d'une île*, Daniel says of his satirical sketches, 'je pratiquais l'ironie du double exact' (2005: 395) ['I was being doubly ironic' (2006: 343–4)]: ironically, no one else realised. Houellebecq's satirical intentions are clear, as are his targets and his cherished, tattered values. He is, as Metzidakis puts it, 'a postmodernist in agony' (2003: 141). As Houellebecq knows only too well, however, the only way he can affirm these values is to insert them as so many small interruptions within the materialism that has all but destroyed them. This means, crucially, that the values in question can no longer be thought of as transcending this materialism: rather, they find themselves entangled with it. When utopia is no longer available as the end point of an ultimately eschatological progressive narrative (all such narratives having supposedly sold themselves out to the individualism of the so-called free market), it can only be configured as an attempt at withdrawal, a sidestep, an interruption, a puncture – a kind of utopia under erasure. Discussing this question in relation to *La Rivière* in Edinburgh in October 2005, Houellebecq pointed out that in this work, he had created a pornographic film in which the principal body part filmed is the face. Somewhere between the reductive body of pornography, and the supposed nobility of the human face, lies Houellebecq's unrepresentable, implosive utopia.[13] But if utopia is only conceivable as a puncture, or as under erasure, then any denunciation of all the misery that surrounds this utopia may well find itself also punctured, semi-effaced, irretrievably in hock to this hegemonic misery. The kind of internal, irreducible opposition to the world he still – just about – associates with the literary certainly does count among the distinctive aims of Houellebecq's work, and deserves to be recognised as such. Whether this aim can ever be said to be realised in this work, however – indeed, whether such an aim can be realised at all in the midst of what is trumpeted as the hegemonic victory of consumer capitalism – is less clear. In the middle of Houellebecq's grim, commercialised, materialistic world – which may well also be ours – there remains, then, the possibility of an island. As every tourist knows, however, the only means we have of reaching this island may be in the process of destroying it for good.

Notes

1　The film in question, *La Rivière* (2001), was broadcast by Canal Plus in 2002, and presents a soft-core bucolic idyll, peopled exclusively by classically beautiful women engaged in remaking the world and the species in a life of generous sensuality.

2　Houellebecq's cultural significance is lucidly presented in Abecassis 2000. A helpful record of Houellebecq's presence in the media (and much more) may be found at www.houellebecq.info.

3　See Cruickshank (2003, 2006, and forthcoming) whose analyses have had a decisive influence on this discussion; and Morrey 2004.

4　Including Arrabal, *Houellebecq* 2005; Demonpion 2005; Naulleau 2005; Patricola 2005. On these debates in the *rentrée littéraire* of 2005, see the *Magazine littéraire*, 445 (September 2005), 26–8.

5　See www.prix-litteraires.net/goncourt.php, accessed 25 November 2005.

6　See Abecassis 2000, and Wassenaar 2001.

7　A handy guide to these occasions is provided for interested readers by Deleu (2002: 114). See also Schuerewegen 2004.

8　On the Houellebecquian penis, see Reader 2006.

9　This is an old argument in discussions of literary pornography, best encapsulated in debates over how to read Bataille's *Histoire de l'œil*, in which the literalism of Andrea Dworkin (1981) finds itself opposed by the contextual subtlety of Susan Rubin Suleiman (1995). For a defence of a kind of literality, see Crowley 2004.

10　For Houellebecq's comments on the pernicious effects of the *second degré* on contemporary communication (effects to which he suggests, as mentioned above, that literature might be singularly resistant), see 1998a: 72–5.

11　Critics who resist this residual structure include Baggesgaard 2006 and Hussey 2006, both of whom equate the residuality in question with a distinction between literary artifice and deep sincerity, before drawing opposite conclusions: for Baggesgaard, the affirmation of residuality sees this artifice as just a deceitful veil, and so equates to an excessive criticism of Houellebecq; for Hussey, the very same affirmation equates to an excessive celebration of this very same artifice. This might suggest that it equates to neither of these positions, but rather describes Houellebecq's characteristic ability to invite and maintain them both.

12 On sex tourism in Houellebecq, see Ní Loingsigh 2005.

13 Thanks to Andrew Hussey for this point, made in the same discussion.

7

The uses and abuses of children: thinking infantile eroticism

Christopher Dare suggests that 'the idea of the sexual abuse of children, usually by an adult or older child, is so assaulting that all of us want immediately to evacuate it and push it away so we don't have to think about it' (Minsky 1998: 167). The extent of the trauma inflicted is literally 'unthinkable', in that for children and adults alike, it can neither be mentally contained nor symbolically processed. The concept of child pornography is equally abhorrent, equally emotive, and furthermore subject to stringent laws; its stigma in society is such that few would openly admit to a desire to see or read such material. And yet, thinking about the relationship between children and sexuality, often in shocking and graphic ways, is intrinsic to so many of the millennium cross-over texts that were part of, or followed in the wake of, the *nouveaux barbares*. Time and again abuse to young children crops up in the texts of Houellebecq and Despentes, while early sexual fantasies and experiences are essential to the artworks of Nimier and Breillat. The question of infantile sexuality has recently provoked in France a whole range of fictional and life writing texts that explore the troubled, damaged past of the central protagonist, subject to bewildering abuse and still seeking some form of redemption or reconciliation, the works of Christine Angot offering something of a paradigm here. Many texts treat this issue sensitively and creatively, but some, in their use of graphic sexual detail (Angot once again exemplary) blur the borderlines between a detailed and provocative exposure of child abuse, and a collapse into the pornographic. On the furthest end of this scale, there have also been some notably controversial texts, such as Nicolas Jones-Gorlin's unpalatable *Rose Bonbon*, whose supposedly sympathetic portrait of a paedophile provoked a huge outcry. Whether it be a question of premature sexual initiation, or the exploration of traumatic abuse, whether children are used as complicit accomplices or unwilling witnesses, whether art exploits adolescent fantasies or underage nightmares, contemporary French writing has displayed a fascination with infantile eroticism that is ambiguous, ethically uncertain, pervasive and utterly persistent.

What makes this fascination ever more complex is that since 2001, France has for the first time marshalled a significant anti-pornography campaign – focused on controlling the transmission of pornographic material on television – in the name of 'protection de la jeunesse'. The need to protect children provides a persuasive standpoint from which to mount a campaign since, as Ruwen Ogien argues, previous attempts had concentrated on the inherent degradation to women, or the offense dealt to certain religions, reasons that affected only a particular category of the population. In those circumstances, 'il n'y avait pas de "scandale public", pas de "problème de société". L'attaque n'aurait eu d'impact qu'à partir du moment où elle se serait faite au nom de la "protection de la jeunesse", c'est-à-dire d'une raison *universelle*' (Ogien 2003: 5). ['there was no "public scandal", no "social problem". The campaign only had an impact once it was mounted in the name of "the protection of youth", in other words, for a universal reason'.] But beyond this philosophical judgement, there exists also a more political reason; Ogien points out that 'c'est, curieusement, la gauche dite "progressiste" qui s'est emparé du thème de la "protection de la jeunesse", auquel "l'opinion publique" est manifestement très sensible' (2003: 6). ['curiously it's the supposedly "progressive" left which has taken hold of the theme of "the protection of youth", towards which "public opinion" is manifestly sensitive'.] One evident manifestation of this current sensitivity was the scandal provoked by the appearance of Jones-Gorlin's text. We can gauge the strength of public opinion in France by the widespread moral outrage that met the publication of *Rose Bonbon*, with two children's rights groups, *L'Enfant bleu* and *La Fondation pour l'enfance*, calling for it to be removed from the shelves. Indeed, the publisher, Gallimard, did bow to legal threats, issuing the book with a warning on the jacket and then deciding not to resupply bookstores. Jones-Gorlin protested his astonishment at the strength of the reaction his novel provoked, not in terms of the issues it raised, but in the personalised nature of the attack. In an interview he described his experience as one akin to persecution: 'Je me suis terré chez moi ... je pense qu'il y aurait eu un vrai lynchage médiatique si je m'étais montré ... Les premiers jours ont vraiment tenu de l'hystérie' (Bontour 2002). ['I went to ground at my home... I think there would have been a real media lynching if I'd shown myself... The first few days it was like a kind of hysteria'.] The author received unexpected support, however, from the League of Human Rights, whose spokesperson for culture, Agnès Tricoire, argued that fact should be understood as separate from fiction, and that just as detective novels did not promote murder, so texts dealing with paedophilia did not equate to an apologia for child abuse. Beyond this defense of narrative, however, Tricoire added that the issue was particularly problematic because nowadays 'L'enfant est le nouveau sacré, la nouvelle cause religieuse' (Joye 2002). ['The child is the new form of the sacred, the new religious cause'.] This curious remark, and the scandal from which it arose, shows how the cultural concept of the child is as conflicted as it has ever been, defended and idealised but simultaneously used and exploited, politically, culturally and aesthetically.

The conflict seems to arise between a culture that demonstrates an intensely emotional response to protecting the idealised vulnerability of children, and cultural artworks that seek to represent with distanced accuracy, exactly what occurs at the heart of the traumatic and abusive encounter. Emma Wilson, writing on contemporary films that deal with sensitive issues surrounding children suggests that: 'Their aim appears not to be to order or organize experience, to establish values or rules, but rather to represent and respond to its mess and pain. This levelling, and suspension of judgement, may be disturbing in a territory where views on right and wrong have tended to be entrenched and absolute' (Wilson 2003: 9). This is particularly the case with contemporary French texts and films that cite the pornographic. While the images and scenarios portrayed are often direct quotations of those whose original purpose was to excite and arouse, they are repeatedly placed in contexts and perspectives that negate the possibility of arousal or else use it to trouble and disquiet the reader or spectator. These texts and films do not construct their own moral universes, preferring to allow disturbing images to speak for themselves. Inevitably, then, such works that use or focus on the sexual experiences of children tread on difficult ethical ground, raising the question of whether it is possible to represent children in this way without sliding into an aestheticisation of the horrific, or encroaching upon morally dubious territory.

While there is a current trend in art towards an amoral consideration of sexual issues, there is also a quasi-obsession within popular culture, promoted essentially by the media, surrounding sexual crimes against children. It is not surprising that Jones-Gorlin's text received such hostile attention when we consider the way that contemporary concerns about paedophilia in France are explored in Cathy Bernheim's curiously hybrid text, *Dors, ange amer*. In this text the author's fictionalisation of her own abused childhood and a dialogue with an eponymous fantasy child, Posthume, sit either side of an alarming collection of statistics and news reports. Bernheim produces a range of figures depicting the rapidly increased number of children at risk, as well as the mounting charges of rape and abuse.[1] Her récit is particularly interested in the case of a teacher, M. K., who abused his pupils throughout his career, but was only denounced when one committed suicide, releasing a deluge of over sixty further charges from fellow sufferers. This case, however, is only one among hundreds brought to prominence in a culture that is now highly sensitised to child abuse. The narrator claims that in one day's paper alone, she reads 'un article consacré aux "7 disparues de l'Yonne". Dans la même page, "Les petits chanteurs accusent les responsables d'une chorale", et un autre titre annonce: "Nice, prof de gym soupçonné de pédophilie"' (Bernheim 2005: 125). ['an article on the "Seven missing in the Yonne". On the same page: "Young singers accuse their choir leader" and another headline proclaims "In Nice, PE teacher suspected of paedophilia"'.] For Bernheim, it seems that this newly acquired sexual conscience has come too late for the victims of M. K. 'Qui parlait de pédophilie à l'époque?'(2005: 128) ['Who spoke about paedophilia at that time?'] one witness asks, and Bernheim finds this comment apt. Yet the excessive newspaper reportage seems to insist that nowadays *no one stops talking* about paedophilia, that the extent of the current media obsession with children at risk might itself be a suspicious response to the problem of child abuse. Bernheim's book is a cautious if sentimental approach to the consequences of childhood trauma, but it embraces the brutality of the *fait divers* without critique, without wondering whether the journalistic appropriation of such trauma is not itself potentially conflicted. The paradoxical media display of violations to child privacy remains unquestioned. If artistic representations of child sexuality are perpetually threatened by a collapse into the exploitative, what are we to make of lurid and sensationalised accounts of sexual attacks on children that risk becoming as emotionally inflammatory as the pornography they would undoubtedly seek to censor? Where to draw a line, then, between healthy and unhealthy, responsible and irresponsible, accounts of child sexual abuse?

This is not germane to France alone, but seems instead to be pervasive throughout the contemporary western world. James Kincaid, an American professor of literature, has produced controversial research on the media representations of child molestation cases, suggesting that while contemporary American society genuinely cares about the mental health of the children concerned, 'we also care about maintaining the particular erotic vision of children that is putting them in this position in the first place'(Kincaid 1998: 246). Kincaid details this particular erotic vision by explaining that from the nineteenth century onwards, children have been equated with a number of 'negative attribute[s]', such as liberty, purity and innocence, which have 'become more and more firmly attached to what was characterized as sexually desirable' (1998: 247). He suggests that, '[t]he physical makeup of the child has been translated into mainstream images of the sexually and materially alluring. We are told to look like children, if we can and for as long as we can', with the result that, 'we are instructed to crave that which is forbidden' (1998: 247–8). Nicolas Jones-Gorlin, too, claimed that one of the main targets of his novel was 'l'obsession du jeunisme, la peur de vieillir' (Bontour 2002). ['the obsession with youth culture, the fear of growing old'.] Such a viewpoint remains, and perhaps not surprisingly, antipathetic to the current media climate, however. Kincaid's book received very hostile reviews in the UK; the *Sunday Times* declared him to be 'a passionate champion of paedophilia' (Carey 1993) and the *Daily Mail* ran an article headed '"Paedophile Book" Should Be Banned' (Verity 1994).

There are, then, any number of conflicting perspectives on child sexuality that help to make the issue hopelessly entangled. On the one hand we have what would seem a perfectly reasonable and ethical desire to protect children from sexual abuse by their elders. Yet the excessive representation of the occurrences and experiences of sexual abuse risks promoting the exploitative climate it would seek to condemn. Furthermore, such representations collide with a culture that privileges youth as a desirable commodity. On the other hand, commentators like Ruwen Ogien have asked exactly what it is that we wish to protect children from, when they themselves must explore and understand their sexuality if they are to make a healthy transition to adulthood. Ogien points to a fundamental confusion in French society over the capabilities of the young adolescent: 'A 13 ans, on n'est pas assez "responsable" pour voir des films porno, mais on l'est assez pour aller en prison' (2003: 132) ['At 13 the child is not sufficiently "responsible" to watch a porn film, but is considered responsible enough to go to prison'], and a lack of research to indicate that what amounts to fleeting glimpses of pornographic material will have any long-term deleterious effects. In conclusion he proposes that the need to protect children from graphic images of sexuality arises from the internal and misplaced projections of adults onto children that do not in fact protect them so much as imply a criminality to their desire: 'On présente les jeunes comme des victimes, alors qu'en vérité on les traite comme des coupables' (2003: 140). ['Young people are presented as victims, while in truth they are treated as criminals'.] How then can we possibly think of the sexuality of children? How can we distinguish between acceptable sexual experience in the child and degrading abuse?

One way to approach this issue is via Adam Phillips' original psychoanalytic perspective on the kind of sexuality that inhabits the child. Rather than constructing a retrospective fiction of sexual development, Phillips explores the mindset of the child 'whom psychoanalysis has mislaid', and this child possesses 'an astonishing capacity for pleasure and, indeed, the pleasures of interest, with an unwilled relish of sensuous experience which often unsettles adults who like to call it affection... I would rather call it a kind of ecstasy of opportunity' (1998: 21). Phillips draws on Freud here, recalling his understanding of children as hedonists whose immense curiosity is akin to a form of appetite. For Freud, this appetite required satisfaction via fantasies and stories, and arose once that child had been displaced by the birth of a sibling. In this sense, the curiosity inspired by such ungraspable acts of displacement is a sign of all that the child has lost; loss that has been transformed into a recognition of the necessity of knowledge. Phillips points out that subsequent theorists – Lacan, Klein, Winnicott – have focused almost exclusively on formative losses and the vulnerability and helplessness they imply. But for Freud, these earliest forays into curiosity and hypothesis creation also held their compensations: 'It is the child's always paradoxical resilience – the inventions born of apparent insufficiency, the refusal of common sense, of the facts of life – that Freud is taken by' (1998: 19). Phillips argues that the insistence on the child as longing to overcome in teleological and rational fashion the unknown that surrounds him is too easily co-opted into an overly adult perspective of progress: 'The child – unlike the adult – is not merely compensating for not being an adult, or for not being self-sufficient. Because there is no purpose to the child's life other than the pleasure of living it. It is not the child, in other words, who believes in something called development' (1998: 21). That childish curiosity, which is, Phillips suggests, always to do with bodies, is a form of intensely pleasurable interest. All subsequent education, in its insistence on telling the child that it really wishes to know about other things, provides a kind of overbearing and relentless distraction. 'This was the real scandal of what Freud called infantile sexuality. Not that it is a (thwarted) warm-up for adult life – and therefore that children are prototypically sexual creatures – but that infantile sexuality with its sole aim of "the gaining of particular kinds of pleasure" is the fundamental paradigm for erotic life' (1998: 26). In other words, children represent the scandal of erotic fecklessness, sexuality unfettered from procreation, released from the demands of community, explorative, inventive and amoral. Phillips is drawing specifically from Freud's paper 'Civilized sexual morality and modern nervous illness', in which Freud details the cost of abandoning such creative sexual freedom and accepting the sublimations of civilisation in its place. For Freud this development brought about 'an increase of anxiety about life and a fear of death', which leaves the subject in a condition that Phillips describes as 'radically imperilled' (1998: 25).

This alternative, and subversive, vision of expansive sexuality in childhood offers significant food for thought. We can see from this version how Oedipal (and legal) barriers protect both children and adults from succumbing to the dangers of free-floating interest. We can also see written into adult accounts of child development both a hopeless nostalgia for the loss of innocent sexual interest, and also, arguably, a directly proportional insistence on linear development to steer the child towards the uncertain compensations of sublimation. What might the outcome be if we were to speculate on the combina-tion of envy and anxiety that might inhabit the adult's retrospective perspective on infantile eroticism? We might at least identify in such a perspective the projection of overly grown-up responses to graphic sexuality, alongside the projection of nostalgic over-evaluations of childish forms of fulfilment. It is not surprising that protecting children from (their own) sexuality becomes such an emotive and fraught issue. However, we can usefully balance the picture given to us by Adam Phillips, with Leo Bersani's rereading of infantile sexuality, again via a creative return to Freud.

Bersani reconsiders Freud's *Three Essays on Sexuality* and *Beyond the Pleasure Principle* with particular attention to the will that children manifest to repeat and even intensify certain unpleasurable experiences. What would it mean to say, Bersani asks, 'that in sexuality, pleasure is somehow distinct from satisfaction, even identical to a kind of pain?' Bersani's answer is based on centralising masochism within the structure of sexuality. He explains that: 'Freud appears to be moving towards the position that the pleasurable, unpleasurable tension of sexual excitement occurs when the body's "normal" range of sensation is exceeded, and when the organization of the self is momentarily disturbed by sensations or affective processes somehow "beyond" those compatible with psychic organization' (1986: 38). Sexuality, in other words, is borne out of an excess of stimuli, out of an event that arouses the self intensely but cannot be understood within the usual frames of reference. Bersani goes on to say that 'From this perspective, the distinguishing feature of infancy would be its *susceptibility to the sexual*. The polymorphously pervasive nature of infantile sexuality would be a function of the child's vulnerability to being shattered into sexuality' (1986: 38). Thought on these lines, Bersani can make his paradoxical claim that 'masochism serves life'; it is an 'evolutionary conquest' whereby the developing self learns to tolerate a period of shattering stimuli for which we are defenceless by finding what we will go on to call sexual pleasure within it. Sexuality would therefore be, according to Bersani, 'a condition of broken negotiations with the world, a condition in which others merely set off the self-shattering mechanisms of masochistic *jouissance*' (1986: 41). If we consider the theories of Bersani and Phillips alongside one another, it might be possible to identify two sexual currents within infantile eroticism; one an 'innocent' creative and explorative pleasure that is linked to the corporeal, and which is increasingly diminished and replaced by education; the other, a developmental tool that translates the possibility of corporeal pleasure into excessive experience, which must be increasingly incorporated into the child's growing subjectivity.

Infantile sexuality would thus be set on a trajectory from hedonis-tically-interested curiosity in the external world towards a learnt, defensive transformation of unbearable externality into internalised pleasure. In short, the child's own experience of sexuality is one of outwardly engaged pleasure being met by brutalising and excessive external forces. From this perspective, we can see how the narrative of child abuse is so fascinating, as it can be seen to symbolise the cross-over point, from infantile eroticism to adult eroticism. It also indicates the extent of the gulf that divides the two. It seems that the difference between the sexuality of adults and that of children is perpetually underemphasised, and that it is indeed from their confu-sion that authentic abuse results.

We need to complicate this picture of infantile sexuality further by situating it within a highly particular contemporary culture. Since the 1960s western civilization has become increasingly sexually permissive, with single mothers, contraception, abortion, homosex-uality and gay marriage becoming commonplace events. Artistic representation has kept step, if not anticipated, such a revolution, with the graphically sexual aesthetic practices of the 1990s onwards presenting a kind of pinnacle of visibility and transparency. The disintegration of paternal authority, the constraining 'no' that instils the first, paradigmatic moral law, has resulted, according to Slavoj Žižek, in a postmodern sexuality that is not the erotic utopia antici-pation might have projected; instead, the situation today is increas-ingly fragile and disillusioned:

> What is undermined today, in our post-Oedipal permissive societies, is sexual jouissance as the foundational 'passionate attachment', as the desired/prohibited focal point around which our life revolves. (From this perspective, even the figure of the paternal 'sexual harasser' looks like a nostalgic image of someone who is still fully able to enjoy 'it'.) Once again the superego has accomplished its task successfully: the direct injunc-tion 'Enjoy!' is a much more effective way to hinder the subject's access to enjoyment than the explicit Prohibition which sustains the space for transgression. (1999: 367)

It is intriguing that Žižek should draw attention to the narrative of abuse as providing, in these fraught contemporary times, a genuine family romance, or at least, a fable of sexual success. He goes on to say that 'The utopia of a new post-psychoanalytic subjectivity engaged in the pursuit of new idiosyncratic bodily pleasures beyond sexuality has reverted to its opposite: what we are getting instead is disinterested boredom – and it seems that the direct intervention of pain (sado-masochistic sexual practices) is the only remaining path to the intense experience of pleasure' (1999: 367). Žižek's remarks can be aligned here to the split between Phillips's and Bersani's theories which we outlined earlier. What is lost in modern society is precisely the sexual curiosity of childlike eroticism, defined and heightened by paternal prohibition, and all that can come to fill its place is excessively masochistic sexuality; the learnt, defensive transformation of overwhelming stimulation into something resembling pleasure.

We can see these dynamics in play in the contemporary texts that explore child sexuality. Narratives of child abuse, alongside a general cultural and aesthetic fascination for the intense experiences of childhood, tap into an ambivalent climate in which the exploitation of infantile sexuality is an ethical outrage, but also a rare experience of genuine, intense sexual excitement. We can see this ambivalence depicted and explored from varying perspectives across a number of texts published since 1990. One particularly clear example of this trend is Caroline Thivel's *Une Chambre après l'autre* (2001). In this narrative, written from the child's perspective in simple, limpid prose, Cécile is abducted from school one day by her estranged father and taken to spend several weeks with him in an isolated chalet in the mountains. This event is the realisation of a fantasy for Cécile who, uncomfortable with her mother's bitterness and distress, longs for her idealised father. However, the time she spends with Richard is equally uncomfortable as the generation gap between them is bridged awkwardly by the romanticised love they have for each other. With nothing to do and nowhere to go, the relationship they both long for takes on inappropriate overtones. Richard does not know what to say to his child and Cécile is unable to formulate the questions she wants to ask. For Cécile is represented as consumed by a curiosity about her father that she does not know how to appease: 'Elle a honte de sa curiosité parce qu'elle sais que Richard est incapable de la satisfaire' (Thivel 2001: 51) ['She is ashamed of her curiosity because she knows that Richard is incapable of satisfying it'], and which translates into the insidiously dangerous will to please the other. Richard, however, sees in his daughter the image of his wife when they first met, and transfers onto her the frustrated desires that he has not managed to negotiate in the wake of their separation. Incest is the inevitable outcome, and is described in terms designed to inhabit the limited comprehension of the child. 'Cécile a enfin eu le courage de le regarder lui, son père, puis le petit animal à l'ombre entre ses jambes. D'étonnement elle a lâché la chose dressée. La main de Richard a récupéré celle de Cécile et l'a ramenée docile au point crucial' (2001: 75–6). ['Cécile finally finds the courage to look at this man, her father, then at the small animal hiding in shadow between his legs. Surprised, she lets go of the erect thing. Then Richard's hand has caught Cécile's and brought it back to the crucial spot.'] We can see here how Cécile's curiosity is rewarded with more than she bargained for, but this moment of transparent confusion at the heart of their sexual encounter is paradigmatic of their entire relationship, structured as it is around a disastrous collision between a child's loving, seeking but unformulated curiosity, and an adult's misplaced, projected erotic desires.

The rest of the narrative follows the trajectory of Cécile's subsequent sexual development, which is oddly familiar within the context of postmodern erotic texts. Far from feeling horrified by what has occurred between herself and her father, 'Cécile l'en aime d'autant plus' (2001: 89). ['Cécile loves him even more for it'.] Richard, by contrast, is consumed with guilt and on the verge of breakdown. They end up in a car crash that has as its consequence their definitive separation. Abandoned and uncomprehending, unable to articulate what happened, still less to find comfort and reassurance in her mother, Cécile is forced to live on her own insufficient resources. Once old enough to be independent, she shuns romantic love but embarks on a series of loveless and damaging sexual encounters that bring her no pleasure but express only her sense of guilt and self-disgust. The terms in which this shallow, self-abusing sexual life is described recall, with uncanny accuracy, the sexual encounters that structure the works of writers like Clothilde Escalle and filmmakers like Catherine Breillat. Male *jouissance* is observed detachedly as something bestial and displeasing: 'Elle se sent ridicule, déteste le rictus de plaisir, le râle de l'autre' (2001: 112) ['She feels ridiculous, despising the rictus of pleasure, the other's groans'], while female pleasure is absented, the act provoked only by the compulsion to couple: 'Elle a agi come un robot, une fille de joie, c'était plus fort qu'elle et maintenant elle regrette' (2001: 115). ['She has acted like a robot, a tart; it was stronger than she was and now she regrets it.'] Divorced from any kind of sentimentalised context, the focus is entirely on the sexual act itself in true pornographic style.

However, significant differences exist between Thivel's heroine and those in the works of Breillat, Escalle, *et al.* Not least that Cécile acknowledges, however hazily, that her behaviour is unhealthy and symptomatic of her own internal damage. She both seeks and fears a conventional romantic attachment in order to effect a cure, which is indeed the happy outcome of the novel. The protagonists of some of the *nouveaux barbares*, by contrast, revel in their masochistic, compulsive sexuality, exploring limit fantasies as a new form of transgression. We can read into both representations a cultural obsession with the erotic as something potentially traumatic. The privileging of (female) protagonists who explore a radical form of pornographic eroticism that focuses on the act and leaves their own subjectivity opaque and unknown, can be read through Hal Foster's understanding of the contemporary subject of trauma as: '*evacuated and elevated at once*' (1996: 168). In psychoanalytic terms the subject of trauma is radically absent from the event, evacuated from their abilities to comprehend and register. In popular culture, however, Foster describes how 'trauma is treated as an event that guarantees the subject, and in this psychologistic register the subject, however disturbed, rushes back as witness, testifier, survivor' (1996: 168). This definition seems entirely apt for these female protagonists who carry the narrative viewpoint in and through their own radical absence from the intense event. What are we to make, then, of Thivel's novel, which recontextualises postmodern sexuality in the framework of child abuse? Does the novel suggest that contemporary images of female sexuality are simply unhealthy, derived from a cultural negativity that is pervasive if unacknowledged?

Rather than read the narrative as a form of cultural reproach (and there seems indeed to be no sign in the novel of such a critique) we could instead return productively here to Žižek's recognition of 'the growing collapse of symbolic efficiency' in contemporary culture, the loss of a secure and defining sense of paternal limit and prohibition, that results in what Žižek terms '*a big Other that actually exists, in the Real*, not merely as a symbolic fiction' (1999: 362). The Oedipus complex traditionally stands for the supreme moment of transition from the real (in terms of a symbiotic attachment to the maternal body) to the symbolic (a recognition that relations must now take place at the distancing level of words rather than corporeal interactions). Žižek draws our attention here to a contemporary transference of power away from the symbolic realm, thanks to a generalised weakening of the moral order, into a personalised real; hence his term 'big Other', which stands for the belief that someone, somewhere is still ultimately in control, managing law and order in what might otherwise seem to be a chaotic universe, enhancing the lure of conspiracy theories among other things. For Žižek, one pertinent example of this return to the real is false memory syndrome, where the figure of the father is seen as an actual seducer of his daughters, rather than 'the embodiment of a symbolic fiction'. Žižek highlights the obstinacy with which the father is understood to have 'really' abused his children as indicative of a cultural need to construct an 'obscene, invisible power structure' (1999: 362) in the absence of a visible, dependable source of authority. In other words, perverse and haunting as such a thought may be, there is a paradoxical security in the belief that free-floating sexual anxiety can be tied down to the real experience of abuse. As such these texts can be understood as differing responses to the same problematic of uncertain, destabilised sexual relations in modern society, with Breillat and Escalle embracing that uncertainty and pushing it to the limit, while Thivel 'solves' it, constructing a narrative of psychic convalescence that romanticizes both the cause and the outcome of abuse.

For all its reconciliatory tone, however, we have to ask how healthy such a narrative may be in its representation of the sexual encounter between father and child as both formatively, overwhelmingly erotic and also an event which can be tamed and overcome. Far more disconcerting and uncomfortable is the work of Christine Angot, which constructs a series of structurally complex texts around the foundational motif of incest. Angot's work belongs to the increasingly popular genre of autofiction, a hybrid practice of textuality that produces an excessive but internally troubled form of autobiography. Marion Sadoux claims that: 'One of the great merits of Angot's works is the way they question, albeit indirectly, the nature of literature in an age in which intimacy, privacy and personal histories are so relentlessly mediatised and exploited, and real lives are packaged, performed and televised for a mass audience' (2002: 174). Angot is working at the heart of contemporary culture's desire for transparency and visibility, for the instant intimacy that can (even if fallaciously) seem to be on offer in the pornographic, and this by way of her own sexual scandals. Yet the incest that is so repeatedly evoked by Angot is never dealt with in a transparent way (although the sexual acts in her texts are often graphic in nature), nor can we make any simple equation between the events in the text and Angot's own personal history, even though we are repeatedly and insistently invited to do so. The figure of incest becomes instead a lure, a trap into which the voyeuristic contemporary reader is encouraged to fall. As Cata and DalMolin argue, 'Elle les appâte avec leur propre désir de faire l'expérience livresque de la violence du sexe ... jusqu'au bout du roman où elle dévoile enfin ce qui n'était qu'un piège et une illusion créée par l'indéniable force du désir pornographique qui anime la culture, d'aujourd'hui' (Cata and DalMolin 2004: 90). ['She entices her readers with their own desire to have a literary experience of sexual violence ... right up to the end of the novel where she finally reveals that it was nothing but a trap and an illusion created by the irrevocable force of pornographic desire which animates contemporary culture'.] Much like Cécile in *Une Chambre après l'autre*, however, the reader's sexual curiosity is met within Angot's text by more than he or she may have bargained for. Instead of a glimpse into an eroticised, transgressive sexual space, the reader is forced into a closer relationship with Angot's damaged and aggressive psyche than is comfortable.

The damage is manifest in Angot's extraordinary sentence structure, where excessive punctuation splits phrases into tiny segments, while the narrative thread leaps between different topics and concepts without explanation or connection. Angot's writing practice in *L'Inceste* manages to be neither metaphoric nor metonymic; at best it may be described as palimpsestic, whereby each thought expressed textually by Angot's stream of consciousness evokes others that lie beneath it in a way that suggests analogy without actually producing it. Angot herself has a more pertinent explanation for it: 'J'atteins la limite, avec la structure mentale que j'ai, *incestueuse*, je mélange tout, ça a des avantages, les connexions, que les autres ne font pas, mais trop c'est trop comme on dit, c'est la limite' (1999: 91). ['I reach the limit, with this mental structure that I have, incestuous, I mix everything up, but that has its advantages; I make connections that others don't, but too much, it's too much, as they say, it's the limit'.] Cata and DalMolin suggest that Angot's work 'calque de façon performative l'écriture de l'inceste sur l'expérience de l'inceste' (2004: 86). ['translates literally, in performative fashion, the writing of incest into the experience of incest'.] The readerly struggle to follow Angot's tortuous prose (watched over it would seem by the narrator herself) leads to a profound engagement with a damaged subjectivity that lacks any sense of *pudeur*, and which leaves the reader without the protection of formal symbolic restraint.

L'Inceste recounts the brief but intense homosexual relationship the narrator had, which was marked by profound ambivalence. It then returns to the past to recall her experience of incest, which lasted until her mid-twenties. Fundamentally, the text revolves around the criminalisation of desire. Whether it be Angot's desire for her lesbian lover, or her desire to explain her sexuality to her young daughter, Léonore, or the reader's desire to know the 'truth' of a text, desire is represented as excessive, damaging and misplaced, satisfied always at an unacceptable cost of violence, in one form or another, to others. We can read into this a formative experience of desire-as-destructive that recalls Adam Phillips' quotation of Freud: 'The sexual behaviour of a human being often lays down the pattern for all his other modes of reacting to life' (1998: 25). Furthermore, the consequences – the aggressive attacks the narrator launches into lovers and readers alike – can equally be explained by Christopher Dare's understanding of certain patterns of behaviour instilled by underage sexual abuse. He suggests that 'the child's shame turns into blame and then may manifest itself in a life of living out the grudge in destructive retribution on others' (Minsky 1998: 167). Or as Angot's lover, Marie-Christine expresses it, 'tu massacres les autres, parce que tu as été massacrée' (1999: 125). ['you massacre other people because you've been massacred'.] Curiously, this text is not about drawing the reader to an understanding of the effects of child abuse; for all its structural opacity, it remains consistently lucid and insightful on Angot's own psychological difficulties. Instead its aim is more concerned with disquieting the reader and troubling the always already intimate relationship between reader and narrator (encouraged to be indistinguishable from the author in modern, trauma-obsessed times). In its linguistic complexities and its claim to offer an unmediated experience of sexual violence, the text plays with the power relations between author and reader, performing the abuse of textual authority on its gullible, because curious, audience. Hence the readerly sense of disorientation when, after a lengthy passage detailing the painful aftermath of her affair, Angot writes that 'Ecrire, c'est peut-être ne faire que ça, montrer la grosse merde en soi. Bien sûr que non. Vous êtes prêts à croire n'importe quoi' (1999: 177). ['Writing is perhaps nothing other than that; showing the great pile of shit inside oneself. But of course it's not. You're ready to believe anything.'] The innocence of the reader is at stake here, the transaction with a text that promises the revelation of absolute truth. Of course, such a reader may well be naïve, if not disingenuous, but the point is to show that incest occurs in all manner of relationships. The eager curiosity of the reader, a curiosity that could easily cross the borderline into appropriative, unethical voyeurism, is repeatedly shown to be seeking an intimacy with the subject of the narrative that is both inappropriate and open to abuse. Angot turns the tables on the erotically questing desire of the reader to know sexual secrets, meeting the reader's curiosity with painful brutality. For the reader who pruriently wishes to know about incest, Angot is ready to offer the textual equivalent.

Of all the paradoxical, conflicted erotic figures that structure postmodern pornographic texts, the figure of incest can be understood as one of the most excessive. Angot's text is uncompromising in its flaunting of incestuous relationships; there can be nothing more intriguing at the heart of the sexual confession than illicit childhood seductions, and at the same time seduction equals abuse, the immeasurable, unthinkable damage wrought upon society's most vulnerable members that can distort sexual experience for the remainder of a lifetime. The texts by Angot and Thivel, despite their differences, represent sexual abuse alongside its severe consequences, installing an ethical perspective within texts that are nevertheless ambivalent about the eroticism inherent in father–daughter relationships. Some of the texts that have been published recently are less coy about exploiting graphic scenarios of underage sex for their erotic power, however, notably the much reviled and highly controversial *Rose Bonbon*. Yet there have been other texts that have slipped beneath the radar of child protection, even though they contain material that might well be considered morally dubious or, even, from some points of view, provocative and offensive. The significant distinction between texts that emphasise an ethical dimension and those that quite blatantly exploit child sexuality would appear to be a couple of year's difference in the age of the (girl) child protagonist. As soon as a child – and in these texts the child is always female – has entered what might be considered adolescence it is notable how the tone of the writing alters to become more salacious. It is also notable that the authors of such eroticised texts tend to be male, as opposed to the female-authored texts of child abuse.

One text of quite self-evident child pornography, first published in 1987, is Jean-Pierre Enard's *Contes à faire rougir les petits chaperons*. In this novel, again issuing from the respectable publishing house of Gallimard just as *Rose Bonbon* did, a male narrator describes a series of pornographic encounters between himself, his girlfriend, the maid and his niece, Alice, a nubile and sexually curious 13–year-old. Essentially this novel provides a kind of 'What Alice did next' after her adventures through the looking glass, with her penetrative sexual initiation as the finale. The text stages a series of sexual acts, each one delayed or interrupted by the narrator recounting a salacious rewrite of a fairy tale, and fairy tale characters provide metaphors throughout the text, with the narrator figuring himself as Sheherezade, the White Rabbit and even Cinderella at various moments. It offers a slick and humorous pornographic fantasy, yet this text could be considered a far more dangerous and subversive text than *Rose Bonbon* precisely because it is so subtly inoffensive. It is interesting that this novel should be quietly acclaimed whereas *Rose Bonbon* in its rather graceless and ludicrous offensiveness should produce such a violent and extreme response. Such distinctions raise questions that need to be considered about representations of a sexual nature concerning adolescents and children: what, for instance, constitutes the borderline between indecent and acceptable material? What are the cultural guidelines governing the reception of the obscene, and this when it involves underage girls in particular? Why is it that in some cases such representations are horrific, and in others, entertainingly titillating? These questions cannot be answered without an exploration of the cultural fantasies that surround the vulnerability and the desirability of children, both those fantasies produced by adults and projected onto children, and those that speak directly to the child in question.

In *Contes à faire rougir les petits chaperons*, the opening scenes of the narrative situate the action in a zone that rests uneasily between fantasy and reality: 'Alice a changé depuis toutes ces histoires au pays des Merveilles. Elle s'enferme dans la salle de bains. Elle se met nue et s'observe dans la glace. Elle voudrait bien voyager encore de l'autre côté du miroir. Passé douze ans, on ne sait plus comment faire' (Enard 1987: 7). ['Alice has changed since all those adventures in Wonderland. She locks herself in the bathroom. She undresses and looks at herself in the mirror. She would still very much like to travel to the other side. Once past 12, it's hard to know how to.'] Alice is still a fantasy character, but her predicament is represented with explicit reality. The Wonderland at stake here, the text implies, is an erotic one, the only possibility left for adults who want to engage on a fantastic journey and emerge transformed. In this way the text indicates the degree of fantasy involved in adult sexuality, but it also keeps a wary distance from the idea of a real 13–year-old girl. Alice sets off in search of her sister's boyfriend, the narrator, and once she finds him, lifts her T-shirt to show him her breasts, removes her knickers, sits on his lap and cannot restrain herself from masturbating. The narrator maintains a veneer of contented victimisation in the face of this sexual assault, wondering if a good spanking would solve the problem and then considering: 'A la réflexion, ce n'est peut-être pas idéal pour la calmer' (1987: 11). ['On reflection it's perhaps not the ideal way to calm her down'.] Repeatedly, the text makes us aware of Alice's strength of will, her unrelenting sexual curiosity, her knowing sexual manipulativeness. As the narrative progresses, Alice manages to become increasingly involved in the sexual games of the adults around her, until the eventual loss of her virginity at the end of the novel. The resolution of Alice's sexual precociousness is presented as a very happy ending indeed. Her sexual education has been comprehensive and satisfactory and there is no shade of guilt, doubt or fear among the protagonists. This is undoubtedly a fairy tale in itself, one written for an audience of men, and while our teenage heroine is called Alice as an appeal to a certain type of humorously fantastic context, she could easily have been named Lolita instead.

We might pause here briefly to consider another text in which classic pornographic fantasies that involve children or at least adolescent girls are knowingly placed centre stage. Roger des Roches' *La Jeune Femme et la pornographie*, discussed earlier for its relationship to the abject, features a lengthy and highly explicit scene in which the female protagonist recounts a fantasy of seducing her younger brother. The text provides a significant comparison with the Enard as its appropriation of pornographic clichés is expressly emphasised, as opposed to *Contes à faire rougir* which *inhabits fantasy without signalling this context*. Des Roches' text highlights the erotic potential of the adolescent girl and exploits it with a clearly articulated gratuitousness. In this scene the protagonist, Hélène B. is recording a video that will be sent to the man she loves with the precise intent of stimulating him sexually. To that end she fixes upon: 'L'inceste: c'est

à tout prix qu'il faut raconter des épisodes affreux ou tremblants'
(2005: 61). ['Incest: at all costs she must recount scenes of fear and
trembling'.] The first scenario she fixes upon, although not the one she
will subsequently elaborate, features herself as a young girl hiding in
a wardrobe while watching her mother masturbate. This consciously
evoked cliché is, intriguingly, closely related to the central scene in
Clotilde Escalle's *Où est il cet amour?*, in which a child locked in a
wardrobe witnesses incestuous sex between her father and grandmother. The self-reflexivity with which the cliché is produced in des
Roches' text asks us to consider retrospectively similar scenes in
other texts that are represented in the absence of irony or distance.
Des Roches' text installs in the distance between his narrative and
the scenes it recounts the recognition that such eroticism appeases
the male erotogenic gaze. Similarly when the narrator reminds
herself: 'Dis que tu en avais treize, Hélène: des seins de femme sur le
corps d'une fillette de treize ans!' (2005: 67). ['Say that you were 13,
Hélène: the breasts of a woman of the body of a 13–year-old girl!'.]
We find the template here for Enard's sexually precocious Alice. Yet,
des Roches' text is troubling in its own way, as the sexual encounter
detailed at length here between Hélène and her younger brother is
one of eye-watering realism that does not trouble to hide the actuali-
ties of childhood. Hélène describes how 'Je tenais ses fesses au creux
de mes mains. Une petite fesse ronde dans chaque main. Son érection
me chatouilla aussitôt le menton. Je levai les yeux: son regard croisa
le mien, et j'y lus plaisir et affolement' (2005: 64–5) ['I held his
buttocks in the palms of my hands. One small round buttock in each
hand. His erection tickled my chin. I lifted my eyes and his gaze met
mine; I read pleasure and panic there'], recognising the ambivalent
drama of sexual initiation. At the same time it insists on the traumatised passivity of the younger brother: 'j'avais une poupée devant
moi, consentante et fragile' (2005: 66). ['I had a doll before me,
consenting and fragile'.] And on the overwhelming drive towards
sexuality that inhabits the adolescent but which does not know how
to be satisfied: 'Quelqu'un qui était moi s'affairait aux commandes,
et je n'avais plus, moi, aucun contrôle. Je m'étendis à côté de mon
frère et l'avalai. Je le suçais, je l'aspirais – je levais mon cul afin
d'y fourrer les doigts – , mais ce n'était pas assez' (2005: 68–9).
['Someone who was me dealt with the orders and I, myself, wasn't in
control any more. I laid down beside my brother. I sucked him and
pumped him – I lifted my arse so as to stick my fingers in – but it

wasn't enough'.] As such, this fantasised scenario draws attention to the highly conflicted dimensions of graphic representations of child sexuality. It is a narrative that recognises the drama of sexual initiation but also its victims and its voyeuristic value. It hovers uncertainly between eroticism and the recognition of the damaging reality that early sexual experience potentially encompasses. It details the child's self-shattering encounter with adult sexuality that lies on the borderline of its transformation into eroticism, and provides a lucid if disturbing contrast to Enard's sugar coating of the sexual realities of adolescence.

Enard's essential strategy for rendering the sexual enlightenment of children more palatable is to process the eroticism of his narrative through the medium of the fairytale, which *Contes à faire rougir les petits chaperons* appeals to repeatedly, if in ironic and distorted fashion. The fairy tale is the traditional medium for transmitting the experience of adults to the naivety of children, and as such is put to use here to minimise the invidious nature of its context. The cunning cleverness of Enard's text lies in its implication that Little Red Riding Hood was also a Lolita-in-waiting. Enard's rewritten fairy tales emphasise an eroticism that is banal and vulgar and playful, but not entirely misplaced. His rewrites include *Pinocchio* (whose growing nose is clearly open to a bawdy interpretation), *Snow White and the Seven Dwarfs*, the *Three Little Pigs* and *Tom Thumb*. There is nothing dark and menacing about the sexuality at play in these tales, even though part of the entertainment involved comes from destroying their sugary tweeness. Instead, as Snow White figures out how to accommodate all seven dwarves at once, or as Tom Thumb pleasures the Ogre's wife, a certain cheery innocence is maintained in tone and register and the sexualisation, while relentless, has a certain bizarre aptness. It is interesting to note that *Red Riding Hood* is not offered as a rewrite, partly perhaps because its own sexual preoccupations are already intrinsic to its organisation. Yet there are other possibilities why this story should be fundamental to the collection, but not retold. One of the earliest versions, that of Charles Perrault, is clearly a tale of sexual precociousness that ends in disaster, as Red Riding Hood is eaten and the story draws to a close with a morality verse. As Jack Zipes argues: 'We tend to forget that Perrault implied that a young girl, who was irresponsible and naïve if not stupid, was responsible for a wolf's behaviour and consequently caused her own rape'

(Zipes 1995: 26). This harsh line has been softened by the time the tale is written by the Grimm brothers, who introduce the rescuing huntsman to save both child and grandmother and help outwit the wolf. This version offers an Oedipal drama for Bruno Bettelheim to interpret, in which the child's premature sexuality is simply checked by the reinsertion of a sheltering, responsible father figure. Bettelheim suggests that it is, 'much better, despite one's ambivalent desires, to settle for a while longer for the protection the father provides when he is not seen in his seductive aspect' (1991: 181). The difference between the two tales seems essentially to be that Perrault considers the child old enough to be responsible for herself, whereas in Grimm she is not.

The question of responsibility becomes an urgent one, when we understand that at the heart of Red Riding Hood we find what Bettelheim calls 'the fascination which sex, and everything surrounding it, exercises over the child's mind'. Or put another way, Djuna Barnes' allusion in *Nightwood* that 'Children know something they can't tell; they like Red Riding Hood and the wolf in bed!'(1961: 79). The tale of Red Riding Hood proposes that sexuality is nascent in all children, and that the fairy tale offers a medium through which this issue can be approached. Hence Enard's saucy *contes* have a certain appropriateness that allows them to pass through cultural censors. Yet the question of Alice's responsibility for her own sexuality is rigorously silenced throughout this novel, while the adults who might be expected to protect her involve her instead in their erotic play. Repeated references to Alice's sexual voraciousness stand as proof of her maturity, and the context of eroticised fairy tales asks the reader's indulgence for what is in any case latent in the child. The tale of little Red Riding Hood, along with the other fairy tales that lie palimpsestically under Enard's text are used to provide an appeal to comfort, fantasy and security in a scenario that would otherwise be fraught with potential trauma; they defuse the demonic nature of the sexuality that would otherwise be apparent here.

Enard also employs another strategy in order to render Alice's sexual initiation harmless and fulfilling. It is a striking feature of his rewritten tales that women feature abundantly as heroic, strong, demanding and sexually alluring. The magical, transformative power in these tales is always erotic, and that power is placed fully in the hands of the female characters. Males here are generally hesitant victims, or else resort to sexuality as a useful, self-protective strategy. This runs counter to the usual organisation of gender roles in the fairy tales. Discussing the rather unfortunate lot of princesses in traditional tales, Jack Zipes points out that, 'The young "heroines", obviously ready for marriage, are humiliated, degraded and besmirched. Their major virtue is patience and, to a certain extent, opportunism. They must wait for the opportune time to make themselves available to a man. Without a man, they are nothing. Only when they find their prince, who comes from outside to rescue them, can their lives assume meaning, and the meaning is marriage and departure for another realm' (1995: 39). Enard's tales cast such humiliation aside and present women as sexually initiatory and powerful through their desirability.

This is not so much a rewrite as a simple, if exaggerated, appeal to a different kind of fictional myth, and one that is also aimed directly at girl children. Valerie Walkerdine points to the musicals of *Gigi*, *My Fair Lady* and *Annie*, in which otherwise disadvantaged working-class girls call upon the transformative power of their innocent desirability. This 'eroticised little girl' as Walkerdine calls her, 'is inscribed as one who can make a transformation, which is also a self-transformation, which is also a seductive allure' (1998: 263). That image is not confined solely to the stage. Walkerdine points to the way that in contemporary culture it has become increasingly pervasive, so that 'popular images of little girls as alluring and seductive, at once innocent and highly erotic, are contained in the most respectable and mundane of locations – broadsheet newspapers, women's magazines, television adverts' (1998: 257). Such images appeal to adults and children alike, informing little girls of the assets they must cultivate if they are to achieve recognition and power in their culture, and presenting children to adults as adorable and admirable in a way that seems entirely without victimisation. What seems to be most at stake here is the pervasiveness of such images throughout our culture, their ultimate invisibility and the unchallenged status of their innocence. Yet to present a child as adorable is to invest in its image either a misplaced sexuality or a misplaced spirituality, both of which are heavy symbolic constructions for a child's narrow shoulders. Our current society, however, prefers to adore children, the message implicit in Agnès Tricoire's remarks on the child as the new divine. Enard's text offers, then, a highly palatable reconstruction of child sexuality because, although it is somewhat extreme, its foundations lie in a collusion with any number of fairy tales that pervade our culture concerning children, girl power, sexuality and happy endings. The way that culture has evolved the fairy tale to diminish the warning they encapsulate for children, to increase the power assigned to female figures, but this through the ever more significant power of their physical desirability, is entirely in keeping with the fantasies that support Enard's profoundly pornographic representation of the adventures of a girl child. Enard's tale must be involved in a work of such cultural legibility that it fails to arouse any dissonant echoes in its readership; it is difficult, otherwise, to understand how such a text could be published with so little outward sign of public concern.

However, we can view this text as extremely dangerous, precisely because of its collusion with some of culture's less healthy fantasies. The idea of the girl child as a 'Lolita' is fraught with difficulty in the policing of relations between children and adults. In Judith Herman's text, *Father–Daughter Incest*, Herman identifies some significantly pervasive myths that help to diminish the responsibility of the offender in sexual abuse cases, one of which is the 'seductive daughter'. This seductive daughter is another appellation for the concept of Lolita, the sexually precocious child who assumes agency and asks for her abusive treatment.[2] The Lolita myth arises out of the uncomfortable but pervasive split between wicked children and innocent children, and perpetuates a misguided, oversimplified cultural belief that children can be only one or the other. Such a split can be understood through adult projections of sexuality onto children, but in this collision of childish curiosity and adult eroticism, the guilt of the encounter leads the adult to a self-reassuring shift of blame. The image of Lolita is thus the perfect symbol of a culture confused over sexual and moral responsibility between the generations. Texts like Enard's only glorify the Lolita role, rendering it highly erotic and titillating in a way that aims to disarm censure, but feeds dangerously into a culture's bank of myths about sexualised children and victimised males.

Emma Wilson highlights another dimension to the sexually abusive relationship, which corresponds to the analysis of the eroticised princess discussed earlier. This is the recognition that in many contemporary films concerning child abuse, 'the sexualisation of children [is seen] as an excessive, distorted image of normative processes of separation, initiation and the acquisition of sexual knowledge' (Wilson 2003: 9). In other words, incest is understood here as a vicious and brutal but ultimately accurate replica of the sexual power relations at large in contemporary society. Hence the fairy-tale image of the princess becomes essential to gendered, sexual society for whether it be Jack Zipes's model of the degraded, opportunistic princess who must win a man for her own safety, or the more contemporary model of the princess whose titillating allure offers her power, the outcome remains the same; female subordination to male sexual desire. This feminist argument suggests that whether girls are forced to offer themselves sexually to imposing men, or whether they choose to offer themselves is a matter of social nicety. If a society organises its sexual power relations on unequal lines, if satisfying male desire still remains the imperative, then a patriarchal family with the father as traditional seat of power becomes a potentially dangerous place for a submissive girl child to be.

This may seem in itself an excessive argument, until we realise the extent to which a child lacks autonomous agency of its own. Children are born into an environment in which they are necessarily submissive because of their own utter helplessness and dependency. It is within such parameters that their sense of being is created. Jessica Benjamin in her psychoanalytic work on domination explores these earliest moments of subjectivity formation for the child, identifying a significant but fragile developmental stage in which a dialectic of reciprocal recognition is negotiated:

> In order to exist for oneself, one has to exist for another. It would seem there is no way out of this dependency. If I destroy the other, there is no one to recognise me, for if I allow him no independent consciousness, I become enmeshed with a dead, not-conscious being. If the other denies me recognition, my acts have no meaning; if he is so far above me that nothing I do can alter his attitude toward me, I can only submit. My desire and agency can find no outlet, except in the form of obedience. (1988: 53)

Benjamin's analysis is intended to explain the reason why victims often collude in their own abuse, but it also explains why children battle so hard for recognition in the daily control struggles which they fight with their parents, and which they are regularly destined to lose. Children will always give in eventually because they must be loved in order to survive; there is no possibility of social or psychic space for them otherwise. It is all too easy to make a child submit, either to the whims of an individual, or to the validating gaze of its surrounding culture. The responsibility that adults bear towards children is thus enormous. The power they possess over the child is already weighted so heavily in their favour, that it takes very little to turn a child into a complicit victim.

From this perspective we could usefully reconsider the fairy tale through Jack Zipes' alternative analysis. Zipes wonders why it is that we so resolutely focus on the happy ending rather than the terrible trials the child must endure in its quest. Neglect, abandonment and abuse are all intrinsic to the child's predicament, and we prefer to treat them in retrospect as didactic tools, rather than consider them as traumatic experiences. Zipes suggests we remember that fairy tales express an adult viewpoint on family relations, and not that of a child. 'To a certain extent,' he argues, 'they were told and written down to reveal the shame and guilt that adults felt over the centuries or to redress wrongs. More than anything, I believe, they reveal what the psychiatrists Alice Miller and James Hoyne have identified as ambivalent feelings many parents have towards their children – their desire to abandon them, and the shame they feel when they actually abuse them' (1995: 219). Fairy tales, then, become part of the strategies that adults have developed to assuage or subli- mate these uncomfortable feelings, part of the structure of uneasy control that asks children to take responsibility for themselves, to mistrust the world, and to rationalise the trauma of abuse. Zipes proposes that: 'We refuse to discuss the trauma in the tales based on children's real experiences of maltreatment because we want to believe that such trauma did not and does not exist. We want desperately to forgive the parent in us and happily resolve what can never be completely resolved' (1995: 222). The happy-ever-after ending protects the adult every bit as much as it intends to protect the child. But what if a tale existed that shattered the coherency and the consistency of the fantasy world of the fairy tale, that exploited a culture's self-contradictory stance on the eroticised child, and played openly to its fears and anxieties for its most vulnerable members? With these thoughts in mind, let us turn our attention to the much- reviled *Rose Bonbon*, by Nicolas Jones-Gorlin

The text opens in the cinema at a showing of *Snow White*, a regular haunt of Simon's where he can watch children. On this occasion he spots a young girl and is overcome with desire. A foolhardy attack on the child in the toilets of a café afterwards leads to a conviction. Rather than be sent to prison, however, he is placed in a form of rehabilitation and given a small caravan in a deserted area. Here he meets le Vieux, an elderly, wealthy man of influence who shares his feelings towards children. Le Vieux rationalises child abuse to Simon: 'Les enfants sont très séducteurs; ils cherchent l'affection des adultes. Il n'y a rien d'anormal à leur répondre' (Jones-Gorlin 2002: 62) ['Children are very seductive; they seek adult affection. There is nothing abnormal in responding to them'], accuses society of hypocrisy, and goes on to prove his power and prowess to Simon by approaching a child in a burger bar and buying an hour of his time from his ambiguously represented parents. Le Vieux takes Simon's career development in hand, and together they decide to make a film ('Un film pour dire que l'amour libre entre une enfant et un adulte, c'est bien' 2002: 83) ['A film to tell people that free love between children and adults is good'], rejecting *La Belle au bois dormant* and *Le Petit Chaperon rouge* in favour of a remake of *Peter Pan*. Needing an actor to play the lead part, le Vieux reinvents Simon as a star, Dany King, by placing him in a bizarre reality show in which contestants must survive in the (simulated) environment of outer space. Simon wins by playing to the audience's need to see pain and suffering on their television screens, and goes on to star in the musical. So far, so ludicrous. He then commits an error by making an assault on a young niece of le Vieux, Rose. He has been warned off, but when he finds her in the bath, he cannot resist indulging in a sexualised rendition of *The Three Little Pigs*. Simon's career suddenly falls apart as he is exposed as a paedophile by the press, and he is forced once again into hiding. He realises that his downfall has been manipulated by le Vieux, just as his success was manufactured by him. In consequence, he sets off on a mission of revenge. This involves trawling provincial France for three other paedophiles, whom he recognises without need of any formal communication, and who all instantly fall in with his plans. They kidnap a scout, Simon disposes of his companions, and he takes the scout to le Vieux, whose predilection for small boys he knows well. However, the child has been wired up as a suicide bomb, ready to explode once he is undressed. In the manner of cartoon heroes, Simon cannot leave well alone and returns to the hotel room because he has not heard the bomb go off; in the subsequent explosion Simon is paralysed as well.

This is clearly not a sensitive and insightful exploration of paedophilia. One of the most striking elements of the text is the increasing derangement of its fantasy frame. What is initially a story of some plausibility quickly veers off into the absurd and fantastic. Equally

the focus shifts from Simon's sexual feelings towards children, to
his murderous feelings towards his one-time patron. This is, we
would suggest, an indication of how alarmed the text is by its own
material. The sheer ludicrousness of the novel, after the initial scene-
setting of the first section, seems to imply a lack of responsibility
towards the issues it raises, and a desire to distance itself from them
through the realm of fantasy. Further evidence of this comes in the
odd coda to the text, a tacked-on *Note de la Rédactrice*, which
displaces the origin of the story from Simon to the journalist who
comes to visit him in hospital, at his request, in order to write his
life history. Having listened to a very particular, very immediate
narrative voice throughout the novel, it is a shock to the reader to
discover that this voice was ventriloquised through a woman, who
then undermines what she has written: 'l'état de santé de Simon,
dès la moitié du livre, s'est profondément degradé. Il ne parvenait
plus à prononcer l'ensemble des mots, ses idées semblaient plus
confuses et leurs enchaînements sans lien évident. La chronologie
et la structure réelle du récit, elles aussi, ont été malmenées' (2002:
169). ['once past the midway point of the book, Simon's health
went severely downhill. He could no longer manage to pronounce
words in their entirety, his ideas seemed muddled and the causal
links between them were missing. The chronology and the structure of the tale were also messed up'.] The reader is left uncertain
how to interpret these remarks; does this therefore mean that the
fantastic second part of the narrative did not occur at all? That it
was an invalid's delusion? Or, that part of it occurred, but not in
the order or the manner in which it was recounted? And if any of
this were true, would it affect in any way the judgement the reader
could carry out on the main protagonist? Having raised so many
questions without offering answers, all we can know for sure is that
this coda seeks to undermine further the plausibility of the narrative, to remove it ever farther from the field of mimesis and absolute
moral interpretation.

   This systematic disruption also occurs at the level of the discourse.
Simon's voice is highly stylised; a peculiar mishmash of street slang,
idiom and English phrases, all combined in a high-octane, breath-
less dash along the sentences. According to the journalist's coda,
this discourse is one which she has attempted to tidy up, but it has
not been possible to excavate an elegant French out of it: 'Il a bien
fallu que ma syntaxe se plie à son désordre mental' (2002: 168)

['In the end I was obliged to alter my syntax to fit the disorder of his mind'], she declares. The discordant, incoherent nature of the language is supposed to be an indication of Simon's psychic disorder, and it is clearly under the banner of mental illness that this text wishes to place paedophilia. Yet if we examine closely the elements that compose Simon's speech, we find a striking absence of emotion, and in its place, a cacophony of advertising slogans, idiom and cultural references. The intention is, we imagine, to make Simon seem inhuman, to displace him from any possibility of subjectivity. But the effect is to put the language of culture itself on trial, to uncouple it from its human origins, put it through the liquidiser and parody it as the source and the manifestation of society's sickness. The text's internal malaise, its ugliness and incoherence cannot truly be attributed to the viewpoint of the paedophile as this character and the world he inhabits are so implausibly represented. Instead this odd, discontinuous textual world presents us with a fractured subjectivity created out of the sordid flotsam and jetsam of popular culture. Simon's narrative voice and the tale it tells become a discordant anthem of jarring notes, a staccato rap that threatens at all moments to descend into senselessness, where it might risk revealing the fundamental discontinuities of cultural ideology itself.

One of the reasons why this text feels so offensive is because it fails to create meaning out of the situations it represents. It wishes to maintain an intention to shock, but cannot quite bring itself to articulate the conclusions to its arguments. The exploitation of fairy tales, focusing on their demonic dimension but failing to link it to an understanding of their rationalisation of childhood trauma is an obvious case in point. The text abounds with disquieting representations of cultural failings whose dangers the narrative seems fearful of outwardly expressing. Instead it remains at the level of anxieties, veering off into implausible fantasy, or disowning its own insights. Yet it represents a sordid, degraded society which treats children as desirable commodities; it represents adults as possessing the causal powers to create reasons for abusing children alongside the moral bankruptcy to actually do so; it represents desire unleashed and catastrophic, lacking any possible framework of comprehension. Its own discontinuities provide, despite itself, a powerful critique of a culture that prefers to run away from its deepest fears and anxieties rather than take responsibility for the dangers it has created. Unable to cohere itself into a penetrating indictment of a culture's malaise,

Rose Bonbon remains a dislikeable, frustrating and unpleasant text, exploiting society's weakest spots without offering the intellectual or emotional framework to assimilate and heal them. Like the crazy discourse that has rebelled against the journalist's attempts to contain it, this narrative remains at the level of threatening fantasy, its jagged and uncomfortable discontinuities repeatedly erupting through its attempts at aesthetic resonance.

Most alarmingly of all, this is a text that contains no children. That is to say, the ones it features are little more than cardboard cut-outs, devoid of personality. Instead its focus is entirely upon the adults and the fantasies, desires and anxieties with which they invest their images of the child. It would seem that one of the most offensive messages that can be transmitted is that adults gain erotic pleasure from looking at children, and that this pleasure is poten- tially dangerous. *Rose Bonbon* makes adults solely responsible for the abuse of children, while *Contes à faire rougir les petits chaperons* goes to some pains to suppress and disarm such a thought, and this is perhaps a significant reason why their public receptions should have been so strikingly different. It is not surprising that such a message would receive a profoundly hostile response; it touches on some of the most powerful and disturbing emotions in adult subjec- tivity, such as unresolved Oedipal issues from childhood, the painful demands of desirability culture places on subjects who long to be validated within it, the blackest and most unacceptable aggressions we harbour towards our own offspring. As our society increasingly adores children, their desirability translating into a need to keep them safe at all times, so the responsibility parents bear towards children becomes ever more difficult to shoulder; it is simply too much to deal with. The hysteria that surrounds issues of paedo- philia in the western world, is bound up with the paradoxical knot of sexual relations within which we bind our children. It represents the intolerable responsibility we bear towards our much-prized children, but its form comes from the implicit eroticisation with which we surround their images. If our culture could find a way to love children less sexually, admire them less erotically, then perhaps it could be less excessively afraid of the threat of the pervert. This is in no way to condone any sexual abuse of children in any form whatsoever, but to propose instead that we reconsider the sexual power relations that structure our culture, and the myths of valida- tion that our culture offers to children. However, the outrage provoked by *Rose Bonbon* is excessive compared to its material; it is undoubtedly a terrible book, but not a really dangerous one, while Enard's novel is more disturbing in its intentions and implications. But rather than attempting to censor such disturbing representations, we should perhaps consider them dispassionately and unflinchingly, as if we had nothing to hide.

Notes

1 'Ainsi en 1997, l'Observatoire national de l'action sociale décentralisée (ODAS) rappelle que "74 000 enfants [ont été] maltraités ou en risque de maltraitance en 1996, soit 14% de plus que l'année précédente". Cette année-là (1997), "le nombre des signalements d'enfants maltraités augmente de 5%, alors que celui d'enfants en risque augmente, lui, de 18%, c'est aussi le taux d'augmentation du nombre d'enfants victimes d'abus sexuels entre 1995 et 1996, date à laquelle ils sont 6 500 à être signalés"' (Bernheim 2005: 120). ['Thus in 1997, ODAS recalled that "74,000 children [had been] mistreated or risked being mistreated in 1996, which represents 14% more than the previous year"'. That year (1997), "the number of reported cases of mistreated children increased by 5 per cent, while those of children at risk rose by 18 per cent, which was also the rate of increase of the number of children who were victims of sexual abuse between 1995 and 1996, at which point 6,500 cases had been reported".']
2 This relationship is explored in more detail, from a sociological perspective, in Vicki Bell's *Interrogating Incest* (Bell 1993).

Bibliography

Filmography

Akerman, C. *La Captive* (2001)
Bonello, B. *Le Pornographe* (2002)
Breillat, C. *Une vraie jeune fille* (1975)
— *Tapage nocturne* (1979)
— *36 fillette* (1987)
— *Sale comme une ange* (1991)
— *Aux Niçois qui mal y pensent* (1995)
— *Parfait amour!* (1996)
— *Romance* (2000)
— *A ma sœur!* (2000)
— *Brève traversée* (2001)
— *Sex Is Comedy* (2002)
— *Anatomie de l'enfer* (2003)
Despentes, V. and Coralie Trinh Thi. *Baise-moi* (2000)
Houellebecq, M. *La Rivière* (2001)
Kahn, C. *L'Ennui* (2000)
Noë, G. *Irréversible* (2003)

Primary bibliographical works

Breillat, C. 1968. *L'Homme facile*. Paris: Christian Bourgois.
— 1970. *Le Silence, après…* Paris: François Wimille.
— 1971. *Les Vêtements de mer*. Paris: François Wimille.
— 1974. *Le Soupirail*. Paris: Guy Authier. (Republished in 2000 as *Une vraie jeune fille* (Paris: Denoël).)
— 1979. *Tapage nocturne*. Paris: Mercure de France.
— 1985. *Police*. Paris: Albin Michel.
— 1987. *36 fillette*. Paris: Carrère.

— 1999. *Romance*. Paris: Cahiers du cinéma.

— 2001a. *A ma sœur!* Paris: Cahiers du cinéma.

— 2001b. *Pornocratie*. Paris: Denoël.

— 2005. *Le Livre du plaisir* (1999). Paris: Livre de poche.

Despentes, V. 2001a. *Baise-moi* (1994). Paris: J'ai lu.

— 2001b. *Les Jolies Choses* (1998). Paris: J'ai lu.

— 2002a. *Les Chiennes savantes* (1996). Paris: J'ai lu.

— 2002b. *Mordre au travers* (1999). Paris: Librio.

— 2002c. *Teen Spirit*. Paris: Grasset.

— 2003. *Baise-Moi (Rape Me)*, tr. Bruce Benderson. New York, NY: Grove Press.

— 2004. *Bye Bye Blondie*. Paris: Grasset.

Des Roches, R. 2005. *La Jeune Femme et la pornographie*. Paris: La Musardine.

Dustan, G. 1996. *Dans ma chambre*. Paris: POL.

— 1997. *Je sors ce soir*. Paris: POL.

— 1998a. *Plus fort que moi*. Paris: POL.

— 1998b. *In My Room*, tr. Brad Rumph. London: Serpent's Tail.

— 2002a. *Génie divin* (2001). Paris: J'ai lu.

— 2002b. *LXiR*. Paris: Balland.

— 2003. *Nicolas Pages* (1999). Paris: J'ai lu.

— 2004. *Dernier roman*. Paris: Flammarion.

— 2005. *Premier essai*. Paris: Flammarion.

Enard, J-P. 1987. *Contes à faire rougir les petits chaperons*. Paris: Gallimard.

Henric, J. 1987. 'Le Diable au corps et l'érection intégrale'. *L'Infini*, 20, 98–108.

— 2001. *Légendes de Catherine M*. Paris: Denoël.

— 2004a. *Catherine M*. Paris: Instantané Editions.

— 2004b. *Comme si notre amour était une ordure!* Paris: Stock.

— 2005. 'Pasolini, la pensée irradiante'. *Le Monde des livres*, 11 November 2005, 3.

Houellebecq, M. 1998a. *Interventions*. Paris: Flammarion.

— 1998b. *Whatever*, tr. Paul Hammond. London: Serpent's Tail.

— 1999. *H.P. Lovecraft: Contre le monde, contre la vie* (1991). Paris: J'ai lu.

— 2000a. *Extension du domaine de la lutte* (1994). Paris: J'ai lu.

— 2000b. *Les Particules élémentaires* (1998). Paris: J'ai lu.

— 2000c. *Lanzarote*. Paris: Flammarion.

— 2000d. *Atomised*, tr. Frank Wynne. London: Heinemann.

— 2001a. *Plateforme*. Paris: Flammarion.

— 2001b. *Rester vivant et autres textes*. Paris: Librio.

— 2003. *Platform*, tr. Frank Wynne. London: Vintage.

— 2005. *La Possibilité d'une île*. Paris: Fayard.

— 2006. *The Possibility of an Island*, tr. Gavin Bowd. London: Phoenix.

Jones-Gorlin, N. 2002. *Rose Bonbon*. Paris: Gallimard.

Millet, C. 2002a. *La Vie sexuelle de Catherine M.* (2001), précédé de *Pourquoi et comment*. Paris: Le Seuil, 'Points'.

— 2002b. *The Sexual Life of Catherine M.*, tr. Adriana Hunter. London: Serpent's Tail.

Moix, Y. 2004. *Partouz*. Paris: Grasset et Fasquelle.

Nimier, M. 2002. *La Nouvelle Pornographie* (2000). Paris: Gallimard, 'Folio'.

Noël, B. 1990. *Le Château de Cène* (1969). Paris: Gallimard, 'L'Imaginaire'.

Rémès, E. 2000. *Le Maître des amours*. Paris: Balland, 'Le Rayon'.

— 2004. *Je bande donc je suis* (1999). Paris: Editions Blanche.

— 2005. *Serial Fucker. Journal d'un barebacker*. Paris: Editions Blanche.

Reyes, A. 1988. *Le Boucher*. Paris: Seuil.

— 2005. *Sept nuits*. Paris: Robert Laffont.

Tordjman, V. 2004. *La Pornographie de l'âme*. Paris: Le Passage.

Zagdanski, S. 2005. *Jouissance du temps*. Paris: Arthème Fayard.

Other works consulted

Abecassis, J. I. 2000. 'The eclipse of desire: l'affaire Houellebecq'. *MLN*, 115:4, 801–26.

Adorno, T. W. 1984. *Aesthetic Theory*, tr. C. Lenhardt. London: Routledge & Kegan Paul.

Amis, C. 2001. 'A rough trade' (online), *Guardian*, 17 March. Available from: www.guardian.co.uk (accessed 28 July 2006).

Anderson, R. 2001. *Hard*. Paris: Grasset.

Angot, C. 1999. *L'Inceste*. Paris: Stock.

Arcan, N. 2002. *Putain* (2001). Paris: Seuil, 'Points'.

Arrabal, F. 2005. *Houellebecq*. Paris: Le Cherche Midi.

Assiter, A. and Carol, A. (eds) 1993. *Bad Girls and Dirty Pictures: The Challenge to Reclaim Feminism*. London: Pluto.

Auboneuil, A. 1999. *Le Rendez-vous du 29 février*. Paris: Double Interligne.

Audé, F. 2001. 'Les Cinéastes françaises hors machisme, toutefois…', *Cinémaction*, 99: *Le Machisme à l'écran*, 233–8.

— 2002. *Cinéma d'elles, 1981–2001*. Lausanne: L'Âge d'homme.

Baggesgaard, M. A. 2006. 'The complexities of honesty: on the prose of Michel Houellebecq', in G. Bowd (ed.), *Le Monde de Houellebecq*. Glasgow: University of Glasgow French and German Publications, pp. 159–70.

Ballard, J. G. 2005. 'Cultiver son jardin', *Les Inrockuptibles*, hors série 22: *Houellebecq*, 36.

Baqué, D. 2002. *Mauvais genre(s): Erotisme, pornographie, art contemporain*. Paris: Editions du regard.

Bardolle, O. 2004. *La Littérature à vif (le cas Houellebecq)*. Paris: L'Esprit des péninsules.

Barnes, D. 1961. *Nightwood*. New York, NY: New Directions.

Barnes, J. 2005. 'Haine et hédonisme: l'art insolent de Michel Houellebecq', *Les Inrockuptibles*, hors série 22: *Houellebecq*, 30–5.

Barthes, R. 1982. 'The metaphor of the eye' in G. Bataille, *The Story of the Eye*, tr. Joachim Neugroschal. London: Penguin, pp. 119–27.

— 2002a. *Le Degré zéro de l'écriture* (1953). In *Œuvres complètes*, I. Paris: Seuil, pp. 169–225.

— 2002b. *Sade, Fourier, Loyola* (1971). In *Œuvres complètes*, III. Paris: Seuil, pp. 699–868.

— 2002c. *Le Plaisir du texte* (1973). In *Œuvres complètes*, IV. Paris: Seuil, pp. 217–64.

— 2002d. *La Chambre claire* (1980). In *Œuvres complètes*, V. Paris: Seuil, pp. 785–892.

— 2002e. 'La Métaphore de l'œil' (1963). In *Œuvres complètes*, II. Paris: Seuil, pp. 488–95.

Bataille, G. 1970. *Œuvres complètes*, I. Paris: Gallimard.

Baudrillard, J. 1988. *De la séduction* (1979). Paris: Gallimard, 'Folio'.

Bazin, A. 1958. *Qu'est-ce que le cinéma?*, I. Paris: Editions du Cerf.

De Beauvoir, S. 1949. *Le Deuxième Sexe*. Paris: Gallimard.

Beigbeder, F. 2003. 'La Fin de la fidélité', in C. Ley, *Voyage au pays de l'échangisme*. Lausanne: Favre, pp. 7–9.

— 2004. *Nouvelles sous ecstasy* (1999). Paris: Gallimard, 'Folio'.

Bell, V. 1993. *Interrogating Incest: Feminism, Foucault and the Law*. London: Routledge.

Bellil, S. 2002. *Dans l'enfer des tournantes*. Paris: Denoël.

Benjamin, J. 1988. *The Bonds of Love: Psychoanalysis, Feminism and the Problem of Domination*. New York, NY: Pantheon Books.

Benjamin, W. 1973. *Understanding Brecht* (1966), tr. Anna Bostock. London: NLB.

— 1992. 'The work of art in the age of mechanical reproduction' (1936), in *Illuminations*, tr. Harry Zohn. London: Fontana, pp. 211–44.

— 1999. *The Arcades Project*, tr. Howard Eiland and Kevin McLaughlin.

Cambridge, MA: Harvard University Press.

Berens, J. 2002. 'The double life of Catherine M' (online), *Observer*, 19 May. Available from: www.books.guardian.co.uk (accessed 26 March 2003).

Bernheim, C. 2005. *Dors, ange amer*. Paris: Seuil.

Bersani, L. 1986. *The Freudian Body: Psychoanalysis and Art*. New York, NY: Columbia University Press.

— 1988. 'Is the rectum a grave?', in D. Crimp (ed.), *AIDS: Cultural Analysis, Cultural Activism*. Cambridge, MA: MIT Press, pp. 197–222.

— 1996. *Homos* (1995). Cambridge, MA: Harvard University Press.

Bettelheim, B. 1991. *The Uses of Enchantment: The Meaning and Importance of Fairy Tales* (1976). London: Penguin.

Beyala, C. 2005. *Femme nue femme noire* (2003). Paris: Livre de poche.

Biron, M. 2005. 'L'Effacement du personnage contemporain: l'exemple de Michel Houellebecq', *Etudes françaises*, 41:1, 27–41.

Blanchot, M. 2000. *L'Espace littéraire* (1955). Paris: Gallimard, 'Folio'.

Blond, P. (ed.) 1998. *Post-Secular Philosophy: Between Philosophy and Theology*. London: Routledge.

Bois, Y.-A. and Krauss, R. E. 1997. *Formless: A User's Guide*. New York NY: 1997.

Boisseron, B. 2003. 'Post-coca et post-coïtum: la jouissance du logo chez Guillaume Dustan et "Seinfeld"', *L'Esprit Créateur*, 43:2, 81–91.

Boldt-Irons, L.-A. (ed.) 1995. *On Bataille: Critical Essays*. Albany, NY: State University of New York Press.

Bontour, B. 2002. 'Nicolas Jones-Gorlin: pédophilie, jeunisme, la figure de Janus' (online). Available from: www.écrits-vains.com (accessed June 2004).

Boulé, J.-P. 2002. *HIV Stories: The Archaeology of AIDS Writing in France, 1985–1988*. Liverpool: Liverpool University Press.

Bourcier, M.-H. 2004. 'Pipe d'auteur: la "nouvelle vague pornographique française" et ses intellectuels (avec Jean-Pierre Léaud et Ovidie, Catherine Millet et son mari et toute la presse)', *L'Esprit Créateur*, 44:3: *After the Erotic*, 13–27.

Bowd, G. 2002. 'Michel Houellebecq and the pursuit of happiness', *Nottingham French Studies*, 41:1, 28–39.

— (ed.) 2006. *Le Monde de Houellebecq*. Glasgow: University of Glasgow French and German Publications.

Braidotti, R. 1994. *Nomadic Subjects: Embodiment and Sexual Difference in Contemporary Feminist Theory*. New York, NY: Columbia University Press.

Bronfen, E. 1992. *Over Her Dead Body: Death, Femininity and the Aesthetic*. Manchester: Manchester University Press.

— 1998. *The Knotted Subject: Hysteria and its Discontents*. Princeton, NJ: Princeton University Press.

Bruckner, P. 2004. *L'Amour du prochain*. Paris: Grasset et Fasquelle.

Butler, J. 1993. *Bodies That Matter: On the Discursive Limits of Sex*. London: Routledge.

— 1999. *Gender Trouble: Feminism and the Subversion of Identity* (1990). London: Routledge.

Cairns, L. 2002a. *Lesbian Desire in Post-1968 French Literature*. Lampeter: Edwin Mellen Press.

— 2002b. 'Le Phallus lesbien (bis): lesbo-erotic French writing of the late 1990s', *Nottingham French Studies*, 41:1, 89–101.

Camus, A. 1965. *Essais*. Paris: Gallimard, 'Bibliothèque de la Pléiade'.

Camus, R. 1987. *Journal romain, 1985–1986*. Paris: POL.

Camy, G. and Montagne, A. 2002. '*Baise-moi*', *Cinémaction*, 103: *50 films qui ont fait scandale*, 217–21.

Canto-Sperber, M. 2001. 'Le Sexe et la vie d'une femme', *Esprit*, 273, 270–89.

Carey, J. 1993. 'The age of innocents', *Sunday Times*, 7 March, pp. 9–11.

Caron, D. 1998. '*Liberté, Egalité, Séropositivité*: AIDS, the French Republic and the question of community', *French Cultural Studies*, 9:27, 281–93.

— 2001. *AIDS in French Culture: Social Ills, Literary Cures*. Madison, WI: University of Wisconsin Press.

— 2003. 'Guillaume Dustan', in D. Eribon (ed.), *Dictionnaire des cultures gays et lesbiennes* (Paris: Larousse), p. 166.

— 2005. 'AIDS/Holocaust: metaphor and French universalism', *L'Esprit Créateur*, 45:3, 63–73.

Carter, A. 2000. *The Sadeian Woman: An Exercise in Cultural History* (1979). London: Virago.

Casey, E. 1997. *The Fate of Place: A Philosophical History*. Berkeley, CA: University of California Press.

Cata, I. and Dalmolin, E. 2004. 'Ecrire et lire l'inceste: Christine Angot', *Journal of Women in French*, 12, 85–101.

Champagne, J. 1995. *The Ethics of Marginality: A New Approach to Gay Studies*. London: University of Minnesota Press.

Chastel, J. 2002. '*Romance*', *Cinémaction*, 103: *50 films qui ont fait scandale*, 214–16.

Cixous, H. and Clément, C. 1975. *La Jeune Née*. Paris: Union Générale des Editions.

Clément, C. 1981. *Vie et légendes de Jacques Lacan*. Paris: Grasset.

Clément, M.-L. 2003. *Houellebecq: Sperme et sang*. Paris: L'Harmattan.

— 2004. 'Masculin versus féminin chez Michel Houellebecq', *L'Esprit Créateur*, 44:3, 28–39.

Clouzot, C. 2004. *Catherine Breillat: Indécence et pureté*. Paris: Cahiers du cinéma.

Clover, C. J. 1993. 'Introduction', in P. C. Gibson and R. Gibson (eds), *Dirty Looks: Women, Pornography, Power*. London: British Film Institute, 1–4.

Colebrook, C. 2002. *Gilles Deleuze*. London: Routledge.

Cooper, S. 2005. 'Reconfiguring sexual–textual space: the seductions of Catherine Cusset's *Jouir*', *L'Esprit Créateur*, 45:1, 38–47.

Cornell, D. (ed.) 2000. *Feminism and Pornography*. Oxford: Oxford University Press.

Crary, J. 1992. *Techniques of the Observer*. Cambridge, MA: MIT Press.

Crowley, M. 2000. *Duras, Writing and the Ethical: Making the Broken Whole*. Oxford: Oxford University Press.

— 2004. 'Bataille's tacky touch', *MLN*, 119:4, 765–80.

Cruickshank, R. 2003. 'L'affaire Houellebecq: ideological crime and *fin de millénaire* literary scandal', *French Cultural Studies*, 14:1, 101–16.

— 2006. 'Sex, shopping and psychoanalysis: Houellebecq and therapy', in G. Bowd (ed.), *Le Monde de Houellebecq*. Glasgow: University of Glasgow French and German Publications, pp. 199–212

— Forthcoming. Fin de millénaire *French Fiction: The Aesthetics of Crisis*. Oxford: Oxford University Press.

Cusset, C. 1997. *Jouir*. Paris: Gallimard.

Dean, C. J. 1996. *Sexuality and Modern Western Culture*. New York, NY: Twayne Publishers.

— 2000. *The Frail Social Body: Pornography, Homosexuality and Other Fantasies in Interwar France*. Berkeley, CA: University of California Press.

Deleu, X. 2002. *Le Consensus pornographique*. Paris: Mango Document.

Deleuze, G. and Guattari, F. 1972. *Capitalisme et schizophrénie: L'Anti-Œdipe*. Paris: Minuit.

Delvaux, M. 2004. 'Catherine Millet: l'archive du sexe', *L'Esprit Créateur*, 44:3, 48–56.

Derrida, J. 1990. *Mémoires d'aveugle: L'Autoportrait et autres ruines*. Paris: Editions de la Réunion des musées nationaux.

— 2000. *Le Toucher, Jean-Luc Nancy*. Paris: Galilée.

Demonpion, D. 2005. *Houellebecq non autorisé: Enquête sur un phéno-mène*. Paris: Maren Sell.

Détrez, C. and Simon, A. 2004. '"Plus tu baises dur, moins tu cogites": littérature féminine contemporaine et sexualité: la fin des tabous?', *L'Esprit Créateur*, 44:3, 57–69.

Devanne, L. 2005. 'Catherine Breillat, cinéaste' (online). Available from: www.arkepix.com (accessed 9 August 2005).

Di Folco, P. (ed.) 2005. *Dictionnaire de la pornographie*. Paris: Presses Universitaires de France.

Di Meo, P. 2001. 'La légende d'un corps', *Magazine littéraire*, 398, 72–4.

Dion, R. and Haghebaert, E. 2001. 'Le Cas de Michel Houellebecq et la dynamique des genres littéraires', *French Studies*, 55:4, 509–24.

Diski, J. 2002. 'Hang on to the Doily', *London Review of Books*, 25 July, 28–9.

Darrieussecq, M. 2004. *Truismes* (1996). Paris: POL, 'Folio'.

Doane, M. A. 2002. *The Emergence of Cinematic Time: Modernity, Contingency, the Archive*. Cambridge, MA: Harvard University Press.

Dufourmantelle, A. 2003. *Blind Date: Sexe et philosophie*. Paris: Calmann-Lévy.

Duras, M. 1982. *La Maladie de la mort*. Paris: Minuit.

Dworkin, A. 1981. *Pornography: Men Possessing Women*. London: Women's Press.

Dyer, R. 1992. *Only Entertainment*. London: Routledge.

Eagleton, M (ed.). 2003. *A Concise Companion to Feminist Theory*. Oxford: Blackwell.

Eakin, E. 2000. 'Le Provocateur' (online), *New York Times*, 10 September 2000. Available from: www.multimania.com/houellebecq (accessed 17 July 2001).

Edelman, L. 2004. *No Future: Queer Theory and the Death Drive*. Durham, NC: Duke University Press.

Eisenstein, S. 1998a. 'The montage of film attractions' (1924), in R. Taylor (ed.), *The Eisenstein Reader*. London: British Film Institute, pp. 35–52.

— 1998b. 'Beyond the shot' (1929), in R. Taylor (ed.), *The Eisenstein Reader*. London: British Film Institute, pp. 82–92.

Eribon, D. 1989. *Michel Foucault (1926–1984)*. Paris: Flammarion.

— 1999. *Réflexions sur la question gay*. Paris: Fayard.

— (ed.) 2003. *Dictionnaire des cultures gays et lesbiennes*. Paris: Larousse.

Escalle, C. 1996. *Pulsion*. Paris: Zulma.

— 2001. *Où est-il cet amour*. Paris: Calmann-Lévy.

Falcon, R. 2001. 'Last tango in Lewisham', *Sight & Sound*, 11:7, 20–4.

Fayard, N. 2005. 'Sadeian sisters: sexuality as terrorism in the work of Virginie Despentes', in S. F. Donachie and K. Harrison (eds), *Love and Sexuality: New Approaches in French Studies* (Oxford: Peter Lang), pp. 101–20.

— 2006. 'The rebellious body as parody: *Baise-moi* by Virginie Despentes', *French Studies*, 60:1, 63–77.

Ferrari, F. and Nancy, J.-L. 2002. *Nus sommes*. Brussels: Yves Gevaert.

ffrench, P. 1999. *The Cut/Reading Bataille's Histoire de l'œil*. Oxford: Oxford University Press, published for the British Academy.

Foster, H. 1996. *The Return of the Real: The Avant-Garde at the End of the Century*. Cambridge, MA: MIT Press.

Foucault, M. 1966. *Les Mots et les choses*. Paris: Gallimard.

— 1976. *Histoire de la sexualité*, I: *La Volonté de savoir*. Paris: Gallimard.

— 1984. *Histoire de la sexualité*, III: *Le Souci de soi*. Paris: Gallimard.

— 1986. 'Of other spaces', tr. J. Maskowiec, *Diacritics*, 16:1, 22–7.

— 1994. *Dits et écrits, 1954–1988*, IV: 1980–1988, ed. Daniel Défert, François Ewald and Jacques Lagrange. Paris: Gallimard.

Frappat, H., and Lalanne, J.-M. 2002. 'Breillat-Parillaud: Auto-frictions', *Cahiers du cinéma*, 568, 34–7.

Frodon, J.-M. 2004. Interview with Catherine Breillat and Christine Angot, Bibliothèque nationale de France, 12 February 2004 (audio document held at Bibliothèque nationale de France).

Gablik, S. 1991. *The Reenchantment of Art*. London: Thames & Hudson.

Gaillac-Morgue. 2005. 'Interview with Catherine Breillat', on UK DVD of *Anatomie de l'enfer* (London: Tartan Films).

Garcin, J. 2000. 'Le Porno, c'est du viol' (interview with Raffaëlla Anderson and Karen Bach) (online), *Le Nouvel Observateur*, 22 June 2000. Available from: www.archives/nouvelobs.com (accessed 13 September 2005).

— 2005. 'Je suis un prophète amateur' (interview with Michel Houellebecq) (online). Available from: www.houellebecq.info (accessed 4 November 2005).

Garréta, A. F. 2001. 'Re-enchanting the Republic: "Pacs", *Parité*, and *Le Symbolique*', *Yale French Studies*, 100, 145–66.

Garsault, A. 2004. 'Sexy est mort', *Positif*, 521–2, 6–8.

Gatens, M. 1996. *Imaginary Bodies: Ethics, Power and Corporeality*. London: Routledge.

Gibson, P. C. (ed.) 2004. *More Dirty Looks: Gender, Pornography and Power*. London: British Film Institute.

— and Gibson, R. (eds). 1993. *Dirty Looks: Women, Pornography, Power*. London: British Film Institute.

Gilbert-Rolfe, J. 1999. *Beauty and the Contemporary Sublime*. New York, NY: Allworth Press.

Gordon, R. S. C. 2000. '"To speak oneself and die": Pasolini and the poet as martyr', in Martin Crowley (ed.), *Dying Words: The Last Moments of Writers and Philosophers*. Amsterdam–Atlanta, GA: Rodopi, pp. 56–68.

Grangeray, E. 2004. 'Virginie Despentes, l'âge de raison sans compromission', *Le Monde*, 22–23 August 2004, p. 15.

Grosz, E. 1994. *Volatile Bodies: Towards a Corporeal Feminism*. Bloomington: Indiana University Press.

— and Probyn, E. (eds) 1995. *Sexy Bodies: The Strange Carnality of Feminism*. London: Routledge.

Harrison, N. 2000. 'Reading Sade through censorship', *Paragraph*, 23:1, 26–37.

Harvey, D. 1990. *The Condition of Postmodernity*. Oxford: Blackwell.

Heath, S. 1981. *Questions of Cinema*. Bloomington, IN: Indiana University Press.

Herman, J. 1981. *Father–Daughter Incest*. London: Harvard University Press.

Hollywood, A. 2002. *Sensible Ecstasy: Mysticism, Sexual Difference and the Demands of History*. Chicago, IL: Chicago University Press.

Hottell, R. A., and Russell-Watts, L. 2002. 'Catherine Breillat's *Romance* and the female spectator: from dream-work to therapy', *L'Esprit Créateur*, 42:3, 70–80.

Howlett, J. and Mengham, R. (eds) 1994. *The Violent Muse: Violence and the Artistic Imagination in Europe 1910–1939*. Manchester: Manchester University Press.

HPG. 2002. *Autobiographie d'un hardeur*. Paris: Hachette Littératures.

Hughes, A. and Ince, K. (eds) 1996. *French Erotic Fiction: Women's Desiring Writing*. Oxford: Berg.

Hussey, A. 2006. '*Présence humaine*: Michel Houellebecq, poet-*chansonnier*', in G. Bowd (ed.), *Le Monde de Houellebecq* (Glasgow: University of Glasgow French and German Publications), pp. 59–70.

Hutton, M-A. 1995. 'Assuming responsibility: Christiane Rochefort's exploration of child sexual abuse in *La Porte du fond*', *Modern Language Review*, 90:2, 333–4.

Ince, K. 2000. *Orlan: Millennial Female*. Oxford: Berg.

— 2004. 'Is sex comedy or tragedy? The cinema of Catherine Breillat', paper presented at the conference of the Society for French Studies, Cambridge, July 2004.

Les Inrockuptibles, 504, 505, 506: *Sexe!* (triple edition, 27 July–16 August 2005).

— hors série 22: *Houellebecq* (May 2005).

Irigaray, L. 1974. *Speculum de l'autre femme*. Paris: Minuit.

— 1977. *Ce sexe qui n'en est pas un*. Paris: Minuit.

— 1984. *Ethique de la différence sexuelle*. Paris: Minuit.

Itzin, C. (ed.) 2001. *Pornography: Women, Violence and Civil Liberties: A Radical New View* (1992). Oxford: Oxford University Press.

Jacob, D. 1999. 'Les nouveaux barbares', *Le Nouvel Observateur*, 26 August 1999, 64–7.

Jameson, F. 1984. 'Postmodernism or the cultural logic of late capitalism'. *New Left Review*, 1:146 (July–August), 53–92.

Jenkins, H. (ed.) 1998. *The Children's Culture Reader*. New York, NY: New York University Press.

Jones, R. 1988. 'Hover culture'. *Artscribe* (summer), 46–51.

Jordan, S. 2002. '"Dans le mauvais goût pour le mauvais goût"?: pornographie, violence et sexualité féminine dans la fiction de Virginie Despentes', in N. Morello and C. Rodgers (eds), *Nouvelles écrivaines: Nouvelles voix?* Amsterdam–New York, NY: Rodopi, pp. 121–39.

Joyce, C. 2005. 'Tainted love' (online). Available from: www.archive.salon.com (accessed 10 August 2005).

Joye, F. 2002. 'La censure plane sur les artistes' (online). Available from: www.LeCourrier.fr (accessed June 2004).

Jung, C. 1998. *Once upon a poulette*. Paris: KTM.

— 2001. *Cul nu*. Paris: KTM.

Kincaid, J. 1998. 'Producing erotic children', in H. Jenkins (ed.), *The Children's Culture Reader*. New York, NY: New York University Press, pp. 241–53.

Kipnis, L. 1993. 'She-male fantasies and the aesthetics of pornography', in P. C. Gibson and R. Gibson (eds), *Dirty Looks: Women, Pornography, Power*. London: British Film Institute, pp. 124–43.

— 1996. *Bound and Gagged: Pornography and the Politics of Fantasy in America*. New York, NY: Grove Press.

Koch, G. 1993. 'The body's shadow realm', in P. C. Gibson and R. Gibson (eds), *Dirty Looks: Women, Pornography, Power*. London: British Film Institute, pp. 22–45.

Kotz, L. 1993. 'Complicity: women artists investigating masculinity', in P. C. Gibson and R. Gibson (eds), *Dirty Looks: Women, Pornography, Power*. London: British Film Institute, pp. 101–23.

Krauss, R. E. 1993. *The Optical Unconscious*. Cambridge, MA: MIT Press.

Krisjansen, I. and Maddock, T. 2001. 'Educating Eros: Catherine Breillat's *Romance* as a cinematic solution to Sade's metaphysical problem', *Studies in French Cinema*, 1:3, 141–9.

Kristeva, J. 1974. *Des Chinoises*. Paris: Des Femmes.

— 1980. *Pouvoirs de l'horreur: essai sur l'abjection*. Paris: Le Seuil

— 1996. *Sens et non-sens de la révolte*. Paris: Librairie Arthème Fayard.

— 2000. *The Sense and Non-Sense of Revolt*, tr. Jeanine Herman. New York, NY: Columbia University Press.

Kuspit, D. 1993. *The Dialectic of Decadence*. New York, NY: Stux Press.

Lacan, J. 1973. *Le Séminaire Livre XI. Les quatre concepts fondamentaux de la psychanalyse, 1964*, ed. Jacques-Alain Miller. Paris: Seuil.

Lane, R. 2000. *Jean Baudrillard*. London: Routledge.

Larcher, J. 2002. 'Repassage à l'acte', *Cahiers du cinéma*, 568, 38–9.

Levy, A. 2005. *Female Chauvinist Pigs: Women and the Rise of Raunch Culture*. London: Simon & Schuster.

Levy, G. 1999. *Refiguring the Muse*. Bern: Peter Lang.

Ley, C. 2003. *Voyage au pays de l'échangisme*. Lausanne: Favre.

'The Limits of Sex'. 2001. *Sight & Sound*, 11:7, 21.

Luckhurst, R. 1996. '(Touching on) tele-technology', in J. Brannigan, R. Robbins and J. Wolfreys (eds), *Applying: To Derrida*. Basingstoke: Macmillan, pp. 171–83.

Macey, D. 1994. *The Lives of Michel Foucault* (1993). London: Vintage.

Macnab, G. 2004. 'Sadean woman', *Sight & Sound*, 14:12, 20–2.

Marcelle, P. 1998. 'Face aux piles: revue de Houellebecq' (online), *Libération*, 9 October 1998. Available from: www.liberation.fr (accessed 17 September 2001).

Marchal, H. 2003. 'Chroniques de la vie sexuelle', *Magazine littéraire*, 426, 56–8.

Marks, L. U. 2000. *The Skin of the Film: Intercultural Cinema, Embodiment and the Senses*. Durham, NC: Duke University Press.

— 2002. *Touch: Sensuous Theory and Multisensory Media*. Minneapolis, MN: University of Minnesota Press.

Martel, F. 1999a. *The Pink and the Black: Homosexuals in France since 1968* (1996), tr. Jane Marie Todd. Stanford, CA: Stanford University Press.

— 1999b. 'C'est ainsi que je fabrique mes livres' (interview with Michel Houellebecq), *Nouvelle Revue française*, 548, 197–209.

Martin, A. 2005. '"X" marks the spot: classifying *Romance*' (online). Available from: www.sensesofcinema.com (accessed 9 August 2005).

Martinek C. 2005. '"Inventer jusqu'au délire dans la danse des anges"?: la sexualité dans *Baise-moi* de Virginie Despentes et *Femme nue, femme noire* de Calixthe Beyala', *L'Esprit Créateur*, 45:1, 48–58.

Marzano, M. 2003. *La Pornographie ou l'épuisement du désir*. Paris: Buchet/Chastel.

— 2005. 'Le Miroir des contradictions de l'Occident', *Magazine littéraire*, 447, 27–8.

Mayné, G. 2001. *Pornographie, violence obscène, érotisme*. Paris: Descartes et Cie.

McGrath, J. E. 1995. 'Trusting in rubber: performing boundaries during the AIDS epidemic', *TDR: The Drama Review*, 39:2, 21–38.

McMahon, L. 2005. 'Touching intact: Sophie Calle's threat to privacy', paper presented at the Cambridge French Graduate Conference, April 2005.

McNair, B. 2002. *Striptease Culture: Sex, Media and the Democratization of Desire*. London: Routledge.

Meltzer, F. 2001. *For Fear of the Fire: Joan of Arc and the Limits of Subjectivity*. Chicago, IL: Chicago University Press.

Merleau-Ponty, M. 1999. *Le Visible et l'invisible* (1964). Paris: Gallimard, 'Tel'.

Merritt, N. 2000. *Digital Diaries*. Cologne: Taschen.

Merrick, J. and Ragan, B. T. Jr. (eds) 1996. *Homosexuality in Modern France*. Oxford: Oxford University Press.

Metzidakis, S. 2003. 'Postmodern neutralizing of nineteenth-century imagery', *Nottingham Journal of French Studies*, 42:2, 128–41.

Miller, D. A. 1993. 'Sontag's urbanity' (1989), in H. Abelove, M. A. Barale and D. M. Halperin (eds), *The Lesbian and Gay Studies Reader*. London: Routledge, pp. 212–20.

Minsky, R. 1998. *Psychoanalysis and Culture: Contemporary States of Mind*. Cambridge: Polity.

Molinier, P. 2003. 'La Pornographie "en situation"', *Cités*, 15: *Politiques de la pornographie: Le sexe, le savoir, le pouvoir*, 61–7.

Morello, N. and Rodgers, C. (eds) 2002. *Nouvelles écrivaines: nouvelles voix?* Amsterdam–Atlanta, GA: Rodopi.

Morgane, C. 2003. *Sex Star*. Paris: Adcan.

Morrey, D. 1998. 'Sida-topies: provocative communities in Guy Hocquenghem's *Eve* and Vincent Borel's *Un Ruban noir*', *French Cultural Studies*, 9:27, 385–98.

— 2004. 'Michel Houellebecq and the international sexual economy' (online). *Portal*, 1:1, available from: http://epress.lib.uts.edu.au/ojs/index.php/portal (accessed 11 November 2005).

Murphy, K. 2005. 'Hells' angels: an interview with Catherine Breillat on *Anatomy of Hell*' (online). Available from: www.sensesofcinema.com (accessed 9 August 2005).

Nancy, J.-L. 2001. *Les Muses*, édition revue et augmentée. Paris: Galilée.

Naulleau, E. 2005. *Au secours, Houellebecq revient!* Paris: Chifflet et Cie.

Nead, L. 1992. *The Female Nude: Art, Obscenity and Sexuality*. London: Routledge.

Nettlebeck, C. 2002. 'Trans-figurations: verbal and visual frissons in France's millennial change', *Australian Journal of French Studies*, 39:1, 86–101.

— 2003. 'Self-constructing women: beyond the shock of *Baise-moi* and *A ma sœur!*' (online), *FULGOR: Flinders University Languages Group Online Review*, 1:3, 58–68. Available from: http://ehlt.finders.edu.au/deptlang/fulgor (accessed 11 November 2005).

Ní Loingsigh, A. 2005. 'Tourist traps: confounding expectations in Michel Houellebecq's *Plateforme*', *French Cultural Studies*, 16:1, 73–90.

Noguez, D. 2001. 'Ce qui compte', *Nouvelle Revue française*, 557, 61–77.

— 2003. *Houellebecq, en fait*. Paris: Fayard.

Nussbaum, M. 2004. *Hiding from Humanity: Disgust, Shame and the Law*. Princeton, NJ: Princeton University Press.

Ogien, R. 2003. *Penser la pornographie*. Paris: Presses Universitaires de France.

O'Toole, L. 1998. *Pornocopia: Porn, Sex, Technology and Desire*. London: Serpent's Tail.

Ovidie. 2002. *Porno manifesto*. Paris: Flammarion.

Pasolini, P. P. 1998. *Heretical Empiricism* (1972), tr. Ben Lawton and Louise K. Barnett. Bloomington, IN: Indiana University Press.

Patricola, J.-F. 2005. *Michel Houellebecq ou la provocation permanente*. Paris: Ecriture.

Pease, A. 2000. *Modernism, Mass Culture and the Aesthetics of Obscenity*. Cambridge: Cambridge University Press.

Perec, G. 1990. *Les Choses* (1965). Paris: Presses Pocket.

Phillips, A. (Adam) 1995. *Terrors and Experts*. London: Faber & Faber.

— 1998. *The Beast in the Nursery*. London: Faber & Faber.

Phillips, A. (Anita) 1998. *A Defence of Masochism*. London: Faber & Faber.

Phillips, J. 1999. *Forbidden Fictions: Pornography and Censorship in Twentieth-Century French Literature*. London: Pluto.

— 2001. 'Catherine Breillat's *Romance*: hard core and the female gaze', *Studies in French Cinema*, 1:3, 133–40.

Pollock, G. 2003. 'The visual', in M. Eagleton (ed.), *A Concise Companion to Feminist Theory*. Oxford: Blackwell, pp. 173–94.

Poster, M. 2001. *Jean Baudrillard: Selected Writings*. Cambridge: Polity.

Pratt, M. 1998. 'The defence of the straight state: heteronormativity, AIDS in France and the space of the nation', *French Cultural Studies*, 9:27, 263–80.

Prendergast, C. 1978. *Balzac: Fiction and Melodrama*. London: Edward Arnold.

Price, B. 2005. 'Catherine Breillat' (online). Available from: www.sensesofcinema.com (accessed 9 August 2005).

Puaux, F. 2001. 'Entretien avec Catherine Breillat', *Cinémaction*, 99: *Le Machisme à l'écran*, 165–72.

Rabinow, P. (ed.) 1984. *The Foucault Reader*. London: Penguin.

Radoilska, L. 2003. 'La Sexualité à mi-chemin entre l'intimité et le grand public', *Cités*, 15: *Politiques de la pornographie: Le sexe, le savoir, le pouvoir*, 31–42.

Read, J. 2000. *The New Avengers: Feminism, Femininity and the Rape-revenge Cycle*. Manchester: Manchester University Press.

Reader, K. 2006. *The Abject Object: Avatars of the Phallus in Contemporary French Theory, Literature and Film*. Amsterdam–New York, NY: Rodopi.

Reynaud, B. 2005. '*Baise-moi*: a personal angry-yet-feminist reaction' (online). Available from: www.sensesofcinema.com (accessed 9 August 2005).

Riddell, M. 2002. 'The fiction of new fiction' (online), *Observer*, 22 September. Available from: www.observer.guardian.co.uk (accessed June 2004).

Roger, A. 2001. 'Le Phallangélus de Millet', *Critique*, 655, 911–28.

Roman, J. 2005. *Marie pleine de larmes*. Paris: Lignes.

Rouyer, P. and Vassé, C. 2004. 'Catherine Breillat: de l'évanescent qui n'est plus de l'ordre du charnel', *Positif*, 521–2, 36–40.

Russell, D. (ed.) 1993. *Making Violence Sexy: Feminist Views on Pornography*. Buckingham: Open University Press.

Rye, G. and Worton, M. (eds) 2003. *Women's Writing in Contemporary France: New Writers, New Literatures in the 1990s*. Manchester: Manchester University Press.

Savigneau, J. 2004. 'Une question de vérité' (interview with Jacques Henric), *Le Monde des livres*, 29 October, p. iv.

Sadoux, M. 2002. 'Christine Angot's *autofictions*: literature and/or reality', in G. Rye and M. Worton (eds), *Women's Writing in Contemporary France: New Writers, New Literatures in the 1990s*. Manchester: Manchester University Press, pp. 171–81.

Schehr, L. R. 1995. *Alcibiades at the Door: Gay Discourses in French Literature*. Stanford, CA: Stanford University Press.

— 2002. 'Writing bareback', *Sites: Journal of Contemporary French Studies*, 6:1, 181–202.

— 2004a. 'Introduction', *L'Esprit Créateur*, 44:3: *After the Erotic*, 3–4.

— 2004b. 'Reading serial sex: the case of Erik Rémès', *L'Esprit Créateur*, 44:3: *After the Erotic*, 94–104.

— 2005. 'Toward a queer cartography of contemporary writing in France', paper delivered at the Cambridge Modern French Research Seminar, November 2005.

Schohr, N. 2001. 'The crisis of French universalism', *Yale French Studies*, 100, 43–64.

Schuerewegen, F. 2004. 'He ejaculated (Houellebecq)', *L'Esprit Créateur*, 44:3: *After the Erotic*, 40–7.

Sedgwick, E. K. 1985. *Between Men: English Literature and Male Homosocial Desire*. New York, NY: Columbia University Press.

Sénécal, D. 2001. Interview with Michel Houellebecq. *Lire*, September, 28–36.

'Sexe et télé: La stratégie des chaînes' (online). Available from: www.leblogtvnews.com (accessed 18 November 2005).

Sobchack, V. 1992. *The Address of the Eye: A Phenomenology of Film Experience*. Princeton, NJ: Princeton University Press.

Sontag, S. 1989. *AIDS and its Metaphors*. New York, NY: Farrar, Straus and Giroux.

— 1994. 'The pornographic imagination' (1967), in *Styles of Radical Will*

(1969). London: Vintage, pp. 35–73.

Spoiden, S. 2002. 'No man's land: genres en question dans *Sitcom, Romance et Baise-moi*', *L'Esprit Créateur*, 42:1, 96–106.

— 2004. 'Clivage', *L'Esprit Créateur*, 44:3: *After the Erotic*, 70–81.

Stoller, R. 1985. *Observing the Erotic Imagination*. New Haven, CT: Yale University Press.

Suleiman, S. R. 1990. *Subversive Intent: Gender, Politics and the Avant-Garde*. Cambridge, MA: Harvard University Press.

— 1994. *Risking Who One Is: Encounters with Contemporary Art and Literature*. Cambridge, MA: Harvard University Press.

— 1995. 'Transgression and the avant-garde: Bataille's *Histoire de l'œil*', in L.-A. Boldt-Irons (ed.), *On Bataille: Critical Essays*. Albany, NY: State University of New York Press, pp. 131–3.

Thivel, C. 2001. *Une Chambre après l'autre*. Paris: Denoël.

Thomas, J. 1989. *Inside the Wolf's Belly: Aspects of the Fairy Tale*. Sheffield: Sheffield Academic Press.

Vallaeys, B. and Armanet, F. 2000. 'Trois femmes s'emparent du sexe' (interview with Catherine Breillat, Virginie Despentes and Coralie Trinh Thi) (online), *Libération*, 13 June 2000, 28–30. Available from: www.liberation.fr (accessed 2 September 2005).

Van Cauwelaert, D. 2004. *Rencontre sous X* (2002). Paris: Livre de poche.

Van Wesemael, S. 2005. *Michel Houellebecq: Le plaisir du texte*. Paris: L'Harmattan.

Vasse, David 2004. *Catherine Breillat: Un cinéma du rite et de la transgression*. Paris: Complexe/Arte.

Vasseleu, C. 1998. *Textures of Light: Vision and Touch in Irigaray, Levinas and Merleau-Ponty*. London: Routledge.

Verity, E. 1994. '"Paedophile Book" Should Be Banned', *Daily Mail*, 8 March, n.p.

Vian, B. 2001. 'Utilité d'une littérature érotique' (1948), in *Ecrits pornographiques* (1980). Paris: Livre de poche, pp. 19–64.

Vincendeau, G. 2001. 'Sisters, sex and sitcom', *Sight & Sound*, 11:12, 18–20.

— 2003. 'What she wants', *Sight & Sound*, 13:5, 20–2.

Waldby, C. 1995. 'Destruction: boundary erotics and refigurations of the heterosexual male body', in E. Grosz and E. Probyn (eds), *Sexy Bodies: The Strange Carnality of Feminism*. London: Routledge, pp. 266–71.

Walkerdine, V. 1998. 'Popular culture and the eroticization of little girls', in H. Jenkins (ed.), *The Children's Culture Reader*. New York, NY: New York University Press, pp. 254–64.

Wassenaar, I. 2001. '*Whatever*: Michel Houellebecq and the future of French literature', paper delivered to the British Academy Postdoctoral Fellowship Symposium, London, April 2001.

Watney, S. 1993. 'The spectacle of AIDS' (1987), in H. Abelove, M. A. Barale and D. M. Halperin (eds), *The Lesbian and Gay Studies Reader*. London: Routledge, pp. 202–11.

Wellershoff, M. and Traub, R. 2005. 'Le Spectacle de la société' (interview with Michel Houellebecq and Bret Easton Ellis) (1999). *Les Inrockuptibles*, hors série 22: *Houellebecq*, 68–71.

Welzer-Lang, D. 2005. *La Planète échangiste: les sexualités collectives en France*. Paris: Payot.

Wicke, J. 1993. 'Through a gaze darkly: pornography's academic market', in P. C. Gibson and R. Gibson (eds), *Dirty Looks: Women, Pornography, Power*. London: British Film Institute, pp. 62–8.

Williams, L. 1993. 'Second thoughts on *Hard Core*: American obscenity law and the scapegoating of deviance', in P. C. Gibson and R. Gibson (eds), *Dirty Looks: Women, Pornography, Power*. London: British Film Institute, pp. 46–61.

— 1999. *Hard Core: Power, Pleasure and the 'Frenzy of the Visible'*. (Expanded edition.) Berkeley, CA: University of California Press.

— 2001. 'Cinema and the sex act', *Cinéaste*, 27:1, 20–5.

— (ed.) 2004. *Porn Studies*. Durham, NC: Duke University Press.

Williams, L. R. 2001. 'Sick sisters', *Sight & Sound*, 11:7, 28–9.

Wilson, E. 2001. 'Deforming femininity: Catherine Breillat's *Romance*', in Lucy Mazdon (ed.), *France on Film*. London: Wallflower, pp. 145–57.

— 2003. *Cinema's Missing Children*. London: Wallflower Press.

— 2005. 'Material Remains: *Night and Fog*', October, 112, 89–110.

Wollen, P. 1998. *Signs and Meaning in the Cinema*. (Expanded edition.) London: British Film Institute.

Worton, M. 1998. 'Looking for kicks: promiscuity and violence in contemporary French fiction', *Nottingham French Studies*, 37:1, 89–105.

Zipes, J. 1995. *Creative Storytelling: Building Community, Changing Lives*. London: Routledge.

Žižek, S. 1989. *The Sublime Object of Ideology*. London: Verso.

— 1992. *Looking Awry: An Introduction to Jacques Lacan through Popular Culture*. Cambridge, MA: MIT Press.

— 1997. *The Plague of Fantasies*. London: Verso.

— 1999. *The Ticklish Subject*. London: Verso

Index

Note: Specific works can be found under the name of their author or director. Page numbers in italic refer to illustrations.